HUMAN DEVELOPMENT AND THE INTERNATIONAL DEVELOPMENT STRATEGY FOR THE 1990s

Human Development and the International Development Strategy for the 1990s

Edited by

Keith Griffin

Professor and Chairman, Economics Department
University of California, Riverside

and

John Knight

Senior Research Officer
Institute of Economics and Statistics, University of Oxford

MACMILLAN in association with
the United Nations

First published 1990

Published by
MACMILLAN ACADEMIC AND PROFESSIONAL LTD
Houndmills, Basingstoke, Hampshire RG21 2XS
and London
Companies and representatives
throughout the world

Printed in Great Britain by WBC Ltd., Bridgend

British Library Cataloguing in Publication Data
Human development and the international development strategy
for the 1990s.
1. Economic development
I. Griffin, Keith *1938*– II. Knight, John
330.9

ISBN 0–333–53512–X (hardback)
ISBN 0–333–53513–8 (paperback)

CONTENTS

FOREWORD

The last decade has brought a sharp deterioration in living conditions in many developing countries, especially in Africa and Latin America. Incomes per capita have declined and social expenditure has been cut, with setbacks in nutrition, school enrolment and health services as a result. The burden of economic adjustment tends to fall most heavily on the poor and on vulnerable groups, such as children. This is not only a tragedy in itself but also a terrible waste of human resources, and it has led to renewed attention to the role of human resources in the process of development.

This is, of course, not a new issue. It has long been understood that the realization of the full potential of human beings is both a means and an end in itself, and that the reduction of poverty should be a primary aim of development. But all too often development tends to bypass the poor unless steps are taken to ensure that they share its benefits; and in times of austerity their position tends to worsen further. Hence, the present search for ways to alleviate poverty, combat hunger and uphold educational and health standards, even in times of economic distress.

This book, containing studies commissioned by the United Nations, focuses on the dynamic interaction between the economic and social variables in development. It presents and develops the case for greater attention to the human factor by identifying and assessing the fundamental role of education, health, work opportunities and social participation in economic and social progress. It is my hope that these essays by distinguished scholars and practitioners in the field will contribute to the lively discussions that will take place in the United Nations about the formulation of a strategy for international co-operation for development in the 1990s, and that they will prove equally valuable to the academic community and the concerned public.

Rafeeuddin AHMED
United Nation Under-Secretary-General for
International Economic and Social Affairs

vii

NOTE ON THE TABLES

The following symbols have been used in the tables throughout:

Two dots (..) indicate that data are not available or are not separately reported.

A dash (—) indicates that the amount is nil or negligible.

A hyphen (-) indicates that the item is not applicable.

A minus (−) sign indicates a deficit or decrease, except as indicated.

A point (.) is used to indicate decimals.

Use of a hyphen (-) between dates representing years, e.g., 1985–1987, signifies the full period involved, including the beginning and end years.

Reference to "dollars" ($) indicates United States dollars, unless otherwise stated.

The term "billion" has been used to signify a thousand million.

Annual rates of growth or change, unless otherwise stated, refer to annual compound rates.

Details and percentage in tables do not necessarily add up to totals because of rounding.

INTRODUCTION

Keith Griffin and John Knight

This volume arises out of the work of the Committee for Development Planning of the United Nations. In 1987 the committee felt that human resource development had been neglected in many countries and that the time had come to investigate the situation and if necessary suggest policy advice. A Working Group on Human Resource Development was therefore established and Keith Griffin was asked to serve as its rapporteur and John Knight as its chief consultant. Our joint paper, which formed the basis of the report of the Working Group, is published below as Chapter 1. The report of the Working Group, in turn, was condensed and incorporated into the 1988 report of the Commitee for Development Planning.[1]

A number of papers were commissioned from recognized scholars to provide background material for the rapporteur and consultant and to assist the deliberations of the Working Group. These papers, along with our own joint paper, were published as a special issue of the *Journal of Development Planning*, the house journal of the United Nations Department of International Economic and Social Affairs.[2]

The story might well have ended there had it not been for the fact that in 1988 the Committee for Development Planning was asked to give its views and make proposals for an International Development Strategy for the 1990s. A Working Group was formed and Keith Griffin was again asked to be the rapporteur. The report of the Working Group emphasized four themes which taken together could constitute the core of an international development strategy for the 1990s. These four themes were: (i) the need to accelerate growth, particularly in those parts of the third world that had suffered from a decline in average living standards in the 1980s; (ii) the need to give high priority to human development; (iii) the need to direct more effort toward the alleviation of poverty, and above all to reduce the absolute numbers of those suffering from acute poverty; and (iv) the need to devote more attention to environmental issues and the sustainability of development in the face of environmental degradation.

The report of the Working Group on the International Development Strategy was accepted and formed part of the 1989 report of the

1

Committee for Development Planning.[3] The importance of human development was thus reaffirmed and human development seems likely to be a major topic of discussion, research and policy initiative in the years ahead.[4]

It is for this reason that it seemed worthwhile to republish the special issue of the *Journal of Development Planning* in a form that makes the papers more accessible to students, academics, the interested public and policy makers. We are delighted that Macmillan agreed to issue the essays in book form and hope that this encourages a wide debate on one of the most fundamental issues in development.

In Chapter 1 we present in some detail the case for renewed emphasis on human development both to foster economic growth and as an end in itself. Policies of human development enhance the "capabilities" of people to be and do things, both by raising their incomes and by improving other components of their standard of living, such as life expectancy, health, literacy, knowledge and control over their destiny. In all parts of the third world there have been long-run improvements in the basic capabilities of people – reflected in GNP per capita, life expectancy, infant mortality, nutrition and school enrolment. However, these long-run trends have been threatened by the severity of the economic problems now facing many developing countries.

Today the pendulum has swung too far towards the neglect of human development. Our object is to provide a counterweight. When governments face a severe dilemma of having to choose between adjusting to short-term economic and fiscal constraints and pursuing long-run human resource goals, there is a danger that the former will dominate the latter. For instance, the costs of neglecting short-term adjustment are more calculable, and more attributable, than the long-run costs to the development process of neglecting human development. Nevertheless, measures adopted in the hope that they will lead to a solution to the short-run problems of the present may contribute to a series of equally pressing short-run problems in the future.

The objectives of policy during periods of structural adjustment, such as characterized the 1980s and are continuing in the present decade, should be to safeguard human development programmes whenever possible and, if curtailment of public expenditure is unavoidable, to ensure that the burdens of adjustment are borne by those most able to do so. In many third world countries the opposite has occurred: human development programmes have been savagely cut and the brunt of the adjustment has fallen on the poor. This has weakened long-run prospects for development while increasing inequality and poverty. It would instead be better to restructure human development programmes to reduce inefficiency, to improve targeting and, where necessary to maintain the existing level of services, to introduce discriminatory user charges.

Human beings are not only the means but also the beneficiaries of economic progress. Economists too often view production as the ultimate concern rather than a means by which to contribute to human lives. Economic progress and the enrichment of human lives are not identical: high income per capita can be accompanied by poor quality of life. Amartya Sen, in Chapter 2, develops the "capability" approach to social evaluation – the notion that people should have the capability freely to choose to be and do things that are valuable. This approach is broader and deeper than the commodity-based and utility-based systems of evaluation: commodities are merely means to, and not themselves, ends, and utility is a subjective perspective which may fail to reflect a person's real deprivation. In very poor societies the crucial capabilities are relatively few and correspond to those addressed in the "basic needs" literature,[5] e.g. the capabilities to be well-nourished, well-sheltered, to escape avoidable morbidity and premature mortality. The advantages of the capabilities approach over more orthodox approaches are illustrated by reference to gender differences in mortality, health, education and literacy.

Amartya Sen provides a theoretical framework within which the subsequent, more specific, contributions to this volume can be understood. He deals with the strategic questions of evaluating development; the subsequent contributors are more concerned with the tactical questions of evaluation procedures for particular issues such as education, health, work opportunities and social participation.

Three papers are devoted to aspects of formal education, the most obvious form of human resource development. John Knight, in Chapter 3, examines some educational policy issues that are relevant to a period of economic stabilization and structural adjustment. There was rapid quantitative expansion of education in the 1960s and 1970s throughout the developing world, reflecting high private rates of return and political pressures for educational provision. Educational progress was slowed or halted in many developing countries by the fiscal squeeze and economic retrenchment of the 1980s. Nevertheless, the high estimated social rates of return to investments in both the quantity and quality of education suggest that education can be important in achieving structural adjustment and economic growth. A possible way out of the impasse, and a means of protecting the quantity and quality of education, is to rely more extensively on levying user charges in publicly provided education. The incidence of taxation is regressive and access to subsidized education unequal in many developing countries. Knight suggests, therefore, that the introduction or raising of user charges at the post-primary levels, especially in higher education, together with targeted subsidies for the children of the poor, would not necessarily be inequitable and might indeed reduce income inequality.

Estimates of the social rates of return to different levels of education generally find the highest return to be at the primary level.

3

However, such estimates are often based on inappropriate samples of workers; less studied, but of crucial importance, is the economic value of primary education to small-scale farmers. Daniel Cotlear, in Chapter 4, investigates the returns to education among farmers, both by surveying the literature and reporting on a study of farm operators in the Peruvian Andes. An important finding of the research is that education cannot be evaluated in isolation: its value depends on the environment in which it is used and the inputs with which it is combined. Thus, in a modernizing environment the use of non-traditional technology imparts considerable value to the skills acquired in school. It facilitates both the adoption and the efficient use of improved practices. Not only formal but also non-formal (agricultural extension programmes) and informal (migration experience) education are shown to be capable of raising productivity among small farmers. The provision of a basic education to all children may well be justified in terms of its personal and social effects; but, in the right conditions, it also has an economic justification.

The quantity of education provided in developing countries has attracted much attention among development economists; the quality of education much less. Yet the quality of education is widely thought to be inadequate in developing countries. Quality-enhancing expenditures could yield economic benefits higher than those from expansion. These two aspects of educational provision compete for limited resources, and it is not obvious that a rational choice will be made between them. It seems to be the case, for instance, that the rapid expansion of subsidized education in response to popular demand, by squeezing the resources available per pupil, has reduced educational quality in many developing countries. John Oxenham and his colleagues, in Chapter 5, survey the evidence on the quality of education in seven selected developing countires, using Japan as a comparator. They examine the quality of inputs – learners, teachers, materials and support systems – and show how poverty itself can stunt the learning process in various ways. They stress the importance of incentive systems for pupils and teachers, and illustrate this by analyzing the effects on the quality of learning or teaching of examination systems, accountability to parents, remuneration, adequate education materials, and a competing private system. Qualitative aspects of education deserve more economic analysis than they have generally received, and this paper helps to prepare the ground.

One of the ingredients of human development, less tangible than formal education yet crucial to industrialization, is the learning of industrial skills in a broad-based process of training, experience, foreign technology transfer and deliberate search and research. In Chapter 6 Sanjaya Lall explores this process, illustrating from the experience of Sub-Saharan Africa, a region of limited industrialization and disappointing industrial progress. What distinguishes Africa from other regions in this respect, he argues, is the relatively small stock of human

4

skills and "industrial capabilities", i.e. the entrepreneurial, organizational and technological capabilities needed for industrialization. Neither physical investment nor "getting prices right" will be sufficient given the shortage of industrial capabilities. The process of learning is a slow but cumulative one, and the "learning curve" can be compressed by attracting or buying foreign capabilities, both to fill gaps and to teach local personnel. Other policies to speed up indigenous learning would include additional formal education to provide general and technical skills, the creation of a pool of technicians who can go into small-scale entrepreneurial activities, help for small enterprises to upgrade their industrial capabilities, fiscal incentives for firms to provide training, and the initial avoidance of industries that use skill-intensive and complex technologies.

Investments in health care and nutritional improvement are no less investments in human resource development than is education. In Chapter 7 Andrea Cornia presents evidence that real health expenditure declined in the 1980s in many developing countries, particularly in Latin America and Africa. This is reflected in the latest information on infant mortality and malnutrition, despite the improvements of previous decades. Yet the evidence he presents suggests that it is now possible to reduce infant and child mortality, and to improve nutrition, through a series of primary health care measures. Pregnancy management programmes, oral rehydration therapy, immunization, essential drugs, water supply programmes, and nutritional interventions such as food fortification or supplementation, can be supplied to the poor at low cost. Technological breakthroughs have reduced the cost of such measures, and the targeting of interventions on the poor now seems feasible. The beneficial short- and long-term effects on production and on curative medical expenditure may well justify these expenditures, quite apart from their effects on personal well-being and poverty alleviation. Cornia recommends a redistribution of resources from high-cost curative to low-cost preventive health care, in which international agencies can play a role.

The straightened circumstances and reduced availability of external resources in developing countries now require them to place greater emphasis on local resources for promoting development. Jacques Gaude and Steve Miller, in Chapter 8, examine ways and means of harnessing local resources – both human capacities and physical inputs – for the creation of rural infrastructure. They concentrate on the use of special public works programmes introduced over the last decade in a number of countries – analyzing forestry schemes in three countries and irrigation schemes in two others. These programmes have the advantages of being labour-intensive and of redistributing income to the poor. The authors find that the successful projects among those studied had several characteristics in common. They were well prepared, involving preliminary studies and local collaboration; they started small, expanding gradually as they succeeded; and they strengthened local institutions, so encouraging local initiative and sustainability. The social rate of return on these projects is difficult to measure as they are recent, still at the pilot stage, and produce longer-term, often intangible, benefits (e.g. environmental improvements, institution building, and demonstration effects), mainly for the rural poor. The authors nevertheless view the successful and sustainable projects as models to be widely emulated.

"Participation" is both a means and an objective of development. In the final chapter Dharam Ghai explains the various possible meanings of participation, and illustrates the participatory approach to development through a study of selective grass-roots group activities in a few Asian and African countries. All aimed at the poor, these take the form of promoting participation through credit programmes, organizing women working in rural slums into trade union-type trade associations, organizing peasant groups to undertake collective initiatives and struggle for their rights, and mobilizing labour and other resources through self-help and mutual-aid initiatives. The study concentrates on success stories, analyzing what can be done and why some schemes succeed rather than why other schemes fail. Nevertheless, the success of these initiatives leads Ghai to present them as models not only for achieving economic development but also for fostering self-reliance, promoting equality, increasing collective strength and enhancing human potential among the poor.

Taken as a whole these nine chapters contain an overview of human resource development. The broad conclusions are clear: human resources have been neglected in many countries, and not only in poor ones; well directed expenditure on human resource development can help to accelerate the growth of output, reduce inequality and alleviate poverty; and above all, by raising the capabilities of people, human development in the final analysis is close to what development is all about. It seemed for a time that we were in danger of losing sight of the obvious fact that people are both the means of development and the end of development. We hope, with the publication of this volume, to put this simple truism back into focus.

NOTES

[1] The Committee for Development Planning Report, 1988, *Human Resources Development: A Neglected Dimension of Development Strategy*, United Nations, Department of International Economic and Social Affairs, New York, 1988, Ch. III.
[2] United Nations (1989). *Journal of Development Planning*, No. 19. Sales No. E.89.II.A.2.
[3] The Committee for Development Planning Report 1989, *Elements of an International Development Strategy for the 1990s*, United Nations, Department of International Economic and Social Affairs, New York, 1989, Ch. III.
[4] Indeed human development has already been the topic of a major international conference, namely, the North South Roundtable on "Human Development: Goals and Strategies for the Year 2000", Amman, Jordan, 3–5 September 1988. The conference

papers were published as Khadija Haq and Uner Kirdar, eds., *Development for People: Goals and Strategies for the Year 2000*, North South Roundtable and UNDP, 1989.

[5] The "basic needs approach" came to prominence during the 1976 World Employment Conference in Geneva. See International Labour Organisation (ILO), *Employment, Growth and Basic Needs*, Geneva, 1976.

1

HUMAN DEVELOPMENT: THE CASE FOR RENEWED EMPHASIS

Keith Griffin* and John Knight**

CONTENTS

Human development

The process of economic development can be seen as a process of expanding the capabilities of people.[1] The ultimate focus of economic development is human development. That is, we are ultimately concerned with what people are capable of doing or being. Can they live long? Can they be well nourished? Can they escape avoidable illness? Can they obtain dignity and self-respect? Are they able to read and write and communicate and develop their minds?

According to this view, development is concerned with much more than expanding the supplies of commodities.[2] The enhancement of capabilities often requires changing technologies, institutions and social values so that the creativity within human beings can be unblocked. This, in turn, results in economic growth, but growth of gross domestic product (GDP) is not the same thing as an expansion of capabilities. The two are, of course, linked but they are not identical.

Economic growth can be seen as a means to the end of enhancing people's capabilities. Yet, economists traditionally have concentrated on the production of goods and services and on its rate of growth.

*Chairman, Department of Economics, University of California at Riverside.
**Senior Research Officer, Oxford University Institute of Economics and Statistics; Fellow of St. Edmund Hall, Oxford.

Increased physical output, in turn, has been assumed to give rise to greater economic welfare.

More recently, it is true, greater emphasis has been placed on the distribution of goods among people and on considerations of need and equity. The philosopher John Rawls defined deprivation in terms of the availability of "primary goods" or "things it is supposed a rational man wants whatever else he wants",[3] and the International Labour Organisation attempted to translate the concept into operational terms with its advocacy of "basic needs".[4] Basic needs, however, remains a goods-oriented view of development, whereas what is wanted is a view that puts people first.

This is the great merit of the human capabilities approach, pioneered by Amartya Sen.[5] The connection between goods and capabilities can readily be illustrated. A bicycle, for instance, is a good; by providing transport, it gives a person the capability of moving from one place to another. It is the concept of capabilities that comes closest to our notion of the standard of living and, more generally, to our notion of development. Goods may provide the basis for a high standard of living, but they are not in themselves constituents of it. A person's standard of living has some components that his money cannot buy. An illiterate person in poor health would not enjoy the same capabilities, and thus the same standard of living, as an otherwise identical person, not only because he would be likely to have a lower income but also because literacy and health directly affect capabilities.

Although there is some relationship between income per capita and human well-being, as the term is commonly understood, the statistical association is not close and divergences from the general tendency are at least as striking as the general tendency itself.[6] Human fulfilment is about whether people live or die, whether people eat well, are malnourished or starve, whether women lead healthy and tolerable lives or are burdened with annual childbearing, a high risk of maternal mortality, the certainty of life-long drudgery, whether people can control their lives at work, whether their conditions of work are tough and unpleasant, whether people have access to work at all, whether people control their political lives, whether they have the education to be full members of society with some control over their destiny. These are all aspects of the standard of living—but only loosely included or not included at all in the measure of GNP per capita.

Any approach that puts people first must come to terms with the fact that in the third world the average age of the population is low, although it is tending to rise slowly. In 1980 in the developing countries as a whole, 39.1 per cent of the population were less than 15 years of age as compared to 23.1 per cent in the developed countries. Conversely, only 4.0 per cent of the population of the third world is over 65 years, whereas in the developed countries 11.3 per cent of the population is older than 65.[7] Thus, human development in the third world is necessarily concerned in large part with enhancing the capabilities of the young.

It is natural to inquire whether economic growth during the past two decades has been accompanied by increased human capabilities. Certainly there has been growth: in no group of countries did per capita income fail to rise during the period 1965-1985. (see table 1). Some groups of countries did much better than others, however. The developing countries as a whole grew faster, than the industrial market economies (3.0 per cent a year compared to 2.4 per cent a year). But within the third world there was a tendency for the poorest countries to fall relatively further behind the less poor. Thus, GNP per capital in the middle-income economies increased 3.0 per cent a year, whereas in India the rate of growth of income per capita was 1.7 per cent and in the "other low-income countries" only 0.4 per cent. China, where GNP per capita increased 4.8 per cent a year, was the great exception. Among the middle-income countries, East Asia did much better than Latin America. As shown below, human capabilities increased relatively most rapidly in both China and East Asia.

TABLE 1. GROWTH OF GNP PER CAPITA, 1965-1985
(Annual percentage)

Low-income economies	2.9
China	4.8
India	1.7
Other low-income	0.4
Middle-income economies	3.0
Lower middle-income	2.6
Upper middle-income	3.3
High-income oil exporters	2.7
Industrial market economies	2.4

Source: World Bank, *World Development Report 1987* (Oxford, Oxford University Press, 1987).

The general rise in average incomes could be a misleading guide to the income gains of the poor. In some countries, including large ones, the incidence of poverty remains high. This often is due in part to a high and even rising degree of inequality in the distribution of income. A large number of cross-sectional studies of countries have been undertaken and these have been used to provide support for the hypothesis of growing inequality.[8] Moreover, a number of studies of individual countries, based on time-series data, have shown that inequality was increased along with a rise in average incomes. Indeed, some authors have attempted to show that not only has inequality increased but that in some countries for quite long periods

11

the absolute standard of living of some sections of the poor has declined.[9] It cannot be assumed, therefore, that the basic human capabilities have risen to the same extent as average incomes.

The debate today is not over whether inequality within countries has increased but whether increased inequality is inevitable. The balance of recent evidence suggests that the degree of inequality is not closely related to the level of income per capita, as was once thought, but to factors dependent upon the strategy of development that is followed. These factors include the distribution of productive assets (particularly land), the distribution of educational opportunities, the employment intensity of the development path and the general policy stance of Government. It is possible, therefore, for Governments successfully to pursue distributive equity objectives as well as growth objectives. Similarly, Governments have it within their power to promote the enhancement of human capabilities by means of their education, health, nutrition, participation and other policies. Moreover, the twin objectives of distributive equity and human development will often involve the same policies.

Taking a long view, there is no doubt that the basic human capabilities have indeed increased in the third world. Perhaps the best indicator of this is the increase in life expectancy at birth since around 1950. In the poorest countries, life expectancy at mid-century was between 30 and 40 years; today it is at least 50 years in most countries and rises to 70 or more for females in such countries as China, Malaysia, Sri Lanka, Chile and Argentina.

The data on infant mortality tell a similar story to that of life expectancy. There has been a long-run decline everywhere and in some countries the decline has been dramatic, with the rate falling by 50 per cent or more. This is true in Latin America for Argentina, Chile and Colombia and in Asia for China, Malaysia, the Philippines and Sri Lanka. However, infant mortality rates remain very high, that is, above 100 per 1,000 infants less than one year old, in Bangladesh, Pakistan, the United Republic of Tanzania and Cote d'Ivoire. As with life expectancy, there is only a weak correspondence between infant mortality rates and per capita incomes.

Data on life expectancy and infant mortality for the period 1965 to 1985 are included in table 2. Figures I and II show similar movements since 1955, but by region, in life expectancy and infant mortality, respectively. The long-run improvements in both indexes are apparent for all regions. However, as with income, averages may overstate somewhat the gains to the poor whose access to health services is marginal in many countries. There is considerable evidence that health delivery systems (oriented towards hospital-based, high-technology, specialized services) provide limited population coverage and contribute to an unequal distribution of health services.

TABLE 2. LIFE EXPECTANCY, INFANT MORTALITY AND GNP PER CAPITA

| | Life expectancy at birth (years) | | | | Infant mortality (deaths per 1,000 aged under one year) | | GNP per capita (US dollars) |
| | Male | | Female | | | | |
	1965	1985	1965	1985	1965	1985	1985
Low-income countries	47	60	50	61	127	72	270
India	46	57	44	56	151	89	270
China	54	68	55	70	90	35	310
Other low-income	44	51	45	53	150	112	200
Middle-income countries	53	60	56	64	104	68	1 290
Lower middle-income	47	56	50	60	132	82	820
Upper middle-income	58	64	62	69	84	52	1 850
High-income oil exporters	48	61	51	65	115	61	9 800
Industrial market economies	68	73	74	79	23	9	11 810

Source: World Bank, *World Development Report 1987* (Oxford, Oxford University Press, 1987).

Turning now to primary education, it is evident that this is one of the great success stories of the third world, at least in quantitative terms (see table 3). It is less certain that there have been improvements in the quality of education. School enrolments have expanded rapidly in the past 20 years and in most countries primary education for boys is universal or nearly so. The position of girls is less good, but even so, in over half the countries more than 90 per cent of girls attend primary school, although they are less likely than boys to complete their primary education. Less favourable treatment in educating young girls continues to be a problem, especially in Pakistan (where twice as many boys as girls attend school) but also in India, Bangladesh, Egypt and Côte d'Ivoire. Although illiteracy rates still are more than 52 per cent in Africa and South Asia, one can anticipate that they will continue to fall as the proportion of the population with a primary school education rises. None the less, the absolute number of illiterate persons will probably increase for years to come.

TABLE 3. PRIMARY AND SECONDARY SCHOOL ENROLMENT RATIOS
(Percentage of age group)

| | Primary | | Secondary | |
	1965	1984	1965	1984
Low-income countries	74	97	21	32
India	74	90	27	34
China	89	118	24	37
Other low-income	44	70	9	23
Middle-income countries	85	104	22	47
Lower middle-income	75	103	16	40
Upper middle-income	96	105	29	56
High-income oil exporters	43	75	10	45
Industrial market economies	107	102	63	90

Source: World Bank, *World Development Report 1987* (Oxford, Oxford University Press, 1987).

13

Figure I.

Life Expectancy

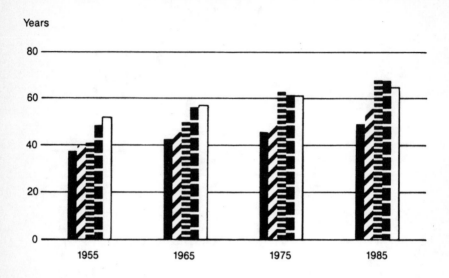

Figure II.
Infant mortality
Deaths per 1,000 live births

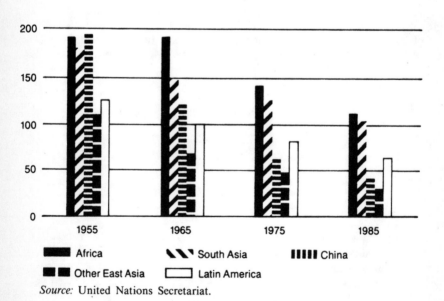

Source: United Nations Secretariat.

14

Secondary education has also grown rapidly, although often from a small base (see table 3). Still, between one third and two thirds of the relevant age group attends a secondary school in most third world countries, including the two largest, India and China. The third largest—Indonesia—has expanded its secondary school system rapidly and has overtaken the two Asian giants. Serious shortcomings remain in Pakistan and Bangladesh (where expansion of the system has been slow) and in sub-Saharan Africa (where, apart from the United Republic of Tanzania, expansion has been fast). Given the difficulties encountered in Asia and Africa at the time of independence, progress in secondary education has been remarkable.

Thus, the indicators suggest that there has been a long-term increase in human capabilities in the third world. The growth not only in output but also in capabilities reflects the application by society of cumulative collective knowledge. Never before has the stock of knowledge in the world increased so rapidly or been so widely disseminated as it has in the past 40 or 50 years. None the less, world-wide access to science and technology is unequal. The diversity of the world's languages is a source of enrichment and cultural plurality and within many countries language is a unifying force. But within some countries linguistic heterogeneity is a source of disunity and conflict and between countries language can act as a barrier restricting access of hundreds of millions of people to world knowledge. Yet, the barriers are slowly being overcome, not least because language teaching has greatly increased the number of people who can speak more than one language.

Nationally and internationally there have been dramatic changes in the ways information and culture are transmitted. There was a time in human history when most education occurred within the family. Gradually, however, the transmission of knowledge became institutionalized, first within the church and other religious organizations and later within state schools and, to a lesser extent, private schools. More recently, superimposed on these inherited means of spreading knowledge, information and cultural values, the mass media have become increasingly prominent. Both deliberately and unintentionally, in both formal and informal ways, the mass media now exercise an enormous influence over what people know, how people interpret and understand the world and what values people adopt and act upon.

Human development in the current economic context

We have seen that, viewed in long-term perspective, there has been remarkable progress in human development in the third world. Recent short-term developments, however, have been unfavourable and in some countries a full-scale crisis has emerged. The most

15

obvious sign of crisis is the dramatic slowing down in the rate of growth of per capita GDP between the last half of the 1970s and the present. The deceleration of growth occurred in all regions of the third world (excluding China), and in every region, except South Asia and East Asia, average incomes fell markedly (see table 4).

TABLE 4. RATE OF GROWTH OF GDP PER CAPITA, 1976-1987
(Annual percentage)

	1976-1980	*1981-1985*	*1986*	*1987*
Africa	1.9	−3.5	−4.9	−2.6
Latin America	2.8	−1.8	1.6	0.4
Western Asia	0.8	−3.9	−0.3	−3.9
South Asia and East Asia	4.1	2.9	3.2	2.7

Source: Department of International Economic and Social Affairs, United Nations Secretariat.

Parallel to the decline in growth rates has been a fall in the rate of growth of the productivity of labour. The phenomenon is widespread throughout Asia, Africa and Latin America and, indeed, in Africa and Latin America, the average level of productivity declined, not just the rate of growth of productivity. During the period 1980-1985, the average productivity of labour declined 1.5 per cent a year in Africa and 2.7 per cent a year in Latin America.[10] This reflects the fact that in Africa and Latin America total output increased less rapidly than the size of the labour force, and in Latin America total output actually declined. A reduction in value added per employed worker is, of course, desirable in a period of recession in so far as it allows large numbers of people to continue to secure a livelihood rather than become openly unemployed. On the other hand, a fall in output per person-year inevitably puts downward pressure on the real wages and incomes of those who remain in employment and on the level of profits (and hence on investment and long-term growth of output and employment).

In practice, rates of urban unemployment in the major cities of Latin America tended to rise (see table 5) and non-agricultural real

TABLE 5. OPEN URBAN UNEMPLOYMENT, 1970-1986
(Percentage)

	1970	*1980*	*1986*
Argentina	4.9	2.9	5.2
Brazil	6.5	6.2	3.6
Chile	4.1	11.7	13.1
Colombia	10.6	9.7	13.8
Mexico	7.0	4.5	4.8
Peru	8.3	10.9	11.8
Venezuela	7.8	6.6	11.8

Source: International Labour Organisation, *Overview of the Employment Situation in the World* (Geneva, November 1987), table 9, p. 39.

16

wages in Africa and parts of Latin America tended to fall (see table 6). In Latin America and the Caribbean the rate of open urban unemployment rose from 6.8 per cent in 1970, to 7.1 per cent in 1980, to an estimated 10.3 per cent in 1986. In some countries, of course, unemployment rates were considerably higher than this, for example, in Colombia, Chile, Peru and Venezuela.

TABLE 6. REAL WAGES IN NON-AGRICULTURAL ACTIVITIES
(*Index: 1980 = 100*)

	Year	Index
Africa		
Kenya	1985	78
Malawi	1984	76
United Republic of Tanzania ..	1983	60
Zambia	1984	67
Zimbabwe	1984	89
Latin America[a]		
Argentina	1986	103.5
Brazil	1986	112.8
Chile	1986	91.9
Colombia	1986	116.5
Mexico	1986	66.1
Peru	1986	65.5
Venezuela	1985	104.6

Source: International Labour Organisation, *Background Document,* High-level Meeting on Employment and Structural Adjustment, Geneva, November 1987, tables 9 and 10, pp. 28 and 32.
[a]The data refer to wages in industry.

In Chile, real industrial wages in 1986 were 7.9 per cent lower than they had been in 1980. In Mexico, the fall was 33.9 per cent and in Peru, 34.5 per cent. The situation in parts of Africa was equally as bad. In Kenya, for example, real non-agricultural wages in 1985 were 22 per cent lower than they had been in 1980, whereas in the United Republic of Tanzania in 1983 the fall was 40 per cent.

Slow growth, declining productivity, rising unemployment and falling real wages and average incomes have resulted in increased poverty and an acceleration in the number of hungry people in the world. According to the World Food Council, between 1970 and 1980, hunger grew by 15 million people, or an average of 1.5 million people a year. The first half of the 1980s added almost 40 million hungry people, or close to 8 million per year—a fivefold increase in the average annual growth rate.[11] The absolute number of undernourished people increased in every region of the third world, but only in Africa did the proportion of undernourished people rise, namely, from 29 per cent in 1979-1981 to 32 per cent in 1983-1985.[12] Changes in nutrition deficiency during the period 1971 to 1985, using data and standards from the Food and Agriculture Organization of the United Nations (FAO), are presented in figure III.

Problems of environmental, ecological and political deterioration exacerbate the long-term economic problem in some parts of the third world. In the Sahel, the Himalayas and the Andes, economic

Figure III.

Nutrition deficiency
Calorie intake below 1.2 BMR threshold

Population (per cent)

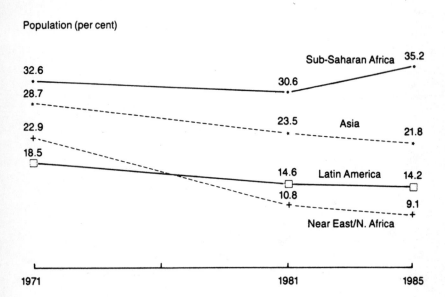

Source: Food and Agriculture Organization of the United Nations.

progress is hampered by desertification or erosion, partly the result of climatic change and partly of population pressure. In other areas, deforestation is upsetting the ecological balance, to the detriment of poor people. In many developing countries, war and political instability exacerbate the poverty problem by withdrawing confidence in the currency, diverting scarce resources, destroying assets, disrupting assistance programmes and sapping incentives and motivation at family and community levels.

The world economy has evidently undergone a profound change in recent years. This change was not planned and in fact has been highly disorderly. World financial markets expanded rapidly for several years and then collapsed in October 1987; remedial measures have brought with them the threat of economic recession; exchange rates have been unstable and have moved in unpredictable ways. These changes have had disruptive consequences for economic progress and have inflicted severe damage on the real economies of many third world countries.

It is important to recognize that the current economic crisis is policy induced. It is not an arbitrary act of nature but a consequence of changes in economic philosophy and in government policies. The policies introduced during the past decade reflect both a revised view of the proper role of the State and changed governmental preferences as between inflation and a higher level of economic activity.

The debt crisis is yet another manifestation of massive world economic imbalances. By 1985 a number of third world countries were deeply in debt to the international banking system and multilateral financial institutions. In absolute terms the largest third world debtors were Brazil ($106.7 billion), Mexico ($97.4 billion), Argentina ($48.4 billion), the Republic of Korea ($48 billion) and Indonesia ($35.8 billion).[13] In per capita terms, however, a great many other countries have very large external borrowings and have

TABLE 7. PER CAPITA INCOME AND PER CAPITA EXTERNAL INDEBTEDNESS
IN 25 COUNTRIES, 1985
(US dollars)

	Per capita GNP	Per capita external debt
Ethiopia	110	44.2
Bangladesh	150	64.9
Mali	150	195.9
Niger	250	180.5
India	270	46.3
Kenya	290	206.8
United Republic of Tanzania	290	162.6
Senegal	370	271.8
Pakistan	380	132.0
Zambia	390	669.1
Bolivia	470	620.6
Indonesia	530	220.5
Philippines	580	478.7
Egypt	610	501.9
Côte d'Ivoire	660	836.2
Zimbabwe	680	255.1
Nigeria	800	184.0
Peru	1 010	735.9
Colombia	1 320	494.5
Chile	1 430	1 671.2
Brazil	1 640	787.1
Mexico	2 080	1 236.4
Argentina	2 130	1 588.3
Republic of Korea	2 150	1 854.3

Source: World Bank, *World Development Report 1987* (Oxford, Oxford University Press, 1987).

been having enormous difficulties servicing their debts. (see table 7). In Mali, Senegal, Zambia, Bolivia, Cote d'Ivoire and Chile, the per capita external debt is greater than the per capita income and in a number of other countries per capita external debt is more than half as large as per capita GNP. Already, several countries have had to suspend payments of interest on the debt and postpone repayment of capital.

The banks find themselves in the position of having to make greater provision in their balance sheets for bad debts, while extending additional loans to the third world so that at least some of the interest can be repaid. The time may come when both creditors and debtors recognize that an orderly programme of debt forgiveness would be to everyone's advantage. Meanwhile, the developing countries have become net suppliers of resources to the rich countries. In 1980 the capital-importing developing countries received a net transfer from the rest of the world of $39.4 billion, but by 1985 resources were flowing in the opposite direction and these developing countries transferred $31 billion to the rich countries.[14]

Many Governments have been forced by an outflow of resources to cut investment, reduce public expenditure and impose a deflationary contraction on the economy. At the same time, in order to service at least part of the debt, attempts have been made to shift resources in favour of the export sectors. This process is described as structural adjustment. It also reflects the need for long-term development strategies that do not assume substantial resource inflows in the future.

Structural adjustment has forced Governments to reveal their expenditure priorities and, unfortunately, many Governments have shown that, in practice, human development receives very low priority. Indeed, in many countries, central government outlays on the social sectors have decreased relative to total government expenditure and in real per capita terms. Education and health have been particularly hard hit. In contrast, the proportion of central government expenditures on general public administration has risen between 1972 and 1985 from 36 to 39 per cent in the low-income countries, from 24 to 36 per cent in the lower middle-income countries and from 18 to 32 per cent in the upper middle-income countries. Some data for selected countries are presented in table 8.

In each of the three groups of countries included in table 8, central government expenditure on education and health in 1985 was proportionately lower then it was in 1972. In the low-income countries, for example, education accounted for 13.2 per cent of central government expenditure in 1972 but only 7.6 per cent in 1985; health accounted for 4.9 per cent in 1972 but only 3.7 per cent in 1985. Expenditure on defence, in contrast, actually rose, from 17.2 per cent of government expenditure in 1972 to 18.6 per cent in 1985. That is, in the latter year, expenditure on the military in the poorest

TABLE 8. CENTRAL GOVERNMENT EXPENDITURE ON EDUCATION AND HEALTH AS PERCENTAGE OF TOTAL GOVERNMENT EXPENDITURE

	Education		Health		Public administration	
	1972	1985	1972	1985	1972	1985
Low-income countries, of which	13.2	7.6	4.9	3.7	36.2	39.1
Burkina Faso	20.6	16.9	8.2	5.5	37.6	37.9
Malawi	15.8	12.3	5.5	7.9	36.7	36.4
Zaire	15.2	0.8	2.3	1.8	56.1	86.2
Kenya	21.9	19.8	7.9	6.7	30.2	35.3
United Republic of Tanzania	17.3	7.2	7.2	4.9	22.6	48.6
Sri Lanka	13.0	6.4	6.4	3.6	37.7	66.2
Lower middle-income countries, of which	16.4	13.8	5.2	3.8	24.0	36.1
Bolivia	31.3	12.2	6.2	1.5	31.2	70.2
Indonesia	7.4	11.3	1.4	2.5	41.2	33.9
Turkey	18.1	10.0	3.2	1.8	18.3	54.1
Tunisia	30.5	14.3	7.4	6.5	25.1	25.7
Chile	20.0	13.2	10.0	6.1	20.0	18.4
Upper middle-income countries, of which	12.3	10.6	7.9	4.6	18.3	32.3
Brazil	8.3	3.2	6.7	7.6	18.3	38.0
Mexico	16.4	12.4	5.1	1.5	15.2	44.4
Argentina	20.0	9.5	0.0	1.8	20.0	21.3
Venezuela	18.6	17.7	11.7	7.6	24.8	31.1

Source: World Bank, World Development Report 1987 (Oxford, Oxford University Press, 1987).
NOTE: Public administration covers expenditure on the general administration of government not included in other categories of economic and social services. Especially in large countries, where lower levels of government have considerable autonomy and are responsible for many social services, central government expenditure on education and health may account for only a small fraction of the total.

countries of the world was nearly 65 per cent higher than spending on education and health combined.

In the low-income countries the share of education in central government expenditure fell 42.4 per cent between 1972 and 1985, whereas the share of health fell 20.4 per cent. The pattern of cuts was reversed in the middle-income countries: in the lower middle-income countries the share of education declined 15.9 per cent compared to a cut of 26.9 per cent in health expenditure, and in the upper middle-income countries there were cuts in shares of 13.8 per cent and 41.8 per cent in education and health, respectively.

The share of education fell in six of the seven low-income countries selected for the table. Indeed, in Zaire, government expenditure on education virtually ceased. The situation regarding health expenditure was as bad or, considering the initial conditions, even worse. In most third world countries, government expenditure on health services was low even in 1972. By 1985 the share of health in total public expenditure had fallen in each of the groups of countries and in almost all the countries listed.

21

Overall, then, the picture is not encouraging. There seems to be a clear bias within the political system towards a reduction of public expenditure on human development in times of distress. This possibly reflects underlying changes in currents of thought about the appropriate role of Government, as mentioned earlier. This change in economic philosophy appears to have originated in the advanced industrial economies, particularly in the United States of America, the Federal Republic of Germany and the United Kingdom of Great Britain and Northern Ireland, and to have spread from there to many developing countries. However, in addition to the change in currents of thought, the reduction in expenditure on human development appears to have been a short-run and, as we shall see, a short-sighted response to the series of crises in which Governments found themselves. Given the need for structural adjustment, many Governments considered it was easier or more expedient to reduce expenditure on human development than on other items in the central government's budget.

The situation, however, is not altogether bleak. Indeed, there has been continued improvement in countries that have been able to maintain economic growth and avoid the worst impact of the 1980s recession. The above average performance of the South Asian and East Asian countries of 2.7 per cent GDP growth per capita per year during the period 1981-1985 was accompanied by continuing progress, and even some acceleration, in health and nutritional trends. Sectoral policies emphasizing the need for accelerating agricultural production in formerly food-importing countries and for expanding low-cost, wide-coverage programmes in health, nutrition and water supply have been important contributory factors.

Moreover, several countries in Africa, other parts of Asia and Latin America have been able to sustain expenditure on human development even while implementing structural adjustment programmes. For instance, targeted programmes in the area of child health and nutrition throughout the 1970s and early 1980s enabled Chile to achieve a continuous decline in infant and child mortality despite serious economic fluctuations; an example of a successful sectoral programme during adjustment was the drought relief programme in Botswana, backed up by a comprehensive system of monitoring nutritional status.[15] Indonesia is one of the countries that managed to expand expenditure on education and health as a proportion of total government expenditure, from 8.8 per cent in 1972 to 13.8 per cent in 1985. (see table 8).

There are policy choices to be made; there are a number of alternative responses open to Governments. Even in times of economic crisis and reduced public resources, Governments can make the following choices:

(a) A reduction in the quantity of services provided, for example, by curtailing the volume of food distributed through public channels such as food-for-work programmes or government-owned ration shops;

(*b*) A deterioration in the quality of services provided, for example, by allowing teacher-pupil ratios to fall sharply or, because of foreign exchange shortages, by reducing expenditure on school textbooks;

(*c*) Reducing inefficiency within the public services, for example, by eliminating the wasteful use of construction materials or by inviting suppliers to tender bids;

(*d*) An improvement in targeting to favour the poor, for example, by switching health expenditure from large urban hospitals to rural clinics or by reallocating educational expenditure from university to primary education;

(*e*) Greater cost recovery of publicly provided services, for example, by introducing tuition fees for university studies (combined with scholarships for the poor) or by charging for certain types of medical care.

In our view, the objectives of policy during periods of structural adjustment should be to safeguard human development programmes whenever possible and, if curtailment of public expenditure is unavoidable, to ensure that the burdens of adjustment are borne by those most able to do so. In many third world countries the opposite has occurred: human development programmes have been savagely cut and the brunt of the adjustment has fallen on the poor. This has weakened long-run prospects for development, while increasing inequality and poverty. It would instead have been much better to restructure human development programmes, to reduce inefficiency, to improve targeting and, where necessary, to maintain the existing level of services, to introduce discriminatory user charges. The case for this approach will be made at greater length below.

Development of human capabilities: scope and definitions

The development of human capabilities should be seen not as an objective with a definitive end-point but as a process continuing in time without end. It is an approach to overall development that puts the well-being of people first and that regards human beings simultaneously as both means and ends of social and economic policy. It is not, of course, a formula that can be applied mechanically, but it does contain ingredients that distinguish it from commodity-centred approaches to development. It places considerable emphasis on local resource mobilization as a way of allowing people to develop their capabilities and on participation as an agent of constructive change.

In many third world countries, Government is highly centralized and authoritarian. The people often are relegated to the status of subjects and come to fear and distrust Government. Particularly in rural areas, and above all among the poor, government officials are seen more as coercive than as persuasive agents. Thus, the relationship between the State and the majority of the people is not conducive to the mobilization of large numbers of people for development. At the very least, a strategy that gives priority to the development of human capabilities requires decentralized administration to the local level and administration at that level by officials who enjoy the confidence and support of the great majority of the population.

Beyond this is the need to organize the population so that it can participate in its own development. Participation, or the opportunity to participate if one wishes, is, of course, an end in itself, but participation also has a number of instrumental values that make it attractive to a process of human development. First, participation in representative community-based organizations can help to identify local priorities, to determine which needs are essential or basic and which are of secondary importance, and to define the content of development programmes and projects so that they reflect accurately local needs, aspirations and demands. Next, having identified priorities and designed the programmes that incorporate them, participation in functional organizations (service co-operatives, land reform committees, irrigation societies, women's groups) can be used to mobilize support for national and local policies and programmes and local projects. Lastly, participation can be used to reduce the cost of public services and investment projects by shifting responsibility from central and local government (where costs tend to be relatively high) to the grass-roots organizations (where costs can be low). In some cases, for example, it may be possible to organize the beneficiaries of an investment project and persuade them to contribute their labour voluntarily to help defray construction costs. In other cases some of the public services (clinics, nursery schools) can be organized, staffed and run by local groups rather than by relatively highly paid civil servants brought in from outside. Thus, in an appropriate context, participation can flourish and in so doing contribute much to development.

The instrumental value of participation and human development is not limited to the economic sphere; they also are of value in other spheres of life. There is, for example, a political dimension to human development. If formal democracy is not to be an empty shell, then people must have an education and information so that all groups in society are aware of the issues facing the country and can participate effectively in the political process.

Human development is of intrinsic value too. In some respects the development of human capabilities is increasingly regarded as a right to which all people are entitled. This right, in many societies, includes the ability to read and write, access to basic health care and

24

freedom from starvation. In addition, certain aspects of human development are akin to consumption goods in the sense that they are sources of satisfaction or pleasure. Education is desired in part for its own sake; employment, too, provides direct satisfaction by giving a person the recognition of being engaged in something worth his while;[16] and a clean and healthy environment can be a source of aesthetic pleasure.

We are particularly concerned, however, with the ability of human development expenditure to increase the productive capacity of an economy and raise the level of material prosperity. There are several ways it can do this.[17] First, human development expenditure can raise the physical, mental and cognitive skills of the population through education and training. Secondly, public policy that focuses on human development can assist in the efficient deployment and full utilization of knowledge and skills; it can increase entrepreneurial and managerial capabilities, and it can transform theoretical knowledge into applied technology through research and development programmes. Thirdly, public policy can establish an institutional framework that enhances incentives, removes impediments to resource mobility and resource mobilization and increases participation in decision-making, which, in turn, can help to improve economic efficiency.[18]

Many programmes could be classified as human development programmes, but in the discussion below we shall restrict consideration to three broad categories: education and training; health services, water supply and sanitation; and food security and nutrition policies. It must be stressed, however, that although these programmes can be listed separately there are in fact a great many complementarities among them.

For example, a programme of school meals, intended to improve the nutrition of young people, often leads to reduced school drop-out rates and hence to an increase in the quality of the education system. Similarly, reduced infant mortality rates combined with greater education for women and greater non-farm employment opportunities for women are associated with lower fertility rates and a lower rate of increase of the population.[19] Women, indeed, play a key role in human development not only because they account for half or more of the total population but also because they have a major responsibility in most societies for ensuring adequate nutrition for the family, caring for the sick and educating the young before they enter the formal education system. In addition, recent research has shown that the weight at birth and the subsequent development of young children are affected by the state of health of the mother during pregnancy. Hence, there is complementarity between the health of the mother and that of the child.

In most developing countries women have substantially less access to education, to jobs, to income and to power than men.

25

Women's levels of health and nutrition are often inferior to men's. Women generally account for the largest proportion of deprived people. The improvement of human capabilities requires in particular that the capabilities of women be improved. In some countries attitudes and customs will have to change; Governments can play a role in this process, for example, through programmes directed at women.

Employment, too, is complementary to many human development programmes. Employment evidently requires and is dependent upon skills being present in the labour force. But employment also generates skills in a process of learning by doing and, conversely, lack of employment can easily lead to the loss of skills. Unemployment represents not only a loss of potential output in the present, but by destroying skills, it represents a loss of future output as well.

In countries where unemployment is high, perhaps because of the way structural adjustment policies have been implemented, there may be scope for the direct mobilization of labour on capital formation projects. Underutilized human resources in the form of unemployed labour can sometimes be transformed into investment which can help to sustain long-run economic growth. Labour-intensive construction projects can be used to expand irrigation facilities, to create reservoirs and sources of safe water, to provide dirt farm-to-market roads, to undertake field terracing, anti-erosion works and tree planting projects, and to build schools, clinics and community centres.[20] In principle, such programmes have the capacity to mobilize local resources that might otherwise remain unused and thereby raise the level of output and the rate of growth. Moreover, if they are properly administered, they do this by creating sources of income, in the form of employment, for some of the poorest members of society and thereby lead to a redistribution of income in favour of those most in need. In this way the creation of employment can lead directly to an enhancement of human capabilities.

Human capital formation, physical investment and economic growth

Expenditures on improving human capabilities have the potential to yield a return to society no less than the return from physical capital formation. Take the example of education. The standard technique for determining priorities for educational expenditure is social rate of return analysis. Some broad conclusions can be drawn from the many studies on this question that have been conducted in developing countries (see table 9). First, the private rate of return to all levels of education is normally extremely high, reflecting in part the government subsidization of education. These high private rates of return help to explain the strength of private demand and of political pressure for education, which in turn have contributed to its

TABLE 9. RETURNS TO INVESTMENT IN EDUCATION, BY REGION, TYPE AND LEVEL

Number of countries reporting	Region	Social			Private		
		Primary	Secondary	Tertiary	Primary	Secondary	Tertiary
16. . .	Africa	28	17	13	43	26	32
10. . .	Asia	27	15	13	31	15	18
10. . .	Latin America	26	18	16	32	23	23
45. . .	Developing countries	24	15	13	31	19	22
15. . .	Developed countries	-	11	9	-	12	12

Source: World Bank, *Financing Education in Developing Countries. An Exploration of Policy Options* (Washington D.C., 1986), p. 7.

rapid expansion in recent decades. Secondly, the social rate of return to all levels of education, although consistently lower than the corresponding private return, is generally no less than average rates of return on fixed capital investments. Thus, despite the rapid expansion, there are many developing countries in which education is still under-provided. Thirdly, the estimated social rate of return is generally highest at the primary level and lowest at the tertiary level of education.

Such estimates have to be treated with caution. There is a limit to what one can learn about the social benefit of educational expansion from cross-section estimates of private earnings streams. The earnings differences between different educational levels may be attributable to various non-causal correlates of education, such as intelligence and determination, rather than, or in addition to, education itself. In so far as this is important, social rate of return estimates are biased upwards. On the other hand, there are various reasons why such estimates may under-state the social value of education. They do not take into account the various "externalities" to which education can give rise, such as the potential effect of educated people on the productivity of those around them or on the health of their families. Nor do they take account of the power of education to enrich the lives and capabilities of people in ways other than by raising the production of goods and services. Moreover, a recognition that investment in human beings makes less use of scarce foreign exchange than does investment in machinery and equipment would similarly favour educational expenditures.

The social return to expansion of primary education depends largely on its effects on the productivity of peasant farmers. The evidence suggests that this in turn depends on whether farmers are operating in a traditional or a modernizing environment—one in which change is rapid. Education assists farmers to obtain and evaluate information about improved technology and new economic opportunities, and thus to innovate.[21] The level of education required depends on the levels of technology currently in use and potentially suitable.[22] Education being complementary to other inputs, its value cannot be assessed in isolation. It depends on the degree of access to

27

credit, extension services, new seeds and other inputs. The greatest impact on rural development can thus be made where education is part of a package of measures.

Perhaps because of the rapid expansion of education in many developing countries, the quality of education is frequently unsatisfactory. The same educational attainment may require more years of schooling in a developing than in a developed economy. In part, this reflects a lack of early environmental stimulation of children and the inadequacy of their health and nutrition. However, it also reflects the quality of teacher training and the strain on resources—often associated with rapid quantitative expansion—such as overcrowded classrooms, high pupil-teacher ratios, lack of textbooks and ill-equipped facilities. In time of fiscal restriction, expenditure on physical inputs is squeezed more than salaries. In some countries there is also a problem of incentives. If the priorities of pupils and their teachers are to perform well in examinations in order to secure good jobs, and if examinations test rote-learning, then repetition, memorization and rigid book-learning are encouraged in the schools—the so-called "diploma disease".[23] Empirical research has suggested that in Brazil the social rate of return on expenditure for improving the quality of primary schooling would exceed that for increasing its quantity.[24]

In a sense, Governments, perceiving a choice between high-quality education for a few and low-quality education for many, have opted for the latter. Indeed, the decision may not have been a conscious one in that educational expansion has often proceeded uncontrolled, impelled along by political pressures. Yet, low educational quality is not inevitable.[25] In the first place, improvements in quality may be possible without raising costs, for example, through curricular and examination reform or less reliance on seniority rules in promotions. Secondly, some expenditures on qualitative improvements may yield high rates of return, for example, training courses in leadership and management for head teachers. Thirdly, the use of pupil fees for particular purposes such as additional textbooks and the involvement of parents and communities in supportive actions may harness the enthusiasm for educational improvements.

There has been a long-run improvement in the various indicators of health in the developing countries over the post-War period. Thus, for instance, the infant mortality rate for the developing countries as a whole fell from 180 per 1,000 in 1950-1955 to 137 in 1960-1965, to 104 in 1970-1975 and to 88 in 1980-1985.[26] However, there is a wide variety of experience, and the gains in many countries have been modest if seen in relation to the improvements that could have been made on the basis of existing knowledge of primary health care and basic nutrition. Progress since 1980 has been more limited. The available evidence suggests that the decline in infant mortality was halted and even reversed during the 1980s in many Latin American

28

and African countries. Indicators of child malnutrition increased in African countries after 1980. By contrast, malnutrition and mortality continued to decline in the majority of South and East Asian countries.

At present, there are economically feasible solutions to most of the health and nutrition problems that afflict many millions of people in the poor countries. The basic ingredients of primary health care would include the following: a simple pregnancy management programme; oral rehydration therapy to cure digestive tract infections and improved water supply, sanitation and health education to prevent them; immunization against the six communicable diseases; and an essential drug programme covering some 15-20 basic products.

The reduction of malnutrition is more difficult: people are hungry because they lack resources to grow enough food or to buy it. The fundamental solution to protein-energy malnutrition may thus require a redistribution of resources, but directed food subsidies and direct feeding schemes can assist. Recent improvements in food technology can help to overcome micronutrient deficiencies, for example, by fortifying the country's salt with iron or iodine.

Studies have shown that improvements in water supply can have dramatic effects on the incidence of diarrhoeal diseases. The cost of providing vaccine doses against six main vaccine-preventable diseases is about $1.20 per child. The per capita cost of 15 essential drugs needed at the village health post level is only some $0.50 -0.60 per year, and an episode of diarrhoea can be treated with oral rehydration salt available commercially at $0.15 - 0.20. The costs of combating micronutrient deficiencies are low: vitamin A capsules cost $0.10, the cost of iodizing salt is $0.05 and iron fortification of salt or centrally processed grains costs $0.05 - 0.09, all per person per year.[27]

The costs of providing primary health care are low, and yet provision is not as widespread as it could be. According to a World Health Organization (WHO) estimate, some three quarters of all health spending in the developing world is being used to provide expensive medical care for a relatively small urban minority.[28] Moreover, modern hospitals and costly medical technology absorb the great majority of health-related foreign aid to developing countries. There is a case for reallocating resources towards low-cost, high-impact primary health care measures.

Health expenditures of this sort can be justified not only by their effect on peoples' capabilities to enjoy life, but also by their effect on productivity. There is evidence that dietary energy improvements have an immediate effect on the performance of workers and that supplementation of micronutrients can have an even more dramatic effect on anaemic workers. Growth retardation at an early age, caused by dietary deficiency or infection, is a powerful mechanism

29

for perpetuating the vicious circle of poverty, malnutrition and stunting. Severe malnutrition of children under five leads to lifelong impairment of cognitive and physical performance. If children can be protected from these harmful effects, their long-run productivity and income could be greatly enhanced, and the resources required for their subsequent health care could be reduced. Moreover, the benefits need not stop there: primary health care lends itself to social mobilization and community participation in the design and delivery of programmes, and this is likely to result in communities being better organized, more self-reliant and more vocal.

The creation of human resources is one thing; their effective utilization is another. It is important that there be the right environment and incentives for human resources to be used fully and productively. Their effective use requires that factor prices reflect their scarcities. The failure of markets to secure this outcome can result in economic inefficiency, associated with, for example, mismatch of supply and demand, unemployment of labour and brain drain. A potential problem is that the free market outcome may well conflict with income distribution objectives of Government. In that case, the better solution may be to pursue income distribution objectives by means of other instruments.

Human capabilities can be dormant, waiting to be tapped, lacking perhaps in organizational initiative. Sometimes these capabilities can be tapped through greater participation of people at the grass-roots level. Obstacles may arise from gross inequalities in power, wealth and incomes between different groups and classes in society. The lack of freedom of association and organization may constitute a barrier in some cases. There are also societies in which discriminatory practices based on gender, race, caste, religion, status etc. effectively preclude equal economic or social participation by some groups. Illiteracy, limited education and knowledge, lack of confidence, passivity and so on also constitute barriers to participation of individuals and groups in society.

Some of these obstacles are more amenable to policy than others. The role of Government has to be examined carefully. Experience suggests that local people will not be motivated if group activities are both controlled and taxed by Government. Perhaps the effective role of Government is to provide information and an organizational framework, to ensure that the incentives are right and let the people do the rest.

Human development and the distribution of income

It is widely believed that expenditure on human development programmes either is distributionally neutral or else discriminates in favour of the poor. This view, however, is not generally correct. Concerning Asia and the Pacific, one study reports that

"Inequality in opportunities to benefit from human resources development is pervasive in the developing countries of the region. There is inequality between sexes, among regions within each country, between rural and urban areas and among persons in different economic and social groups."[29]

What is true of Asia and the Pacific is equally true of Africa and Latin America. The major beneficiaries of human development programmes tend to be males, households living in the large urban areas and people with middle or high incomes. Females, residents in the rural areas and those with relatively low incomes benefit proportionately less than others from the resources allocated to human development. This is due in part to "urban bias" in the provision of services, in part to a failure, for cultural and sociological reasons, of some of the intended beneficiaries to use the public services and facilities that are provided, but above all to a pattern of unequal subsidies among programmes that effectively favours upper-income groups. The per capita subsidy of human development programmes used disproportionately by the relatively better off (such as university education) tends to be much higher than the per capita subsidy of programmes used largely by the poor (such as health clinics in rural areas). Consequently, the potential of expenditure on human development to reduce social rigidities, increase social mobility and thereby ameliorate inequality remains large.

There is thus a need, particularly in times of structural adjustment, for Governments to change the composition of their human development expenditure programmes to ensure that, on balance, most of the benefits accrue to those in the lower half of the income distribution.[30] This can be done, for example, by switching resources from expenditure on urban hospitals to expenditure on primary health care (particularly in countries where hospitals account for 50-60 per cent of government health funds), and by switching resources from university education to primary and secondary education (particularly since expenditure per university student often is 30-40 times greater than expenditure per primary school student).

In addition to a change in the composition of public expenditure, there may be a case in some countries for introducing user charges to help cover part of the cost of human development programmes. If the tax system were optimal and progressive, and if the benefits of public expenditure programmes were equitably distributed, the case against user charges would be quite strong and the case in favour of universal free education and health services would be attractive. But since tax systems in the developing countries often are in practice regressive, and since the benefits of many human development programmes are reaped disproportionately by the better off, there may be an argument on grounds of equity for charging for services. In addition, where the alternative to imposing charges is to cut services, there may be an argument on grounds of long-term development for requiring users to cover at least part of the cost.

It is, of course, essential that if user charges are introduced they are designed in such a way that they do not add to the regressivity of the tax system. This can be done in several ways. First, user charges should be avoided as much as possible on services largely used by the poor, for example, primary education, primary health care and public water points. Secondly, in the case of services and facilities used by both the poor and the rich, for example, secondary education, non-basic health services and piped water, user charges should be selective, discriminating among users according to per capita income. Thirdly, full-cost charges should be imposed on services used largely by upper-income groups, for example, university education and sophisticated medical treatment available only to a few. But, fourthly, where full-cost charges are imposed, low-income groups should be entitled to scholarships (e.g., for university education) or exempted from the charge or subject to only a nominal charge. In this way, a system of user charges can actually be used to create a more egalitarian society.

No system of user charges, however, can counteract discrimination in access to services. This is something that requires positive intervention by the State. One of the clearest cases of discrimination is that against women. In some countries, namely, Bhutan, Nepal, India and Pakistan, discrimination is so blatant that, contrary to the pattern everywhere else, the life expectancy of women is less than that of men. This reflects in part a lower regard for the health of female infants than for male infants. In education, too, there is great discrimination. On average, the illiteracy rate among females in the developing countries is 75 per cent higher than among males, that is, 48.9 per cent illiteracy among women as compared to 27.9 per cent among men.[31] In primary school, women account for 44 per cent of the pupils in the developing countries; in secondary schools, 39 per cent; in tertiary education, 36 per cent. In the least developed countries, the situation is even worse: women account for only 20 per cent of those studying in tertiary education and 11 per cent of the teaching staff in tertiary education.

In addition to discrimination based on sex, there is discrimination based on race (as in South Africa, Fiji and Malaysia) and on religion (as in the Islamic Republic of Iran). Finally, there are specific problems associated with people of a particular age. In some countries the problem takes the form of child labour, that is, of some children entering the labour force, for example, in the carpet-making industry, before they have received primary and secondary education. In others it is reflected in a disproportionately high incidence of unemployment among the urban youth, a high incidence of long-term unemployment and consequently of unemployability among some sections of the young and, partly as a result of this, a sense of hopelessness accompanied by social disorders such as criminality and drug addiction.

32

The distribution of the benefits of human development programmes among the social classes is slightly paradoxical. Most of the absolute benefits of public services in health, nutrition, education, housing and transport accrue to the non-poor, but even so, public subsidies and benefits in kind account for a higher proportion of the total income of the poor than of the non-poor. Everything else being equal, therefore, a reduction in public expenditure is likely to fall most severely on the poor.

To avoid this, we have suggested that Governments alter the composition of public expenditure and, possibly, introduce discriminatory user charges. In the next section we shall discuss the possibility of more accurate targeting of benefits in favour of the poor. It must be recognized and confronted squarely, however, that a redistribution of public resources in favour of the poor may in some circumstances be at the expense not of the rich but of the lower-middle classes. This could easily occur, for example, as a by-product of a switch of expenditure from urban to rural areas. Such a reallocation of resources might well be politically difficult to achieve, particularly if the urban population is more vociferous and better organized than the scattered rural population. In other words, the political economy of public expenditure cannot be ignored when designing human development programmes—politics do impose constraints on policy makers—but at the same time it must be recognized that in many developing countries large sections of the poor have been denied an equitable share of the benefits of government programmes.

Human development and the alleviation of poverty

There is a temporal dimension to the alleviation of poverty. It is important to know whether policies that alleviate poverty in the short term do so at the expense of long-term alleviation or whether they make it easier to achieve long-term success. Sustained economic growth is crucial to reducing poverty in the long run. Among the decisive factors will be the rates at which resources such as physical and human capital accumulate and technical progress occurs, in relation to the growth of the population and labour force. The converse relationship may also be true, however. That is, immediate poverty alleviation may be good for growth. For instance, in so far as measures to enhance human capabilities through improved knowledge and health help people to escape from a vicious circle of poverty, they may make possible further, long-run improvements in their condition. The normal view that capital expenditures promote growth whereas current expenditures raise only current welfare need not hold for such measures.

While economic growth is not sufficient to ensure human development, sustained growth is likely to be central in the long run to policies intended to expand the capabilities of all people in the third world. The austerity currently experienced in many parts of Latin America and Africa is likely, if continued for much longer, to be incompatible with the maintenance of democratic political processes and with the continuation of human development programmes at acceptable levels. In Latin America, for example, the debt crisis has forced countries to undergo a massive contraction in aggregate demand, substantial depreciation of exchange rates and often, after more than a decade of trade liberalization, a reimposition of non-tariff barriers to trade and very high tariffs on imports. The result has been a decline in the real value of imports by more than 45 per cent between 1980 and 1985 (as well as a fall in the real value of exports because of lower commodity prices). Employment, investment and growth have all suffered severely. Unfortunately, the adjustment measures that have had to be adopted in many parts of Africa and West Asia have been even more deleterious. A revival of growth is essential in all three of these regions.

None the less, it may be possible to adopt medium-term measures to contain poverty during the period of financial and economic crisis. One way to do this is to target the benefits of human development programmes to favour the poor. Targeting presupposes, of course, that it is possible to identify the poor in general or those with specific needs, for example, for improved nutrition. This, in turn, requires that data be available and in a form that permits analysis in terms of relevant social categories, for example, by level of income, occupational group, social class and age.

The difficulties and costs of accurate targeting should not be underestimated and in some cases it may be cheaper and more efficient to provide a universal service rather than attempt to discriminate in favour of particular groups. Moreover, there is a danger, indeed a virtual certainty, that every targeted programme will fail to reach some of the intended beneficiaries while providing services to some unintended beneficiaries. A study of the Indian integrated rural development programme, for example, showed that 20 per cent of the actual beneficiaries had incomes above the poverty line and hence, in principle, were not eligible for participation in the scheme.[32]

Targeted programmes that rely on the exercise of discretion by government officials are vulnerable to corruption and abuse. Programmes targeted at people with an income below some arbitrary minimum or with food consumption below some arbitrary daily caloric minimum fall into this category. More likely to be successful are programmes that rely on self-targeting or else are universally available within a restricted category. Examples of the latter include free lunches to all primary school children or rationed food supplies available only to inhabitants of rural areas. The chances of corruption in such cases are pretty low, but conversely the chances of providing benefits to many who are not poor are pretty high.

Self-selection of beneficiaries has great appeal because in principle it is possible to offer universal coverage while in practice designing the programme in such a way that it is attractive primarily to those most in need of assistance. Food-for-work programmes, for instance, can be open to all, yet it is obvious that they will appeal primarily to the unemployed from households where average food consumption and incomes are low. Similarly, it is possible to design a limited food rationing system to which everyone has access but which in practice favours the poor, the rest of the community voluntarily obtaining its supplies elsewhere.[33] The easiest way to do this is by concentrating on varieties of foodgrains and qualities of products that are of special interest to low-income groups and that are characterized by low or even negative income elasticities of demand.

The general point is that it may be possible to redesign human development programmes, for example, by better targeting, to ensure that, particularly in times of increased hardship, a higher proportion of total benefits accrues to the poor. This general point can be extended by considering whether it is possible within a context of falling public expenditure to change the composition of public expenditure in order to give higher priority to reducing poverty. This, of course, raises the issue of the importance given by policy makers to human development as compared to the claims for spending by other government services.

Military expenditure can be used to illustrate the choices facing Governments. In extreme cases, expenditure on defence is a multiple of expenditure on education and health. The data must be interpreted with caution as statistical conventions appear to vary from one country to another, but the figures may provide a rough indication of orders of magnitude (see table 10). In the low-income countries as a whole, average expenditure on defence was 18.6 per cent of total central government expenditure, whereas education and health combined accounted for 11.3 per cent of government spending. In the lower middle-income countries the proportions were 14.2 and 17.6 per cent respectively.[34]

Governments need to ask themselves whether reduced expenditure on the military would lead to reduced national security. In many cases, perhaps a majority, it is doubtful that it would. Governments should also consider whether slack and inefficiency in the armed services is greater than in other areas of public expenditure. Anecdotal evidence suggests that it often is. Similarly, defence procurement policies could be reconsidered: the market for military equipment is in general oligopolistically organized and hence not very competitive and the price mark-up on supplies is high. The scope for financial savings in the defence budget may be much greater than in other areas of public spending and, if so, it may be

TABLE 10. DEFENCE EXPENDITURE AS PERCENTAGE OF TOTAL CENTRAL
GOVERNMENT EXPENDITURE IN SELECTED COUNTRIES, 1972 AND 1985

	1972	1985
Low-income countries	17.2	18.6
Burkina Faso	11.5	18.2
Nepal	7.2	6.2
Malawi	3.1	5.7
Zaire	11.1	5.2
Burma	31.6	18.5
Kenya	6.0	12.9
United Republic of Tanzania ..	11.9	13.8
Ghana	7.9	7.5
Pakistan	39.9	32.3
Sri Lanka	3.1	2.6
Uganda	23.1	16.7
Lower-middle-income countries ...	15.7	14.2
Bolivia	18.8	5.4
Indonesia	18.6	12.9
Morocco	12.3	14.9
Philippines	10.9	11.9
Dominican Republic	8.5	8.4
Thailand	20.2	20.2
El Salvador	6.6	20.3
Paraguay	13.8	10.2
Turkey	15.5	10.9
Mauritius	0.8	0.8
Ecuador	15.7	11.3
Tunisia	4.9	7.9
Costa Rica	2.8	3.0
Chile	10.0	11.5
Upper-middle-income countries ...	14.4	9.7
Brazil	8.3	4.0
Uruguay	5.6	10.8
Yugoslavia	20.5	54.8
Mexico	4.2	2.7
Argentina	10.0	8.8
Republic of Korea	25.8	29.7
Venezuela	10.3	6.1
Israel	40.0	27.8
Oman	39.3	43.0
Singapore	35.3	20.1

Source: World Bank, *World Development Report 1987* (Oxford, Oxford University Press, 1987).

possible to release resources for human development programmes without impairing a country's ability to defend itself.

Finally, it may be possible, particularly during a relatively short period of economic crisis, to use some of the resources allocated to the military services to support human resources, anti-poverty and public investment programmes. It is common for the armed forces to be used to help the civilian population when natural catastrophes such as floods and earthquakes occur. The question being raised here is whether the armed forces could play a constructive role over a longer period when economic catastrophes occur. The manpower and construction equipment of the armed forces might be used to sustain public investment in infrastructure (roads, bridges) and to construct the physical facilities needed for human resource programmes (rural clinics, primary schools). Equally, the training facilities of the armed forces could be used to train the civilian labour force in useful skills (electricians, mechanics). In this way, the conflict in priorities between military expenditure and human resource development could at least be reduced.

There may also be opportunities to reduce poverty by mobilizing slack local resources. The ease with which this can be done depends in part on the degree of grass-roots participation, a topic that was briefly discussed earlier. Particularly in the rural areas, and particularly during the off-peak seasons, the supply of labour is likely to be highly elastic and its opportunity cost low. If this labour is combined with technology of low capital intensity, it should be possible to generate substantial employment, raise the incomes of the working poor and produce productive assets of lasting value. The organizational intensity of a strategy of local resource mobilization, however, is likely to be high. In effect, the mobilization of labour is used as a substitute for physical capital. But again, the cost of mobilizing slack local resources can be kept to a minimum if the local population already has been organized around institutions intended to promote their well-being.

The capability of small-scale, locally based development to be self-sustaining is often underestimated. If resource mobilization is successful in raising rural incomes, experience shows that a significant proportion of the additional income may be ploughed back into investment, which then raises incomes further in the next period. In other words, marginal savings rates are potentially quite high even among very low-income households. Thus, human development programmes based in rural areas should not be regarded as income transfers to the poor but as an efficient way of raising the incomes of the poor on a sustained basis.

In the urban areas, particularly in what is known as the informal sector, it may be possible to mobilize slack resources and release entrepreneurial initiative simply by removing government-imposed obstacles to progress. Quite often government policy towards the urban informal sector contains too few elements of positive support and promotion, and too many elements of inaction, restriction and harassment.[35] The punitive demolition of squatter settlements merely destroys the housing of the poor; it does not result in better health or a more sanitary environment. Similarly, trade licensing systems create monopoly rents for licence holders while discouraging investment in the informal sector. The effect of this is to harm the lower-income groups by reducing employment as well as the supply of goods and services originating in the informal sector which the poor consume. From Kenya to Peru,[36] the informal economy is usually thought of as a problem rather than as a reservoir of frustrated

37

initiative and untapped talent and a way out of underdevelopment for many of the poor.

Yet, especially at a time when public expenditure is falling, and expenditure on human development is falling faster than average, a strong case can be made for removing laws and regulations that make it difficult for the poor to help themselves, to put a roof over their heads, to obtain a job, to establish a small shop or enterprise. If the ability of the State to help the poor in a time of economic crisis is declining, the least that can be done is to make certain that the State does not aggravate the problem of poverty or obstruct the efforts of low-income groups to improve their situation through their own exertions.

Conclusions

The peak of enthusiasm for "investment in human beings" occurred during the 1960s. Since the first oil crisis, the pendulum has swung in the other direction. The question has become: how to manage the economic crisis and return to economic growth? There is again a tendency to consider education, health and social services as consumer goods—luxuries to be afforded in good times but not in bad. The pendulum has swung too far towards the neglect of human resource development.

Our object has been to provide a counterweight. When Governments face a severe dilemma of having to choose between adjusting to short-term economic and fiscal constraints and pursuing long-run human resource goals, there is a danger that the former will dominate the latter. For instance, the costs of neglecting the former are more calculable, and more attributable, than the long-run costs to the development process of neglecting the latter. Nevertheless, the solution to the short-term problems of the present may contribute to a series of equally pressing short-run problems in the future.

We advocate that a broader view be taken of the development process than is normal—a view that encompasses not only the growth of national income per head and improvements in its distribution but also the enhancement of the capabilities of people to be and to do more things and to lead fuller lives. Education, health and nutrition have an important role to play in helping people to develop their capabilities. The enhancement of human capabilities is both an end in itself and a means to higher production and income. There is evidence that the economic returns for expenditures on education and health can be high. There is thus a good case for protecting such expenditure against the fiscal squeeze that generally accompanies economic recession and structural adjustment programmes.

Although the distributional effects of government taxation and expenditure are often regressive, with richer households receiving larger benefits, it is the poor who may suffer most from public expenditure cuts, in that the smaller absolute benefit to the poor is nevertheless a more important part of their income. The basic public services, such as primary education and basic health care, in particular need to be protected, for reasons both of efficiency and of equity. There is a case for greater targeting of subsidized public services on the poor, for example, by concentrating on poor rural areas and using self-selective schemes such as food-for-work. If it is naïve to expect that, in a period of curtailment, additional funds will be provided or that funds will be diverted from other activities, such as defence, for those activities that enhance human capabilities, then at least the basic services should continue to be generally provided free and, where it would not be a regressive move, selective cost recovery might be introduced to maintain and enlarge programmes providing non-basic services.

NOTES

[1] Amartya Sen, "Development: which way now?", *Economic Journal,* vol. 93, No. 372 (December 1983), p. 755.

[2] Amartya Sen, "Goods and people", in *Resources, Values and Development* (Oxford, Basil Blackwell, 1984), pp. 510 and 511.

[3] John Rawls, *A Theory of Justice* (Cambridge, Harvard University Press, 1971), p. 92.

[4] International Labour Organisation, *Employment, Growth and Basic Needs: A One-World Problem* (Geneva, 1976).

[5] Amartya Sen, *Resources, Values and Development . . .*, pp. 315-316.

[6] See Amartya Sen, "Public action and the quality of life in developing countries", *Oxford Bulletin of Economics and Statistics,* vol. 43, No. 4, (November 1981); and Keith Griffin, *Alternative Strategies for Economic Development* (London, Macmillan, 1988), chap. I.

[7] World Bank, *World Development Report 1984* (Oxford, Oxford University Press, 1984), table 4.2, p. 67.

[8] See, for example, Felix Paukert, "Income distribution at different levels of development: a survey of evidence", *International Labour Review,* vol. CVIII, Nos. 2-3 (August-September 1973); and Montek S. Ahluwalia, "Inequality, poverty and development", *Journal of Development Economics,* vol. 3, No. 3 (September 1976).

[9] Keith Griffin and Azizur Rahman Khan, "Poverty in the world: ugly facts and fancy models," *World Development,* vol. 6, No. 3 (March 1978); and Irma Adelman and Cynthia Taft Morris, *Economic Growth and Social Equity in Developing Countries* (Stanford, Stanford University Press, 1973).

[10] International Labour Organisation, *Overview of the Employment Situation in the World* (Geneva, November 1987), p. 2.

[11] World Food Council, *The Global State of Hunger and Malnutrition and the Impact of Economic Adjustment on Food and Hunger Problems* (April 1987), p. 3.

[12] *Ibid.,* table 1, p. 16.

[13] World Bank, *World Development Report 1987* (Oxford, Oxford University Press, 1987), table 16, pp. 232-233.

[14] United Nations Children's Fund, *Adjustment with a Human Face* (Oxford, Oxford University Press, 1987). The net transfer is calculated as the difference between loans, direct investments and grants received and profit repatriation, interest and capital repayments.

[15] United Nations Children's Fund, *Adjustment with a Human Face . . .*, vol. 1, pp. 289-294.

[16] Amartya Sen, *Technology, Employment and Development* (Oxford, Clarendon Press, 1975), p. 5.

[17] See Louis Emmerij, "The human factor in development", *Human Development: The Neglected Dimension* (United Nations publication, Sales No. 86.III.B.2), p. 20.

[18] For evidence that participation raises the return on physical capital and increases the productivity of labour, see Conrad Phillip Kottak, "When people don't come first: some sociological lessons from completed projects" (Washington, D.C., World Bank, 1985); and David C. Korten, "Community organization for rural development: a learning process approach", *Public Administration Review* (September-October 1980).

[19] Robert Cassen, "Population and development: a survey", *World Development,* vol. 4, Nos. 10/11 (1976), pp. 788-796.

[20] See J. Gaude and others, "Rural development and labour-intensive schemes: impact study of some pilot programmes", *International Labour Review* (July-August 1987).

[21] M. E. Lockhead, D. T. Jamison and L. J. Lau, "Farmer education and farm efficiency: a survey", *Economic Development and Cultural Change,* vol. 29 (1980), pp. 37-76.

[22] Daniel Cotlear, "The effects of education on farm productivity: a case study from Peru" (1987).

[23] R. P. Dore, *The Diploma Disease. Education, Qualification and Development* (London, George Allen and Unwin, 1976).

[24] Jere Behrman and Nancy Birdsall, "The quality of schooling: quantity alone may be misleading", *American Economic Review,* vol. 73, No. 5 (1983), pp. 928-946.

[25] Jocelyn Dejong and John Oxenham, "The quality of education in developing countries" (1987).

[26] *World Population Prospects. Estimates and Projections as Assessed in 1984* (United Nations publication, Sales No. E.86.XIII.3).

[27] Figures from G. A. Cornia, "Investing in human resources: health, nutrition and development for the 1990s" (November 1987).

[28] Cited in Cornia, *op. cit.,* p. 23.

[29] *Economic and Social Survey of Asia and the Pacific 1986* (United Nations publication, Sales No. E.87.II.F.1), part two, p. 171.

[30] See G. A. Cornia, "Social policy making during adjustment", in *Human Development, Adjustment and Growth,* Khadija Haq and Uner Kirdar, eds. (Islamabad, North-South Round-table, 1987), pp. 85-88.

[31] United Nations Educational, Scientific and Cultural Organization, Office of Statistics, *The Current Literacy Situation in the World* (Paris, May 1987), p. 4.

[32] N. J. Kurian, "IRDP—how relevant is it?" (May 1987), p. 7.

[33] See Keith Griffin and Jeffrey James, *The Transition to Egalitarian Development* (London, Macmillan, 1981), chap. 4.

[34] World Bank, *World Development Report 1987 . . .*

[35] International Labour Organisation, *Employment, Incomes and Equality: A Strategy for Increasing Productive Employment in Kenya* (Geneva, 1972), p. 226.

[36] See Hernando de Soto, *El Otro Sendero: La Revolución Informal* (Lima, Editorial El Barranco, 1986). See also Victor Tokman, "The informal sector today: a policy proposal", paper presented to the Round-table in Managing Human Development, Budapest, 6-9 September 1987.

2

DEVELOPMENT AS CAPABILITY EXPANSION

*Amartya Sen**

CONTENTS

Introduction

In his *Grundlegung zur Metaphysik de Sitten,* Immanuel Kant argues for the necessity of seeing human beings as ends in themselves, rather than as means to other ends: "So act as to treat humanity, whether in thine own person or in that of any other, in every case as an end withal, never as means only."[1] This principle has importance in many contexts—even in analysing poverty, progress and planning. Human beings are the agents, beneficiaries and adjudicators of progress, but they also happen to be—directly or indirectly—the primary means of all production. This dual role of human beings provides a rich ground for confusion of ends and means in planning and policy-making. Indeed, it can—and frequently does—take the form of focusing on production and prosperity as the essence of progress, treating people as the means through which that productive progress is brought about (rather than seeing the lives of people as the ultimate concern and treating production and prosperity merely as means to those lives).

Indeed, the widely prevalent concentration on the expansion of real income and on economic growth as the characteristics of successful development can be precisely an aspect of the mistake against which Kant had warned. This problem is particularly pivotal in the assessment and planning of economic development. The

---

*Lamont University Professor, Harvard University.

problem does not, of course, lie in the fact that the pursuit of economic prosperity is typically taken to be a major goal of planning and policy-making. This need not be, in itself, unreasonable. The problem relates to the level at which this aim should be taken as a goal. Is it just an intermediate goal, the importance of which is contingent on what it ultimately contributes to human lives? Or is it the object of the entire exercise? It is in the acceptance—usually implicitly—of the latter view that the ends-means confusion becomes significant—indeed blatant.

The problem might have been of no great practical interest if the achievement of economic prosperity were tightly linked—in something like a one-to-one correspondence—with that of enriching the lives of the people. If that were the case, then the pursuit of economic prosperity as an end in itself, while wrong in principle, might have been, in effect, indistinguishable from pursuing it only as a means to the end of enriching human lives. But that tight relation does not obtain. Countries with high GNP per capita can nevertheless have astonishingly low achievements in the quality of life, with the bulk of the population being subject to premature mortality, escapable morbidity, overwhelming illiteracy and so on.

Just to illustrate an aspect of the problem, the GNP per capita of six countries is given in table 1, along with each country's respective level of life expectancy at birth.

TABLE 1. ECONOMIC PROSPERITY AND LIFE EXPECTANCY, 1985

Country	GNP per capita	Life expectancy at birth
China	310	69
Sri Lanka	380	70
Brazil	1 640	65
South Africa	2 010	55
Mexico	2 080	67
Oman	6 730	54

Source: World Development Report 1987 (New York, Oxford University Press, 1988), table 1.

A country can be very rich in conventional economic terms (i.e., in terms of the value of commodities produced per capita) and still be very poor in the achieved quality of human life. South Africa, with five or six times the GNP per capita of Sri Lanka or China, has a much lower longevity rate, and the same applies in different ways to Brazil, Mexico, Oman, and indeed to many other countries not included in this table.

There are, therefore, really two distinct issues here. First, economic prosperity is no more than one of the means to enriching the lives of people. It is a foundational confusion to give it the status of an end. Secondly, even as a means, merely enhancing average economic opulence can be quite inefficient in the pursuit of the really valuable ends. In making sure that development planning and general policy-making do not suffer from costly confusions of ends and

42

means, we have to face the issue of identification of ends, in terms of which the effectiveness of the means can be systematically assessed.

This paper is concerned with discussing the nature and implications of that general task.

The capability approach: conceptual roots

The particular line of reasoning that will be pursued here is based on evaluating social change in terms of the richness of human life resulting from it. But the quality of human life is itself a matter of great complexity. The approach that will be used here, which is sometimes called the "capability approach", sees human life as a set of "doings and beings"—we may call them "functionings"—and it relates the evaluation of the quality of life to the assessment of the capability to function. It is an approach that I have tried to explore in some detail, both conceptually and in terms of its empirical implications.[2] The roots of the approach go back at least to Adam Smith and Karl Marx, and indeed to Aristotle.

In investigating the problem of "political distribution", Aristotle made extensive use of his analysis of "the good of human beings", and this he linked with his examination of "the functions of man" and his exploration of "life in the sense of activity".[3] The Aristotelian theory is, of course, highly ambitious and involves elements that go well beyond this particular issue (e.g., it takes a specific view of human nature and relates a notion of objective goodness to it). But the argument for seeing the quality of life in terms of valued activities and the capability to achieve these activities has much broader relevance and application.

Among the classical political economists, both Adam Smith and Karl Marx explicitly discussed the importance of functionings and the capability to function as determinants of well-being.[4] Marx's approach to the question was closely related to the Aristotelian analysis (and indeed was apparently directly influenced by it).[5] Indeed, an important part of Marx's programme of reformulation of the foundations of political economy is clearly related to seeing the success of human life in terms of fulfilling the needed human activities. Marx put it thus: "It will be seen how in place of the wealth and poverty of political economy come the rich human being and rich human need. The rich human being is simultaneously the human being in need of a totality of human life-activities—the man in whom his own realization exists as an inner necessity, as need."[6]

Commodities, functionings and capability

If life is seen as a set of "doings and beings" that are valuable, the exercise of assessing the quality of life takes the form of evaluating these functionings and the capability to function. This valuational exercise cannot be done by focusing simply on commodities or incomes that help those doings and beings, as in commodity-based accounting of the quality of life (involving a confusion of means and ends). "The life of money-making", as Aristotle put it, "is one undertaken under compulsion, and wealth is evidently not the good we are seeking; for it is merely useful and for the sake of something else."[7] The task is that of evaluating the importance of the various functionings in human life, going beyond what Marx called, in a different but related context, "commodity fetishism".[8] The functionings themselves have to be examined, and the capability of the person to achieve them has to be appropriately valued.

In the view that is being pursued here, the constituent elements of life are seen as a combination of various different functionings (a "functioning n-tuple"). This amounts to seeing a person in, as it were, an "active" rather than a "passive" form (but neither the various states of being nor even the "doings" need necessarily be "athletic" ones). The included items may vary from such elementary functionings as escaping morbidity and mortality, being adequately nourished, undertaking usual movements etc., to many complex functionings such as achieving self-respect, taking part in the life of the community and appearing in public without shame (the last a functioning that was illuminatingly discussed by Adam Smith[9] as an achievement that is valued in all societies, but the precise commodity requirement of which, he pointed out, varies from society to society). The claim is that the functionings are constitutive of a person's being, and an evaluation of a person's well-being has to take the form of an assessment of these constituent elements.

The primitive notion in the approach is that of functionings—seen as constitutive elements of living. A functioning is an achievement of a person: what he or she manages to do or to be, and any such functioning reflects, as it were, a part of the state of that person. The capability of a person is a derived notion. It reflects the various combinations of functionings (doings and beings) he or she can achieve.[10] It takes a certain view of living as a combination of various "doings and beings". Capability reflects a person's freedom to choose between different ways of living. The underlying motivation—the focusing on freedom—is well captured by Marx's claim that what we need is "replacing the domination of circumstances and chance over individuals by the domination of individuals over chance and circumstances".[11]

Utilitarian calculus versus objective deprivation

The capability approach can be contrasted not merely with commodity-based systems of evaluation, but also with the utility-based assessment. The utilitarian notion of value, which is invoked

44

explicitly or by implication in much of welfare economics, sees value, ultimately, only in individual utility, which is defined in terms of some mental condition, such as pleasure, happiness, desire-fulfilment. This subjectivist perspective has been extensively used, but it can be very misleading, since it may fail to reflect a person's real deprivation.

A thoroughly deprived person, leading a very reduced life, might not appear to be badly off in terms of the mental metric of utility, if the hardship is accepted with non-grumbling resignation. In situations of long-standing deprivation, the victims do not go on weeping all the time, and very often make great efforts to take pleasure in small mercies and to cut down personal desires to modest—"realistic"—proportions. The person's deprivation, then, may not at all show up in the metrics of pleasure, desire-fulfilment etc., even though he or she may be quite unable to be adequately nourished, decently clothed, minimally educated and so on.[12]

This issue, apart from its foundational relevance, may have some immediate bearing on practical public policy. Smugness about continued deprivation and vulnerability is often made to look justified on grounds of lack of strong public demand and forcefully expressed desire for removing these impediments.[13]

Ambiguities, precision and relevance

There are many ambiguities in the conceptual framework of the capability approach. Indeed, the nature of human life and the content of human freedom are themselves far from unproblematic concepts. It is not my purpose to brush these difficult questions under the carpet. In so far as there are genuine ambiguities in the underlying objects of value, these will be reflected in corresponding ambiguities in the characterization of capability. The need for this relates to a methodological point, which I have tried to defend elsewhere, that if an underlying idea has an essential ambiguity, a precise formulation of that idea must try to capture that ambiguity rather than attempt to lose it.[14] Even when precisely capturing an ambiguity proves to be a difficult exercise, that is not an argument for forgetting the complex nature of the concept and seeking a spuriously narrow exactness. In social investigation and measurement, it is undoubtedly more important to be vaguely right than to be precisely wrong.[15]

It should be noted also that there is always an element of real choice in the description of functionings, since the format of "doings" and "beings" permits additional "achievements" to be defined and included. Frequently, the same doings and beings can be seen from different perspectives, with varying emphases. Also, some functionings may be easy to describe, but of no great interest in the relevant context (e.g., using a particular washing powder in doing the washing).[16] There is no escape from the problem of evaluation in selecting a class of functionings as important and others not so. The evaluative exercise cannot be fully addressed without explicitly facing questions concerning what are the valuable achievements and freedoms, and which are not. The chosen focus has to be related to the underlying social concerns and values, in terms of which some definable functionings and capabilities may be important and others quite trivial and negligible. The need for selection and discrimination is neither an embarrassment nor a unique difficulty for the conceptualization of functioning and capability.[17]

In the context of some types of welfare analysis, for example, in dealing with extreme poverty in developing economies, we may be able to go a long distance in terms of a relatively small number of centrally important functionings and the corresponding capabilities, such as the ability to be well-nourished and well-sheltered, the capability of escaping avoidable morbidity and premature mortality and so forth.[18] In other contexts, including more general problems of assessing economic and social development, the list may have to be much longer and much more diverse.[19] The task of specification must relate to the underlying motivation of the exercise as well as dealing with the social values involved.

Quality of life, basic needs and capability

There is an extensive literature in development economics concerned with valuing the quality of life, the fulfilment of basic needs and related matters.[20] That literature has been quite influential in recent years in drawing attention to neglected aspects of economic and social development. It is, however, fair to say that these writings have been typically comprehensively ignored in the theory of welfare economics, which has tended to treat these contributions as essentially *ad hoc* suggestions. This treatment is partly the result of the concern of welfare theory that proposals should not just appeal to intuitions but also be structured and founded. It also reflects the intellectual standing that such traditional approaches as utilitarian evaluation enjoy in welfare theory, and which serves as a barrier to accepting departures even when they seem attractive. The inability of utility-based evaluations to cope with persistent deprivations was discussed earlier, but in the welfare-economic literature the hold of this tradition has been hard to dislodge.

The charge of " *ad hoc*-ness" against the development literature relates to the different modes of arguing that are used in welfare theory and in development theory. As far as the normative structure is concerned, the latter tends to be rather immediate, appealing to strong intuitions that seem obvious enough. Welfare theory, on the other hand, tends to take a more circuitous route, with greater elaboration and defence of the foundations of the approach in question. To bridge the gap, we have to compare and contrast the foundational features underlying the concern with quality of life, basic needs etc. with the informational foundations of the more traditional approaches used in welfare economics and moral philosophy, such as utilitarianism. It is precisely in this context that the advantages of the capability approach become perspicuous. The view of human life seen as a combination of various functionings and capabilities, and the analysis of human freedom as a central feature of living, provide a differently grounded foundational route to the evaluative exercise. This informational foundation contrasts with the evaluative bases incorporated in the more traditional foundations used in welfare economics.[21]

The "basic needs" literature has, in fact, tended to suffer a little from uncertainties about how basic needs should be specified. The original formulations often took the form of defining basic needs in terms of needs for certain minimal amounts of essential commodities such as food, clothing and shelter. If this type of formulation is used, then the literature remains imprisoned in the mould of commodity-centred evaluation, and can in fact be accused of adopting a form of "commodity fetishism". The objects of value can scarcely be the holdings of commodities. Judged even as means, the usefulness of the commodity-perspective is severely compromised by the variability of the conversion of commodities into capabilities. For example, the requirement of food and of nutrients for the capability of being well-nourished may greatly vary from person to person, depending on metabolic rates, body size, gender, pregnancy, age, climatic conditions, parasitic ailments and so on.[22] The evaluation of commodity-holdings or of incomes (with which to purchase commodities) can be at best a proxy for the things that really matter, but unfortunately it does not seem to be a particularly good proxy in most cases.[23]

Rawls, primary goods and freedoms

The concern with commodities and means of achievement, with which the motivation of the capability approach is being contrasted, happens to be, in fact, influential in the literature of modern moral philosophy as well. For example, in John Rawls' outstanding book on justice (arguably the most important contribution to moral philosophy in recent decades), the concentration is on the holdings of "primary goods" of different people in making interpersonal comparisons. His theory of justice, particularly the "difference principle", is dependent on this procedure for interpersonal comparisons. This procedure has the feature of being partly commodity-based, since the list of primary goods includes "income and wealth", in addition to "the basic liberties", "powers and prerogatives of offices and positions of responsibility", "social bases of self-respect" and so on.[24]

Indeed, the entire list of "primary goods" of Rawls is concerned with means rather than ends; they deal with things that help to achieve what we want to achieve, rather than either with achievement as such or even with the freedom to achieve. Being nourished is not a part of the list, but having the income to buy food certainly is. Similarly, the social bases of self-respect belong to the list in a way self-respect as such does not.

Rawls is much concerned that the fact that different people have different ends must not be lost in the evaluative process, and people should have the freedom to pursue their respective ends. This concern is indeed important, and the capability approach is also much involved with valuing freedom as such. In fact, it can be argued that the capability approach gives a better account of the freedoms actually enjoyed by different people than can be obtained from looking merely at the holdings of primary goods. Primary goods are means to freedoms, whereas capabilities are expressions of freedoms themselves.

The motivations underlying the Rawlsian theory and the capability approach are similar, but the accountings are different. The problem with the Rawlsian accounting lies in the fact that, even for the same ends, people's ability to convert primary goods into achievements differs, so that an interpersonal comparison based on the holdings of primary goods cannot, in general, also reflect the ranking of their respective real freedoms to pursue any given—or variable—ends. The variability in the conversion rates between persons for given ends is a problem that is embedded in the wider problem of variability of primary goods needed for different persons pursuing their respective ends.[25] Hence, a similar criticism applies to Rawlsian accounting procedure as applies to parts of the basic needs literature for their concentration on means (such as commodities) as opposed to achievements or the freedom to achieve.

Freedom, capability and data limitations

The capability set represents a person's freedom to achieve various functioning combinations. If freedom is intrinsically important, then the alternative combinations available for choice are all relevant for judging a person's advantage, even though he or she will eventually choose only an alternative. In this view, the choice itself is a valuable feature of a person's life.

On the other hand, if freedom is seen as being only instrumentally important, then the interest in the capability set lies only in the fact that it offers the person opportunities to achieve various valuable states. Only the achieved states are in themselves valuable, not the opportunities, which are valued only as means to the end of reaching valuable states.

The contrast between the intrinsic and the instrumental views of freedom is quite a deep one, and I have discussed the importance of the distinction elsewhere.[26] Both views can be accommodated within the capability approach. With the instrumental view, the capability set is valued only for the sake of the best alternative available for choice (or the actual alternative chosen). This way of evaluating a capability set by the value of one distinguished element in it can be called "elementary evaluation".[27] If, on the other hand, freedom is intrinsically valued, then elementary evaluation will be inadequate, since the opportunity to choose other alternatives is of significance of its own. To bring out the distinction, it may be noted that if all alternatives other than the chosen alternative were to become unavailable, then there would be a real loss in the case of the intrinsic view, but not in the instrumental, since the alternative chosen is still available.

In terms of practical application, the intrinsic view is much harder to reflect than the instrumental view, since our direct observations relate to what was chosen and achieved. The estimation of what could have been chosen is, by its very nature, more problematic (involving, in particular, assumptions about the constraints actually faced by the person). The limits of practical calculations are set by data restrictions, and this can be particularly hard on the representation of capability sets in full, as opposed to judging the capability sets by the observed functioning achievements.

There is no real loss involved in using the capability approach in this reduced form if the instrumental view of freedom is taken, but there is loss if the intrinsic view is accepted. For the latter, a representation of the capability set as such is important.

In fact, neither the instrumental view nor the intrinsic view is likely to be fully adequate. Certainly, freedom is a means to achievement, whether or not it is also intrinsically important, so that the instrumental view must be *inter alia* present in any use of the capability approach. Also, even if we find in general the instrumental view to be fairly adequate, there would clearly be cases in which it is extremely limited. For example, the person who fasts, that is, starves out of choice, can hardly be seen as being similarly deprived as a person who has no option but to starve because of penury. Even though their observed functionings may be the same, at least in the crude representation of functionings, their predicaments are not the same.

In practice, even if in general the capability approach is used in the reduced form of concentrating on the chosen functioning combination, some systematic supplementation would be needed to take care of cases in which the freedom enjoyed is of clear and immediate interest. There may be no great difficulty in doing this supplementation in many cases, once the problem is posed clearly enough and the data search is made purposive and precise. Sometimes it would be useful to redefine the functionings in what is called a "refined" way, to take note of some of the obviously relevant alternatives that were available, but not chosen. Indeed, fasting is an example of a "refined" functioning, and contrasts with the unrefined functioning of "starving", which does not specify whether or not this was by choice.[28] The important issue does not concern the existence or not of some actual word (such as fasting) that reflects the refined functioning (that is largely a matter of linguistic convention), but assessing whether or not such refining would be central to the exercise in question, and if central, deciding how this might be done.

As a matter of fact, the informational base of functionings is still a much finer basis of evaluation of the quality of life and economic progress than various alternatives more commonly recommended, such as individual utilities or commodity holdings. The commodity fetishism of the former and the subjectivist metric of the latter make them deeply problematic. Thus, the concentration on achieved functionings has merits over the feasible rivals (even though it may not be based on as much information as would be needed to attach intrinsic importance to freedom). And in terms of data availability, keeping track of functionings (including vital ones such as being well-nourished and avoiding escapable morbidity or premature mortality) is typically no harder—often much easier—than getting data on commodity use (especially divisions within the family), not to mention utilities.

The capability approach can, thus, be used at various levels of sophistication, and how far we can go would depend much on the practical consideration of what data we can get and what we cannot. In so far as freedom is seen to be intrinsically important, the observation of the chosen functioning bundle cannot be in itself an adequate guide for the evaluative exercise, even though the freedom to choose a better bundle rather than a worse one can be seen to be, in some accounting, an advantage even from the perspective of freedom.[29]

The point can be illustrated with a particular example. An expansion of longevity is seen, by common agreement, as an enhancement of the quality of life (though, strictly speaking, I suppose one can think of it as an enhancement of the quantity of life). This is so partly because living longer is an achievement that is valued. It is also partly because other achievements, such as avoiding morbidity, tend to go with longevity (and thus longevity serves also as a proxy for some achievements that too are intrinsically valued). But greater longevity can also be seen as an enhancement of the freedom to live long. We often take this for granted on the solid ground that given the option, people value living longer, and thus the observed achievement of living longer reflects a greater freedom than was enjoyed.

The interpretative question arises at this precise point. Why is it evidence of greater freedom as such that a person ends up living longer rather than shorter? Why can it not be just a preferred achievement, but involving no difference in terms of freedom? One

50

answer is to say that one always does have the option of killing oneself, and thus an expansion of longevity expands one's options. But there is a further issue here. Consider a case in which, for some reason (either legal or psychological or whatever), one cannot really kill oneself (despite the presence in the world of poisons, knives, tall buildings and other useful objects). Would we then say that the person does not have more freedom by virtue of being free to live longer though not shorter? It can be argued that if the person values, prefers and wishes to choose living longer, then the change in question is in fact an expansion of the person's freedom, since the evaluation of freedom cannot be dissociated from the assessment of the actual options in terms of the person's evaluative judgments.[30]

The idea of freedom takes us beyond achievements, but that does not entail that the assessment of freedom must be independent of that of achievements. The freedom to live the kind of life one would like to live has importance that the freedom to live the kind of life one would hate to have does not. Thus, the temptation to see more freedom in greater longevity is justifiable from several points of view, including noting the option of ending one's life and being sensitive to the evaluative structure of achievements which directly affect the metric of freedom. The bottom line of all this is to recognize that the use of the capability approach even in the reduced form of concentrating on the achieved functionings (longevity, absence of morbidity, avoidance of undernourishment etc.) may give more role to the value of freedom than might have been initially apparent.

Inequality, class and gender

The choice of an approach to the evaluation of well-being and advantage has bearings on many exercises. These include the assessment of efficiency as well as inequality. Efficiency, as it is normally defined, is concerned with noting overall improvements, and in standard economic theory, this takes the form of checking whether someone's position has improved without anyone's position having gone down. A situation is efficient if and only if there is no alternative feasible situation in which someone's position is better and no one's worse. Obviously, the content of this criterion depends crucially on the way individual advantage is defined. If it is defined in terms of utility, then this criterion of efficiency immediately becomes that of "Pareto optimality" (or "Pareto efficiency", as it is sometimes—more accurately—called). On the other hand, efficiency can be defined also in terms of other metrics, including that of the quality of life based on the evaluation of functionings and capabilities.

Similarly, the assessment of inequality too depends on the chosen indicator of individual advantage. The usual inequality measures that can be found in empirical economic literatures tend to

51

concentrate on inequalities of incomes or wealth.[31] These are valuable contributions. On the other hand, in so far as income and wealth do not give adequate account of quality of life, there is a case for basing the evaluation of inequality on information more closely related to living standards.

Indeed, the two informational bases are not alternatives. Inequality of wealth may tell us things about the generation and persistence of inequalities of other types, even when our ultimate concern may be with inequality of living standard and quality of life. Particularly in the context of the continuation and stubbornness of social divisions, information on inter-class inequalities in wealth and property ownership is especially crucial. But this recognition does not reduce the importance of bringing in indicators of quality of life to assess the actual inter-class inequalities of well-being and freedom.

One field in which inequalities are particularly hard to assess is that of gender differences. There is a great deal of general evidence to indicate that women often have a much worse deal than men do, and that girls are often much more deprived than boys. These differences may be reflected in many subtle as well as crude ways, and in various forms they can be observed in different parts of the world—among both rich and poor countries. However, it is not easy to determine what is the best indicator of advantage in terms of which these gender inequalities are to be examined. There is, to be sure, no need to look for one specific metric only, and the need for plurality of indicators is as strong here as in any other field. But there is still an issue of the choice of approach to well-being and advantage in the assessment of inequalities between women and men.

The approach of utility-based evaluation is particularly limiting in this context, since the unequal deals that obtain, particularly within the family, are often made "acceptable" by certain social notions of "normal" arrangements, and this may affect the perceptions of women as well as men of the comparative levels of well-being they respectively enjoy. For example, in the context of some developing countries such as India, the point has been made that rural women may have no clear perception of being deprived of things that men have, and may not be in fact any more unhappy than men are. This may or may not be the case, but even if it were so, it can be argued that the mental metric of utility may be particularly inappropriate for judging inequality in this context. The presence of objective deprivation in the form of greater undernourishment, more frequent morbidity, lower literacy etc. cannot be rendered irrelevant just by the quiet and ungrumbling acceptance of women of their deprived conditions.[32]

In rejecting utility-based evaluations, it may be tempting to go in the direction of actual commodities (enjoyed by women and men, respectively) to check inequalities between them. There is here the problem, already discussed earlier in this paper, that commodity-based evaluations are inadequate because commodities are merely means to well-being and freedom and do not reflect the nature of the lives that the people involved can lead. But, in addition, there is the further problem that it is hard—sometimes impossible—to get information on how the commodities belonging to the family are divided between men and women, and between boys and girls.

For example, studies on the division of food within the family tend to be deeply problematic since the observation needed to see who is eating how much is hard to carry out with any degree of reliability. On the other hand, it is possible to compare signs of undernourishment of boys and girls, to check their respective morbidity rates etc., and these functioning differences are both easier to observe and of greater intrinsic relevance.[33]

There are indeed inequalities between men and women in terms of functionings, and in the context of developing countries the contrast may be sharp even in basic matters of life and death, health and illness, education and illiteracy. For example, despite the fact that when men and women are treated reasonably equally in terms of food and health care (as they tend to be in the richer countries, even though gender biases may remain in other—less elementary—fields), women seem to have a greater ability to survive than men, in the bulk of the developing economies, men outnumber women by large margins. While the ratio of females to males in Europe and North America tends to be about 1.06 or so, that ratio is below 0.95 for the Middle East (including countries in Western Asia and North Africa), South Asia (including India, Pakistan and Bangladesh) and China.[34] This crude figure of the ratio of survived females to survived males already tells a story that has much informational value in judging inter-gender inequalities. Sometimes there are sharp contrasts even within a country (e.g., the ratio of females to males varies within India all the way from 1.03 in Kerala to 0.87 or 0.88 in Haryana and Punjab). From the point of view of studying both the actual situations and the causal influences operating in the generation of inter-gender inequalities, these regional contrasts may be particularly important.

Being able to survive is of course only one capability (though undoubtedly a very basic one), and other comparisons can be made with information on health, morbidity etc. The ability to read and write is also another important capability, and here it can be seen that the ratio of female to male literacy rates is often shockingly low in different parts of the world. The combined effects of low literacy rates in general (a deprivation of a basic capability across genders) and gender inequalities in literacy rates (unequal deprivation of this basic capability for women) tend to be quite disastrous denials for women. It appears that even leaving out many countries for which no reliable data exist, in a great many countries in the world, the female literacy rate is still below 50 per cent. In fact, it is below even 30 per cent for as many as 26 countries, below 20 percent for 16 and below 10 percent in at least five.[35]

In general, the perspective of functionings and capabilities provides a plausible approach to examining inter-gender inequalities. It does not suffer from the type of subjectivism that makes utility-based accounting particularly obtuse in dealing with entrenched inequalities. Nor does it suffer from the over-concentration on means that commodity-based accounting undoubtedly does, and in fact it has better informational sources in studying inequalities within the family than is provided by guesswork on commodity distributions (e.g., who is eating how much?). The case of inter-gender inequality is, of course, only one illustration of the advantages that the capability approach has. But it happens to be an illustration that is particularly important on its own as well, given the pervasive and stubborn nature of inequalities between women and men in different parts of the world.

Conclusion

The assessment of achievement and advantage of members of the society is a central part of development analysis. In this paper, I have tried to discuss how the capability approach may be used to substantiate the evaluative concerns of human development. The focus on human achievement and freedom, and on the need for reflective—rather than mechanical—evaluation, is an adaptation of an old tradition that can be fruitfully used in providing a conceptual basis for analysing the tasks of human development in the contemporary world. The foundational importance of human capabilities provides a firm basis for evaluating living standards and the quality of life, and also points to a general format in terms of which problems of efficiency and equality can both be discussed.

The concentration on distinct capabilities entails, by its very nature, a pluralist approach. Indeed, it points to the necessity of seeing development as a combination of distinct processes, rather than as the expansion of some apparently homogeneous magnitude such as real income or utility. The things that people value doing or being can be quite diverse, and the valuable capabilities vary from such elementary freedoms as being free from hunger and undernourishment to such complex abilities as achieving self-respect and social participation. The challenge of human development demands attention being paid to a variety of sectoral concerns and a combination of social and economic processes.

In the collection of papers of which this one is a part, there are a number of specific studies dealing with such matters as education, health and nutrition, as well as the processes of agricultural expansion and industrial development. The problems of resource mobilization and participatory development are also addressed. Some of the subjects thus covered deal with variables that are direct determinants of human capability (e.g., education and health), while others relate to instrumental influences that operate through economic or social processes (e.g., the promotion of agricultural and industrial productivity). The uniting feature is the motivating concern with human development and its constitutive characteristics.

In the distinction between functionings and capabilities, emphasis was placed on the importance of having the freedom to choose one kind of life rather than another. This is an emphasis that distinguishes the capability approach from any accounting of only realized achievements. However, the ability to exercise freedom may, to a considerable extent, be directly dependent on the education we have received, and thus the development of the educational sector may have a foundational connection with the capability-based approach.

In fact, educational expansion has a variety of roles that have to be carefully distinguished. First, more education can help productivity. Secondly, wide sharing of educational advancement can contribute to a better distribution of the aggregate national income among different people. Thirdly, being better educated can help in the conversion of incomes and resources into various functionings and ways of living. Last (and by no means the least), education also helps in the intelligent choice between different types of lives that a person can lead. All these distinct influences can have important bearings on the development of valuable capabilities and thus on the process of human development.

There are also other interconnections between the different areas covered in the collection; for example, good health is an achievement in itself and also contributes both to higher productivity and to an enhanced ability to convert incomes and resources into good living. In focusing on human capabilities as the yardstick in terms of which successes and failures of human development are to be judged, attention is particularly invited to addressing these social interconnections. Given clarity regarding the ends (avoiding, in particular, the pitfall of treating human beings as means), the social and economic instrumentalities involved in the ends-means relations can be extensively explored.

One of the most important tasks of an evaluative system is to do justice to our deeply held human values. The challenge of "human development in the 1980s and beyond" cannot be fully grasped without consciously facing this issue and paying deliberate attention to the enhancement of those freedoms and capabilities that matter most in the lives that we can lead. To broaden the limited lives into which the majority of human beings are willy-nilly imprisoned by force of circumstances is the major challenge of human development in the contemporary world. Informed and intelligent evaluation both of the lives we are forced to lead and of the lives we would be able to choose to lead through bringing about social changes is the first step in confronting that challenge. It is a task that we must face.

———

NOTES

[1] *Grundlegung* (1785), sect. II; English translation, *Fundamental Principles of the Metaphysics of Morals,* in *Kant's Critique of Practical Reason and Other Works on the Theory of Ethics,* 6th edition, T. K. Abbot, ed. (London, Longmans, 1909), p. 47.

[2] Amartya Sen, "Equality of what?", in *Tanner Lectures on Human Values,* S. M. McMurring, ed., vol. I (Cambridge, Cambridge University Press, 1980, reprinted in *Choice, Welfare and Measurement* (Oxford, Blackwell; and Cambridge, Massachusetts, MIT Press, 1982)); *Resources, Values and Development* (Oxford, Blackwell; and Cambridge, Massachusetts, Harvard University Press, 1984); *Commodities and Capabilities* (Amsterdam, North-Holland, 1985); "Well-being, agency and freedom: the Dewey lectures 1984", *Journal of Philosophy,* 82 (April 1985); and "Capability and well-being", WIDER conference paper, 1988.

[3] Aristotle, *The Nicomachean Ethics,* book I, sect. 7; in the translation by David Ross, *World's Classics* (Oxford, Oxford University Press, 1980), pp. 12-14. Note that Aristotle's term "eudaimonia", which is often misleadingly translated simply as "happiness", stands for fulfilment of life in a way that goes well beyond the utilitarian perspective. Though pleasure may well result from fulfilment, that is seen as a consequence rather than the cause of valuing that fulfilment. For an examination of the Aristotelian approach and its relation to recent works on functionings and capabilities, see Martha Nussbaum, "Nature, function and capability: Aristotle on political distribution", *Oxford Studies in Ancient Greek Philosophy,* supplementary volume 1988.

[4] See Adam Smith, *An Inquiry into the Nature and Causes of the Wealth of Nations* (1776), vol. I, book V, sect. II; republished, R. H Campbell and A. S. Skinner, eds. (Oxford, Clarendon Press, 1976), pp. 869-872; and Karl Marx, *Economic and Philosophic Manuscripts of 1844* (1844); English translation (Moscow Progressive Publishers, 1977).

[5] See G. E. M. de Sainte Croix, *The Class Struggle in the Ancient Greek World* (London, Duckworth, 1981); and Martha Nussbaum, "Nature, function and capability . . ."

[6] Karl Marx, *Economic and Philosophic Manuscripts of 1844* . . .

[7] Aristotle, *op. cit.,* book I, sect. 5; in the translation by David Ross, p. 7.

[8] Karl Marx, *Capital,* vol. I, English translation by S. Moore and E. Aveling (London, Sonnenschein, 1887), chap. 1, sect. 4, pp. 41-55; see also Karl Marx, *Economic and Philosophic Manuscripts of 1844* . . .

[9] See Adam Smith, *op. cit.,* vol. II, book V, chap. II (section entitled "Taxes upon Consumable Commodities"); republished . . . , pp. 469-471.

[10] There are several technical problems in the representation of functioning n-tuples and of capability as a set of alternative functioning n-tuples, any one n-tuple of which a person can choose. In this paper, I shall not be particularly concerned with these formal matters, for which see *Commodities and Capabilities* . . . , especially chaps. 2, 4 and 7.

[11] Karl Marx and Friedrich Engels, *The German Ideology* (1846). The quoted passage is taken from the translation by David McLellan, *Karl Marx: Selected Writings* (Oxford, Oxford University Press, 1977), p. 190.

[12] See Amartya Sen, "Well-being, agency and freedom . . ."; and *Commodities and Capabilities* . . .

[13] It is sometimes presumed that to depart from a person's own actual desires or pleasures as the measuring rod of assessment would be to introduce paternalism into the evaluative exercise. This view overlooks the important fact that having pleasure and desiring are not themselves valuational activities, even though the latter (desire) can often result from valuing something, and the former (pleasure) can often result

from getting what one values. A person's utility must not be confused with his or her own valuations, and thus tying the evaluative exercise to the person's own utility is quite different from judging a person's success in terms of the person's own valuation. The important distinction to note in this context is that a person may not have the courage to desire a big social change weighed down by the circumstances in which he or she lives, and yet given the opportunity to evaluate the situation, which is essentially a political exercise in this context, the person may well value a change. One advantage of valuing as opposed to feeling is that a proper evaluation has to be a reflective exercise—open to critical examination—in a way that feelings need not be (the requirement of critical examination does not apply in the same way to feelings as it does to reflective evaluations). These and related issues are discussed in "Well-being, agency and freedom . . ."

[14] In many contexts, the formal representations will take the form of partial orderings, or of overdetermined rankings, or of "fuzzy" relations. This is, of course, not a special problem with the capability approach, and applies generally to conceptual frameworks in social theory; see Amartya Sen, *Collective Choice and Social Welfare* (San Francisco, Holden-Day, 1970; republished, Amsterdam, North-Holland, 1979); and *On Ethics and Economics* (Oxford, Blackwell, 1987); see also "Social choice theory", in *Handbook of Mathematical Economics*, K. J. Arrow and M. Intriligator, eds. (Amsterdam, North-Holland, 1985). The formal problems can be dealt with at different levels of precision (i.e., with varying extent of precise representation of ambiguities). The important general point to note here is that it may be, for substantive social theories, both terribly limiting and altogether unnecessary to shun ambiguities.

[15] See Amartya Sen, *Choice, Welfare and Measurement* . . . , essays 17-20.

[16] Bernard Williams raises this issue in his comments on the Tanner Lectures on the standard of living; see *The Standard of Living*, Tanner Lectures of Amartya Sen, with discussions by John Muellbauer, Ravi Kanbur, Keith Hart and Bernard Williams, edited by Geoffrey Hawthorn (Cambridge, Cambridge University Press, 1987), pp. 98-101 and 108-109.

[17] I have tried to discuss some of the general methodological issues involved in description in "Description as choice", *Oxford Economic Press*, 32 (1980); reprinted in *Choice, Welfare and Measurement* . . .

[18] See Amartya Sen, *Resources, Values and Development* . . . , chaps. 15, 19 and 20; and "The concept of development", in *Handbook of Development Economics*, H. Chenery and T. N. Srinivasan, eds. (Amsterdam, North-Holland, forthcoming).

[19] The range of functionings and capabilities that may be of interest for the assessment of a person's well-being or agency can be very wide indeed; see Amartya Sen, "Well-being, agency and freedom . . ."

[20] See, among other contributions, Michael Lipton, *Assessing Economic Performance* (London, Staples Press, 1968); Paul Streeten, *The Frontiers of Development Studies* (London, Macmillan, 1972); Irma Adelman and Cynthia Tuft Morris, *Economic Growth and Social Equity in Developing Countries* (Stanford, Stanford University Press, 1973); Amartya Sen", "On the development of basic income indicators to supplement GNP measures", *Economic Bulletin for Asia and the Far East* (United Nations publication, Sales No. E.74.II.F.4); H. Chenery and others, *Redistribution with Growth* (London, Oxford University Press, 1974); Irma Adelman, "Development economics: a reassessment of goals", *American Economic Review*, Papers and Proceedings, 66 (1975); James P. Grant, *Disparity Reduction Rates in Social Indicators* (Washington, D.C., Overseas Development Council, 1978); Keith Griffin and Azizur Rahman Khan, "Poverty in the third world: ugly facts and fancy models", *World Development*, 6 (1978); Paul Streeten and S. J. Burki, "Basic needs: some issues", *World Development*, 6 (1978); Morris D. Morris, *Measuring the Conditions of the World's Poor: The Physical Quality of Life Index* (Oxford, Pergamon, 1979); Paul Streeten, *Development Perspectives* (London, Macmillan, 1981); Paul Streeten and others, *First Things First: Meeting Basic Needs in Developing Countries* (New York, Oxford University Press, 1981); S. R. Osmani, *Economic Inequality and*

Group Welfare (Oxford, Clarendon Press, 1982); and Frances Stewart, *Planning to Meet Basic Needs* (London, Macmillan, 1985).

[21] This general question of foundations and informational bases is discussed in Amartya Sen, "Informational analysis of moral principles", in *Rational Action,* Ross Harrison, ed. (Cambridge, Cambridge University Press, 1979); and "Well-being, agency and freedom . . ." In the latter analysis, some distinctions are drawn (especially between agency and well-being and between achievement and freedom) that may be worth pursuing in a more elaborate treatment of this matter, but I shall resist the temptation to go into these issues here.

[22] On this general question and on the relation between commodities, characteristics and functionings, see Amartya Sen, *Commodities and Capabilities* . . . , chap. 2.

[23] On this question, see Amartya Sen, *Resources, Values and Development* . . . , essays 19 and 20; and Paul Streeten, "Basic needs: some unsettled questions", *World Development,* 12 (1984).

[24] John Rawls, *A Theory of Justice* (Oxford, Clarendon Press; and Cambridge, Massachusetts, Harvard University Press, 1971), pp. 60-65.

[25] See Amartya Sen, "Equality of what?" . . . . , and *Resources, Values and Development* . . .

[26] See Amartya Sen, "Freedom of choice: concept and content", Alfred Marshall Lecture at the European Economic Association, *European Economic Review,* 1988.

[27] See Amartya Sen, *Commodities and Capabilities* . . . , pp. 60-67.

[28] See Amartya Sen, "Well-being, agency and freedom . . ."; and "Freedom of choice: concept and content . . ."

[29] On the question of the relation between achieved states and the extent of freedom and liberty, see Amartya Sen, "Liberty and social choice", *Journal of Philosophy,* 80 (1983).

[30] Indeed, not to take note of the person's own evaluations of states of affairs in providing a measure of freedom can yield a very peculiar view of freedom, which would be seriously at odds with the tradition of seeing freedom as important. On this, see Amartya Sen, "Liberty as control: an appraisal", *Midwest Studies in Philosophy,* 7 (1982); and "Liberty and social choice . . ."

[31] See, for example, A. B. Atkinson, *Unequal Shares: Wealth in Britain* (London, Penguin, 1972); and *The Economics of Inequality* (Oxford, Clarendon Press, 1975).

[32] I have discussed this question in *Commodities and Capabilities* . . . , appendix B, and also in *Resources, Values and Development* . . . , essays 15 and 16. The importance of perception biases in the continuation of inter-gender inequalities is discussed in "Gender and cooperative conflicts", WIDER working paper, in *Persistent Inequalities,* Irene Tinker, ed. (forthcoming).

[33] For an attempt to make such functioning-based comparisons between men and women, see Jocelyn Kynch and Amartya Sen, "Indian women: well-being and survival", *Cambridge Journal of Economics,* 7 (1983).

[34] See Jocelyn Kynch, "How many women are enough: sex ratios and the right to life", *Third World Affairs 1985* (London, Third World Foundation for Social and Economic Studies, 1985). The ratios of life expectancy seem to have turned in favour of women *vis-à-vis* men, according to reported statistics in most countries (see United Nations Children's Fund, *The State of the World's Children 1988* (New York, Oxford University Press, 1988), table 7), but the undoing of past biases against women in the sex composition of the population tends to be a slow process over the years.

[35] United Nations Children's Fund, *The State of the World's Children 1988* . . . , table 4.

3

EDUCATIONAL POLICY ISSUES IN A PERIOD OF STABILIZATION AND STRUCTURAL ADJUSTMENT

*John Knight**

CONTENTS

Introduction

During the past quarter century many developing countries have, by historical standards, made rapid progress in the development of their human resources. Today, however, the pace has slowed, along with a decline in economic growth and a fiscal squeeze. The case for human resource development has not diminished: in part this is tied to the rate of population growth. Nor is the popular demand for education, health and other human resource-improving services any the less. Governments are thus posed with a severe dilemma of having to choose between adjusting to the short-run economic and fiscal constraints and pursuing the long-run human resource goals. There is a danger that the former will dominate the latter. For instance, the costs of neglecting the former are more calculable, and more attributable, than the long-run costs to the development process of neglecting the latter. Nevertheless, the solution to the short-run problems now may contribute to a series of equally pressing short-run problems in the future.

This paper takes a broad look at the main educational policy issues that face developing countries over the next decade. The following section briefly documents the substantial progress that has been made over the previous two decades, and the reasons for that

*Senior Research Officer, Oxford University Institute of Economics and Statistics; Fellow of St. Edmund Hall, Oxford.

progress. The next section examines the nature of the squeeze on education brought about by recent adverse macro-economic developments. Then, alternative methods of financing public education are considered and the efficiency and equity issues to which they give rise. The next section reviews the evidence available for establishing priorities among primary, secondary and tertiary education. Education can be productive in various ways, and not only through human capital acquisition by the immediate recipient: the penultimate section considers the human resource externalities to which education can give rise, for instance in the fields of health and demography.

The paper draws its evidence from comparative international statistics and, by way of illustration, from individual countries where it is the case that the experience of, or research in, a particular country has general interest.

Educational expansion

There has been a remarkable explosion in the quantity of education over the past two decades (see table 1). Between 1965 and 1984, in the 35 poorest countries (other than China and India), which the World Bank classifies as "low-income" countries, the primary enrolment ratio rose from 44 to 70 per cent and the secondary enrolment ratio from 9 to 23 per cent. In 1984, the proportion of children of primary school age who attended primary school was less than half in only 12 countries on the World Bank's list of 100 countries: Ethiopia, Burkina Faso, Bhutan, Burundi, Niger, Somalia, Sudan, Guinea, Sierra Leone, Pakistan, Chad and Mauritania. Another 17 countries had enrolment ratios of between 50 and 80 per cent, and the remaining 71 countries, including 13 in the low-income group, over 80 per cent. In both the groups of 36 "lower middle-income" and 23 "upper middle-income" countries, the most recent primary enrolment ratio exceeded 100 per cent. There is a strong positive correlation between GNP per capita and enrolment ratios. For instance, the 1984 secondary enrolment ratio rose from 23 to 40 to 56 per cent as group income rose. The casual nature of the positive relationship is complex, but it is as likely to reflect the demand for education, and the resources to pay for it, as to reflect the long-run effect of human capital acquisition on productivity. Some countries are clearly well away from the line of best fit. For instance, Ethiopia has remarkably little education and Pakistan less than countries at comparable income levels; the secondary system of the United Republic of Tanzania appears to be the smallest of all (the enrolment ratio being 3 per cent). By contrast, Sri Lanka, with roughly the same income level as the United Republic of Tanzania, has a secondary enrolment ratio of 61 per cent—well above the line. The secondary enrolment ratio in the Republic of Korea (at 91 per cent) is the highest in the developing world, and the upper middle-income

TABLE 1. ENROLMENT RATIOS, 1965 AND 1984
(Percentage)

	Primary		Secondary		Tertiary	
	1965	*1984*	*1965*	*1984*	*1965*	*1984*
India	74	90	27	34	5	9
China..........................	89	118	24	37	0	1
Other low income	44	70	9	23	1	3
Lower middle income	75	103	16	40	5	12
Upper middle income	95	105	29	56	7	15
High income oil exporters	43	75	10	45	1	10
Unusually low:						
Ethiopia	11	32	2	12	0	0
Bangladesh	49	62	13	19	1	5
United Republic of						
Tanzania	32	87	2	3	0	0
Pakistan	40	42	12	15	2	2
Unusually high:						
Sri Lanka	93	103	35	61	2	4
Philippines	113	107	41	68	19	29
Republic of Korea	101	99	35	91	6	26

Source: World Bank (1987), table 31.

countries as a group have a tertiary enrolment ratio (15 per cent) similar to that of the industrial market economies in 1960 (17 per cent).

Not only does this progress reflect the importance that many Governments attach to human capital formation in promoting economic development, but it also represents widespread popular pressures on Government for provision of subsidized education, pressures that stem from perceived high private rates of return. In some cases a pattern is apparent. Initial demand for primary schooling is met with a response that in time creates many primary school graduates; the pressure then turns on secondary education, which is expanded, and so on.

Lack of educated and qualified manpower may well be a crucial constraint to the economic development of sub-Saharan Africa in particular. At the time when most African countries gained independence from colonial rule, the region lagged far behind the rest of the world on nearly every indicator of educational development. In percentage terms, African educational expansion has subsequently been more rapid than that of other regions. Yet, despite remarkable educational progress—between 1960 and 1983 the median enrolment ratio in sub-Saharan Africa rose from 36 to 75 per cent at the primary and from 3 to 20 per cent at the secondary level, and enrolment in higher education rose from 21,000 to 437,000—the education gap remains wide (World Bank, 1988, p. 13).

The fiscal squeeze on education

For a sample of 55 developing countries during the three successive five-year periods 1965-1970, 1970-1975 and 1975-1980, the average growth of real public educational expenditure outstripped both that of real GNP and of school-age population (see table 2). However, the gap between GNP and educational expenditure growth narrowed over the three periods, the excess being 3.6, 1.7 and 1.1 percentage points respectively. Moreover, the number of countries in which educational expenditure lagged behind GNP increased from 13 in 1965-1970 to 16 in 1970-1975, and to 22 in 1975-1980. In this last period, growth of educational expenditure fell short of growth in school-age population in 15 countries.

The world economic slowdown since 1975 and the severe world recession of 1980-1983 have had a harmful effect on trade and thus on developing countries' incomes, tax revenues and indebtedness. Between 1981 and 1985, the real per capita growth rate of all developing market economies taken together was − 1.1 per cent per annum, and of Africa − 3.1 per cent per annum. No fewer than 49 out of 82 developing countries experienced a fall in income per capita over the period 1980-1985 (Cornia and others, 1987, p. 16).

TABLE 2. ANNUAL GROWTH RATE, 55 DEVELOPING COUNTRIES AS A GROUP

	1965-1970	1970-1975	1975-1980
Real GNP	5.1	5.1	5.1
Real public educational expenditure	8.7	6.8	6.2
School-age population	3.0	2.9	2.4

Source: World Bank (1986), appendix table 1.

With a large proportion of the public budget devoted to education in many developing countries, education is prone to be a victim of budget cuts. Not only the quantity but also the quality of education suffers—teacher-pupil ratios, educational materials and equipment, and teachers' morale all decline. To illustrate from particular countries: between 1979 and 1983 real public expenditure on education fell in Argentina by 9 per cent, Bolivia by 14 per cent, Costa Rica by 17 per cent, El Salvador by 8 per cent, Ghana by 10 per cent, the Sudan by 17 per cent and Tunisia by 16 per cent; in almost all of these countries GDP per capita also fell during that period (Cornia and others, 1987, p. 76). Measuring vulnerability by the percentage change in real expenditure, for a sample of 57 developing countries, education was second, after economic services, as the most vulnerable sector of government expenditure, defence and general public services being the least vulnerable. Only in the group of 16 African countries was education the least vulnerable sector, health being the most vulnerable.

Further evidence of this process of squeezing education is obtained from a comparison of education in central government expenditure in 1972 and 1985 (see table 3). For all groups of countries, and particularly for the poorest group, the share of the social services, that is, education and health, declined significantly. The fall was particularly marked in the group of highly indebted countries. However, in sub-Saharan Africa, the educationally most deficient region, the share managed to rise a little.

TABLE 3. PERCENTAGE OF TOTAL CENTRAL GOVERNMENT EXPENDITURE DEVOTED TO EDUCATION AND HEALTH, 1972 AND 1985

	Education		Health	
	1972	*1985*	*1972*	*1985*
35 low-income countries (excluding India and China)	13.2	7.6	4.9	3.7
36 lower middle-income countries	16.4	13.8	5.2	3.8
23 upper middle-income countries	12.3	10.6	7.9	4.6
4 high-income oil exporters	15.2	11.1	5.5	6.4
Memorandum items:				
Highly indebted countries	14.0	9.9	8.5	4.6
Sub-Saharan Africa	13.2	14.5	5.1	5.7

Source: World Bank (1987), table 23.

Despite the relative protection of education in Africa, a recent survey of that region paints a picture of stagnating enrolment at the primary level and deteriorating quality at all levels since 1980 (World Bank, 1988). The quality of education appeared to fall as educational funds were squeezed, a squeeze often directed particularly at educational materials. As a short-run response this is understandable, but unless the trend can be reversed, the long-run consequences could be serious for a region still crucially short of educated and qualified manpower.

Financing of education

In recent years, there has been an increasing tendency to prescribe user charges for publicly provided social services. The argument is sometimes that they are desirable in themselves, and sometimes that they are a solution to the problem of the fiscal squeeze on education that may be preferable to restricting the quantity and quality of public education.

This prescription has to be evaluated from the viewpoints of both efficiency and equity. The standard argument against school fees is that they will deter able but poor children, that is, both efficiency and equity will suffer. However, that response is too simple. Evaluation requires distinguishing between the different levels of education, examining the evidence of each case and judging the practicability of alternative schemes.

Table 4, based on data for 27 countries, indicates that cost recovery is generally low in public education. In Africa, the percent-

63

age of unit cost recovered is smallest at the tertiary level, but in all regions the differences in unit costs between educational levels ensure that the absolute size of the public subsidy increases with educational level. In part this reflects the inability of all but a small minority to find the full cost of higher education in poor countries, in part a response to demands for subsidies from articulate socio-economic groups. Quite often the subsidy for the living expenses of a university student will be many multiples of the total subsidy of a primary school pupil.

TABLE 4. EXTENT OF COST RECOVERY IN PUBLIC EDUCATION

| | Percentage of unit cost recovered | | |
	Primary	Secondary	Tertiary
East Africa	6.3	16.6	2.6
West Africa	11.3	9.8	3.1
Asia	1.7	16.0	11.5
Latin America	0.9	1.7	6.6

Source: World Bank (1986), p. 10.

Not only is public education heavily subsidized, particularly at the higher level, but also it is the richer households that benefit disproportionately from the subsidies. They are over-represented at all levels of education, but especially at the higher level. Thus, for instance, the children of white-collar workers appropriate 1.2 times their "share" of public educational expenditure in developed countries but 3.5 times their share in developing countries, the highest ratio (5.9) being found in Francophone Africa (World Bank, 1986, p. 15).

Can the degree of educational subsidization be reduced without harmful consequences for equity or efficiency? User charges at the primary level are least to be recommended: they might interfere with universal coverage and eliminate some of the talented before their talent has been discovered. The sort of use to which fees might be put is to finance additional textbooks, of which many primary schools are woefully short.

There are various reasons to choose higher education when embarking on a programme of cost recovery: the heavy subsidization per student, the existing inequality of access, the excess demand in many countries and the greater feasibility of student loans at this level. To overcome imperfections of the capital market, government-administered loans would be a necessary condition for charging for higher education. With fewer numbers and larger sums involved in higher education, the administration and collection costs of a loan scheme are lower than for secondary education. However, the commitments and risks involved in loans may deter some poor families: a loan scheme should be combined with a selective scholarship scheme for which the criteria would be financial need and academic potential.

Starting instead with secondary education carries the danger that a financial hurdle at one level followed by heavy subsidization at the next would be particularly regressive. However, given the evidence of excess demand for secondary education in many countries, there may well be a case for extending cost recovery from the higher to the secondary level.

The issues can be clarified by means of the figure below. Assume that cost recovery takes the form of school fees, denoted on the vertical axis by p, and that the number of pupils enrolled is denoted on the horizontal axis by q. There is a downward sloping demand curve for secondary education, D, and a horizontal average cost curve, AC. Assume that schooling is initially free and that the number of school places is oc: there is excess demand and the system is supply-constrained. The total cost of secondary education is abco. A rise in fees to oe would eliminate excess demand for places, but enrolment would not fall below oc. If full-cost fees were charged (oa), the system would be demand-constrained and enrolment would be of. Assume that the Government is willing to subsidize secondary education to the extent of abco, that is, fee revenue has the effect of adding to the number of places available. The curve S traces out the increases in school places made available as p is raised. The system would become demand-constrained at fee og and enrolment oh. The policy implication of this analysis is that fees can be raised (to og or to oe depending on the use made of the revenue) without an overall deterrent effect. A scholarship scheme could be used to protect those poor but able children who are part of the excess demand and who would otherwise be squeezed out by the fees.

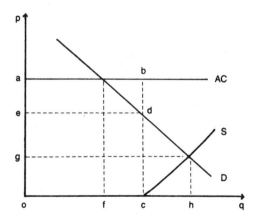

As an illustration of the equity issues involved in educational policy, I draw on a comparative analysis of Kenya and the United Republic of Tanzania (Knight and Sabot, 1987). This is based on two specially designed and rigorously comparable urban labour market surveys, each containing some 2,000 employees. In both countries there is now almost universal primary education: in 1984, the enrolment ratios were 97 per cent in Kenya and 87 per cent in the United Republic of Tanzania. Both have very small higher educational systems. The big contrast is at the secondary level: the secondary enrolment ratio was 19 per cent in Kenya but only 3 per cent in the United Republic of Tanzania.

The Tanzanian Government severely restricted the growth of secondary enrolment in state schools and discouraged the private sector. The former policy was pursued because the Government wished to give priority to primary education, and for budgetary and manpower planning reasons. The latter policy was pursued for reasons of equity: access to secondary education on the basis of ability to pay was to be discouraged. For the same reason, places in the state secondary schools were heavily subsidized and meritocratic selection criteria were applied. There was substantial excess demand for places in state schools. In 1980, only 4 per cent of those completing primary school continued to secondary school—one of the lowest progression rates in the world.

In Kenya, state secondary schools were also highly subsidized and meritocratic criteria were used to ration scarce places. The important policy difference between the two countries was that the government system grew more rapidly in Kenya and restrictions were not imposed on the private sector. This permitted the Harambee system of community secondary schools to mushroom.

The hope that meritocratic selection criteria would prove sufficient to ensure that the various income groups were represented in secondary schools in proportion to their numbers was disappointed in the United Republic of Tanzania. In part, this resulted from the pressures to subvert the selection system which inevitably flowed from the high wage form of education associated with extreme rationing of places. But there is a second and probably more important reason for unequal access to secondary school, even less avoidable than corruption. It stems from the phenomenon, observed in many countries, that children from educated backgrounds are at an advantage in academic competition. In East Africa the children of more educated parents tend to be in the higher quality primary schools. Children from educated homes also have better opportunities to acquire cognitive skills and appropriate attitudes in the home. This effect may be particularly powerful in East Africa because education is often entirely new to a family: no less than half of the urban wage labour force in both countries had parents with no education at all. Accordingly, a disproportionate number of the children of the educated are able to clear the meritocratic hurdle into government secondary school.

It might be expected that the greater importance of private schools in Kenya would produce greater inequality of access than in the United Republic of Tanzania. The surveys suggest otherwise. For the year 1975, in Kenya the probability of access to secondary school among primary school completers was 0.89 for children if one parent had at least secondary and the other at least primary education, and 0.73 for children if both parents were uneducated. In the United Republic of Tanzania, on the other hand, the two probabilities were 0.83 and 0.21 respectively. The difference between the two countries is to be explained by the difference in size of their secondary systems. Inequality of access diminished sharply as Kenyan secondary enrolments expanded rapidly. In Kenya there were places left over for the children of the uneducated after the children of the educated had claimed "their" places, but not in the United Republic of Tanzania. Our survey indicated that many of the poorer families were willing and able to pay private school fees. The frustrated demand for secondary education that resulted from government policy was concentrated among the poor.

Interestingly, it is Kenya that has the more unequal access to higher education among secondary school completers. In the United Republic of Tanzania the few children from uneducated backgrounds—the extraordinary few—who are admitted to secondary school are at least as well qualified as their more privileged peers; and they can compete on equal terms with them in secondary schools, most of which involve boarding away from home. Being larger, the Kenyan system is less selective and the variance in entry qualifications is greater. The children of the educated are found disproportionately in the high-quality, subsidized government schools, whereas the children of the uneducated tend to be found in the low-quality, little subsidized Harambee schools. Access to higher education is sharply differentiated according to education of parents among Kenyan secondary school completers but not among Tanzanians. In Kenya, therefore, the phenomenon of differential access is not avoided but is merely postponed.

Owing to heavy subsidization of places in government secondary schools, the private costs of enrolment in a government school in Kenya are less than those of enrolment in a Harambee school. Moreover, the private benefits—as measured by subsequent earning power—are also greater, reflecting the higher quality of schooling provided. The private rate of return to investment in secondary schooling is therefore far higher in government schools. This explains the substantial excess demand for government school places. Even the social returns (estimated with government subsidies added to costs) are higher in government schools, suggesting that the state schools are the more efficient system for society.

One justification for introducing heavy subsidies in government secondary schools in Kenya was the belief that, in their absence, children from poor families could not afford to attend. Yet, those with the greatest ability to bear the cost of their children's education are the most likely to receive large subsidies. These results for Kenya probably have general application.

Educational priorities

The standard technique for determining priorities for expenditure, both among different educational levels and between them and other forms of investment, is social rate of return analysis. The broad conclusions from such studies are:

(*a*) That the private rate of return to all levels of education is normally extremely high; this in turn helps to explain the high private demand and the political pressures for education;

(*b*) That the social rate of return to all levels of education, although consistently lower than the corresponding private return, is generally no less than average rates of return on fixed capital investments; thus, despite the rapid expansion, education is still not over-provided;

(*c*) That the social rate of return is generally highest at the primary level and lowest at the tertiary level of education.

Table 5, from a World Bank source, is representative of the literature and it reflects the prevailing policy view (see also Psacharopoulos and Woodhall, 1985).

TABLE 5. RETURNS TO INVESTMENT IN EDUCATION, BY COUNTRY, TYPE AND LEVEL

Number of countries reporting	Region	Social			Private		
		Primary	Secondary	Tertiary	Primary	Secondary	Tertiary
16	Africa	28	17	13	45	26	32
10	Asia	27	15	13	31	15	18
10	Latin America	26	18	16	32	23	23
45	Developing countries	24	15	13	31	19	22
15	Developed countries	-	11	9	-	12	12

Source: World Bank (1986), p. 7.

Such estimates have to be treated with caution. There is a limit to what one can learn about the social benefit of educational expansion from cross-section estimates of private earnings streams. It is difficult to know how far the earnings differences between different educational levels are attributable to the education and how far they are attributable to various non-causal correlates of education such as intelligence and determination. These points are illustrated below and their relevance to policy is drawn out.

Consider the argument that the higher income of the educated would accrue even if they had not received the education, and that it merely reflects the natural talents of those selected for or opting for education. It is sometimes claimed that education is used by employers as a "screening" device to identify the more able workers, or that education provides a "credential" which is rewarded, particularly but not exclusively in the public sector, for reasons of custom, status, or class collusion, and does not reflect higher productivity. These hypotheses are extremely difficult to test against the "human capital" hypothesis. Some progress can be made if there is information not only on the education but also on the cognitive skill and reasoning ability of workers, and if the research concentrates on the private sector. Such an approach was possible in the comparative analysis of Kenya and the United Republic of Tanzania referred to in the previous section (Knight and Sabot, 1987). To assess the value of secondary education, samples of both primary school completers and secondary school completers were given tests of their numeracy, their literacy and their reasoning ability. Scores on the numeracy and literacy were combined to yield a measure of cognitive skill.

When cognitive skill and reasoning ability are introduced as variables in the earnings function, as well as secondary school attendance, the coefficient on secondary school is much reduced. The returns to reasoning ability are small, but the returns to cognitive skill are large and statistically significant. There is considerable variance in the cognitive skill score at any given educational level, and this is positively correlated with earnings. Mere attendance at secondary school is no guarantee of higher wages: it is necessary to learn your school lessons (Boissiere, Knight and Sabot, 1985; Knight and Sabot, 1987).

These various survey results, applicable to both Kenya and the United Republic of Tanzania, are a vindication of the view that secondary education can be socially valuable. However, by comparison with many developing countries, the secondary school systems of Kenya and the United Republic of Tanzania have maintained a relatively high quality. Secondary education may not be as productive in countries where, possibly in response to uncontrolled expansion, quality is very low and is characterized by lack of materials and equipment, too many children per teacher, demoralized teachers and the so-called "diploma disease" (Dore, 1976). Recent research (reviewed by Fuller, 1986, pp. 6-9) suggests that there is a trade-off between school expansion and school quality. For instance, over the decade 1970-1980, real expenditure per pupil declined in those countries that had the fastest growth in enrolments.

Whereas estimates of the rate of return to educational expansion abound, there are far fewer estimates of the rate of return to educational improvement. Nevertheless, studies suggest that the rate of return to investments in improving school quality with unchanged enrolment are comparable with returns from increasing enrolment with unchanged quality (for instance, Behrman and Birdsall, 1983, for Brazil). A recent African survey concluded that, at the primary level, the best investment in educational quality is to ensure that there are enough books and supplies—an input almost invariably underfunded yet shown to be effective in raising test scores (World Bank, 1988, p. 4).

It is possible that some of the estimated rates of return to primary schooling are misleadingly high. A number of estimates are based on dated surveys in which primary school completers tended to be in urban wage employment and the uneducated in peasant farming, and at a time when the income gap between urban wage earners, protected by minimum wages or trade unions, and peasant farmers was large. Rates of return estimated in this way are liable to be a poor guide to the returns to expanding primary education to reach the majority of children, who will remain in agriculture all their lives. What is required to estimate the returns to primary education at the margin is production function-type analysis of the effect of primary education on farmer efficiency, of the sort surveyed and conducted by Cotlear (see Daniel Cotlear, "The effects of education on farm productivity", in the present issue).

Although the limitations of much rate of return methodology and data do not permit confident policy prescription, the evidence suggests that in many countries more education at most levels is a good economic investment. In addition, there is a non-economic case for widespread primary education, as a means of improving the lives of the poor.

Linkages with education

There is likely to be a nexus of interrelationships among education, health, fertility, nutrition and income, each assisting and reinforcing the other. For instance, healthy, well-nourished children learn more effectively: school health and feeding programmes have been recommended as potentially productive where sickness and malnourishment impair learning (World Bank, 1988, p. 45). Similarly, educated parents are likely to have fewer but healthier and better-nourished children. In so far as education raises income, it is also likely to improve health and nutrition, and vice versa. The value of education can depend on the availability of other "basic needs" goods: a package may well be more valuable than its components. It is unfortunately inherent in these interrelationships that they are difficult to isolate empirically. Nevertheless, some evidence has been accumulated.

Education can improve health in various ways. Not only can it raise the income of the recipient and so improve the health of his or her family by means of improved food consumption, housing and health care etc., but it can also raise the recipient's knowledge of health care. The education of women may be particularly important in improving the nutrition and health care of children. There is empirical evidence that maternal education is closely related to child health, whether measured by nutritional status or infant and child mortality (Cochrane and others, 1980; World Bank, 1988, p. 24). Bivariate analysis of infant and child mortality indicates that, on the average, an additional year of schooling for mothers results in a reduction of 9 per 1,000 in the mortality of their offspring. Multivariate analysis implies that about a third of this effect results from the fact that more educated women tend to be married to more educated men. The exact mechanisms through which education acts to affect child health are unclear but the evidence suggests that knowledge is no less important than income.

One of the indirect benefits of education in developing countries can be a decline in fertility (Cochrane, 1979). We would expect education to alter attitudes and perceptions in such a way as to reduce the perceived benefits and increase the perceived costs of having children. School-attenders' potential for work is reduced and their schooling may be costly: the possibility of education makes parents more concerned about the "quality" rather than the "quantity" of their children, and the spread of education may erode customary values about family size. In practice, however, the relationship is more complicated. In countries where more than 60 per cent of the population is literate, individuals with some education have lower fertility than those with no education. The relationship holds more strongly for urban than for rural areas and for the education of women than of men. However, in countries where less than 40 per cent of the population is literate, education appears to increase fertility. In these, generally poorer, countries the uneducated may be unable to afford larger families.

Conclusion

There is a danger that investments in human resources, such as expenditure on education, will suffer in a period of macro-economic stabilization and fiscal retrenchment. Nevertheless, the high estimated social rates of return to investments in both the quantity and the quality of education suggest that education can be important in achieving structural adjustment and long-run economic growth. A possible way out of what appears in many countries to be an impasse is the more extensive levying of user charges at post-primary levels. Because the current system of subsidizing education appears to be regressive in many cases, higher user charges, if accompanied by appropriate scholarship schemes, would not necessarily be inequitable and might indeed reduce income inequality.

REFERENCES

Behrman, J. and N. Birdsall (1983). The quality of schooling: quantity alone is misleading. *American Economic Review,* vol. 73, no. 5, pp. 928-946.

Boissiere, M., J. B. Knight and R. H. Sabot (1985). Earnings, schooling, ability and cognitive skills. *American Economic Review,* vol. 75, no. 5, pp. 1016-1030.

Cochrane, Susan H. (1979). *Fertility and Education: What Do We Really Know?* Baltimore: Johns Hopkins University Press.

Cochrane, Susan H., Joanne Leslie and Donald H. O'Hara (1980). The effects of education on health. World Bank Staff Working Paper No. 405. Washington, D.C.

Cornia, G. A., R. Jolly and F. Stewart (1987). *Adjustment with a Human Face. Vol. I. Protecting the Vulnerable and Promoting Growth.* Oxford: Clarendon Press.

Dore, R. P. (1976). *The Diploma Disease: Education, Qualification and Development.* London: Allen and Unwin.

Fuller, Bruce (1986). Raising school quality in developing countries. What investments boost learning? World Bank Discussion Paper No. 2. Washington, D.C.

Knight, J. B. and R. H. Sabot (1987). *Educational Expansion, Productivity and Inequality. A Comparative Economic Analysis of the East African Natural Experiment* (to be published jointly by the World Bank and Oxford University Press).

Psacharopoulos, George and Maureen Woodhall (1985). *Education for Development. An Analysis of Investment Choices.* New York: Oxford University Press.

World Bank (1986). *Financing Education in Developing Countries. An Exploration of Policy Options.* Washington, D.C.

——— (1987). *World Development Report 1987.* Washington D.C.

——— (1988). *Education in Sub-Saharan Africa. Policies for Adjustment, Revitalization and Expansion.* Washington, D.C.

4

THE EFFECTS OF EDUCATION ON FARM PRODUCTIVITY

*Daniel Cotlear**

CONTENTS

Introduction

The purpose of the study is to explore the relation between the formal, non-formal and informal education farmers have received and their subsequent efficiency as farm operators in Peru.[1] A monograph by Jamison and Lau (1982) reviews the literature in this area up to 1978 and develops a thorough theoretical and methodological framework for examining the role of education in production. Later, in an article designed to ascertain further the relation between education and farmer efficiency, Jamison and Moock (1984) provided an excellent exposition of the issues involved, and developed a useful framework for the examination and presentation of results. The present paper is written in that tradition. The data for testing aspects of the causal relationships between education and efficiency were obtained in the Peruvian Andes as part of a larger study into technological change in peasant agriculture and its determinants (see Cotlear, 1986a).

This paper is divided in the following way. The following section presents a general discussion of the determinants of agricultural productivity, with special focus on the role of education, and describes some results previously found in the literature. The discussion is summarized in the form of a set of testable empirical hypotheses. The third section describes briefly the data collection methodology and presents data that will be used to test the

---

*Adviser to the Minister of Agriculture, Government of Peru, on issues related to rural development in the Peruvian highlands.

73

hypotheses. In the fourth section, the determinants of agricultural productivity are examined using production function analysis. The last section provides a general summary and conclusions.

Theory

Three different types of education are often distinguished in the literature: "formal", which consists mainly of schooling; "non-formal", which includes different kinds of extension and organized apprenticeships; and "informal", which refers to a wide definition of learning-by-doing, including not only direct experience in a particular job but the multi-dimensional processes of learning that arise from being exposed to different circumstances (Coombs and Ahmed, 1974; Figueroa, 1986).

Education can have "cognitive" and "non-cognitive" effects. The cognitive effects consist of the development of general reasoning skills and the transmission of specific knowledge. The non-cognitive effects modify attitudes and beliefs.[2] In the cognitive area there exist strong interactions between developing a generalized capacity for thinking and learning, on the one hand, and the specific subjects learned, on the other.

It has been argued that the greater structure, longer duration and specific age group of school attendance makes formal education best suited for the "formation of competences", while the greater flexibility of non-formal services, which allow them to deliver a message closer to the work place, makes this type of education best suited for the "transmission of information" (Bowman, 1976; Jamison and Moock, 1984, p. 69). Informal education can provide either aspect of the cognitive effects depending on the specific type of experience. For example, a migration experience as an urban street seller may improve the numeracy capabilities of a peasant, facilitating future calculations of costs and returns on the farm, whereas his experience as a farm wage-labourer can put him in touch with specific information about new technologies that he can then apply to his own farm.

Many of the non-cognitive effects of education—receptivity to new ideas, competitiveness and willingness to accept discipline—are directly relevant to productive economic activity. Others—tolerance, self-confidence, social and civic responsibility—are more personal or political in nature.[3] Formal and informal education are likely to be the most important processes for the change of attitudes and beliefs.

What are the mechanisms through which education can have an effect on output and income? Education may have productive value because it enables the farmer to produce larger output quantities from the same quantities of inputs and because it helps the farmer to allocate resources in a cost-efficient manner, choosing which and how much of each output to produce, and in what proportions to use

74

inputs in their production (Jamison and Moock, 1984, p. 68). Welch (1970) has labelled these effects of education as the "worker" effect and the "allocative" effect. The former is related to the enhanced capacity of production with a given set of inputs, and the latter has to do with the farmer's ability to acquire and decode information about costs and productive characteristics of other inputs. A central aspect of the allocative effect is the capacity to evaluate and adopt profitable new technologies.

Many variables must be taken into consideration when assessing the new technologies. Imposing order on the existing evidence and understanding the results is a difficult process, and here education may be expected to play an important role. Schooling can facilitate the process in several ways. Increased numerical skills are likely to be of importance. A greater capacity for abstraction will make it easier for an educated farmer to uncover causal relations between technology and outputs which—because of long lags between application and results and weather-related randomness influencing the results—may remain obscure to less educated farmers. Well-designed extension programmes are also likely to help the farmer through this process by demonstrating technologies under conditions that are similar to the farmer's own, by pointing out the causality between the use of new inputs and specific results and by facilitating the calculations of profitability. Also crucial in this phase are the non-cognitive roles of education, which can make the farmer more receptive to new ideas and more self-confident and, consequently, more willing to innovate.

We have referred to adoption as a process largely consisting of the identification of "superior technologies". However, education itself can be a crucial complementary input in the new technological package. The superiority of the new technology over the traditionally used ones may require the presence of high levels of education. The productivity levels obtained with the new technology may crucially depend on the farmer's education.

The use of some modern technologies may involve a large number of alternative procedures, and the choice of a particular one may depend on the conditions of the natural environment or the market. When this is the case, recourse to memory may be insufficient and personalized transmission of information inefficient. In this situation, literacy may be needed to facilitate the storage of the large amounts of information involved and ease its depersonalized transmission. When chemical inputs are introduced, numeracy may be required to calculate the correct proportions in their use. All this suggests that there may exist high costs to learning the use of the new techniques, and these costs are likely to be smaller for the more educated farmers. The level of education required for the efficient use of inputs could depend on the sophistication of the new technologies. For the simpler ones, no formal education might be necessary, or basic literacy might be enough. For the more complex technologies, higher levels of education will be needed.

An implication of this is that when modern technologies are in use, education is likely to have a positive effect on productivity. Thus, education may favour adoption not only because of the role it can play in the faster discovery and assessment of the new technologies but also because it acts as a complementary input for the appropriate use of the new technologies. Hence, adoption will be more profitable for the more educated peasants. In other words, a major reason for the early adoption of the more educated farmers may be that the gain in productivity that can be obtained from the new technologies is larger for them.

The main hypothesis that derives from the preceding discussion is straightforward. Education helps people to obtain and evaluate information about improved techniques and new economic opportunities, to keep track of past events and estimate the returns to potential innovations. Education also helps people to use the new techniques adequately, with a lower learning-cost. In consequence, we expect to observe education to be associated with higher productivity.

Several studies have attempted to test this hypothesis. Lockheed, Jamison and Lau reviewed studies from 37 regions which tested the effects of farmers' schooling on agricultural productivity. Most of these studies used production function analysis to test the hypothesis: output was regressed against physical inputs and education indicators. The survey summarized the results and found that in 15 cases education had a significantly positive coefficient at the 0.05 level, in 6 cases the sign was negative but not significant and in 16 cases the sign was positive but not significant (Lockheed and others, 1980).[4] For the Latin American countries, only 4 out of 13 coefficients were positive and significant. These ambiguous results demonstrate the need for a more precise specification of the hypotheses to be tested.

Schultz has argued that the value of education is likely to be greater in a modern environment. In traditional environments, technology and markets change very slowly. Here, discovery of optimal economic behaviour in the use of technology and the allocation of resources has occurred by a long process of trial and error and the results of this process can be replicated over the years and even from generation to generation. By contrast, a modern environment is characterized by continuous changes in technology and market situations. Facing a dynamic environment of this sort, farmers constantly need to adjust to new opportunities by taking decisions concerning new options which did not exist before. Thus, changes in the technological environment increase the value of a farmer's "ability to deal with disequilibrium", and it is here that education may play a major role.[5] Evidence generally consistent with this hypothesis has been found in previous studies. When the results summarized by Lockheed, Jamison and Lau were classified according to whether the regions are modern or traditional, they found that the effects of education are much more likely to be positive in modernizing agricultural environments than in traditional ones. However, the classification used in this survey utilized *ad hoc* variables to define modernizing agriculture, and it was not possible to examine whether the regions vary in other ways which may mediate the relationship between education and productivity.

A recent paper by Figueroa (1986) compares the results from four Latin American country studies (one of which is the report with the initial results obtained in our Peru study) and concludes that education's contribution to productivity is greatest in modernizing regions. This survey of the more recent literature is unusual in that it describes in some detail the economic and social context of each region under examination before presenting the econometric results. The review of the Brazil and Mexico studies shows the problems of comparisons that include modern and traditional regions that also differ in ecological and economic characteristics.

In Mexico, the study included two traditional regions that were suffering from drought, together with two modern regions that had a good agricultural year. This introduces a problem given that the impact of education is being measured by gaps in the productivity obtained by farmers with high and lower educational levels. These gaps are reduced in a drought year when the regional variance of yields tends to fall. Figueroa recognizes that there are also difficulties in the comparison arising from differences in cropping patterns: education has an effect on the production of maize in regions where this is the most important crop, but has no distinguishable effect on maize where it is a secondary crop. The Brazil study suffers from a similar problem: its authors conclude that education has its greatest effect in modernizing regions, but arrive at this conclusion by comparing a modern region that has a widespread irrigation system with a rainfed traditional region suffering from intense drought. An important methodological lesson arising from Figueroa's review is that, to be valid, the comparison of traditional and modern regions must ensure that the observed differences in the contribution of education to productivity are not mediated by other features that distinguish the regions.

By way of summarizing the above discussion, a number of hypotheses concerning the effects of education on productivity can be presented: (*a*) formal, non-formal and informal education have a positive effect on adoption and productivity; (*b*) the role of education is likely to be stronger in modern, dynamic regions than in traditional regions; (*c*) the required level of education for the efficient use of inputs is likely to depend on the degree of sophistication of the new technologies; (*d*) since agricultural extension is more concerned with "the transmission of information" than with the "formation of competences" and given that the value of having received specific information about the use of new agricultural practices is likely to diminish with time as newer technologies are introduced, the value of extension contacts will diminish with time.

Below we are able to present results that enrich those obtained in previous research. We use data specifically collected with the above issues in mind, and hence in several respects are more precise than those used in some of the other studies. Also, we include in the analysis new variables previously overlooked in the literature. Possibly the most important improvement of this study over the previous ones, however, is that our sample was designed to include regions that are at different levels of development but that are otherwise comparable. The sample design therefore allows us to relate our findings to various specific contexts.

The interpretation of the potential correlation between education and productivity that we favour is that education functions to enhance the productive capacity of workers and the allocative ability of managers. An alternative explanation suggests that education does not make workers more productive but merely identifies those who were more productive to begin with. This argument, usually identified as the "screening hypothesis", was originally used to explain the correlation between education and earnings among employees. According to this hypothesis, employers find it difficult to identify the ability of employees and therefore need a screening mechanism to differentiate them. Workers acquire education as a mechanism to signal their ability to potential employers.[6]

Since in self-employment there are no employers and employees, there is no need for signals of the employee's ability. However, the screening hypothesis cannot be totally ruled out by the finding of a correlation between education and earnings among the self-employed, although it is weakened by it.[7] A defendant of the screening hypothesis might argue that, if the self-employed believe that education enhances their productive capacity, they may demand education in the same way as workers anticipating wage employment. The argument would be that workers in all sectors believe that education enhances their productive capacity. Even if it does not, in the wage sector it signals ability, and ability-blind employers are forced to use education as a signal for ability, and pay according to education. This behaviour reinforces the belief that education adds to productive capacity. The same cycle of belief leading to action reinforcing the belief may occur in self-employment. Since it is easier for the more able people to obtain more education, these two variables will be correlated among the self-employed and it may be impossible to discern which one affects income.

The screening argument is weakened by the fact that in self-employment there are no penalties against those with high ability and little education, and no bonuses for those with low ability and

78

(exceptionally obtained) high education levels. The relationship will therefore be weaker than in wage-employment and will tend to break down as people realize that education has no economic returns.[8]

Care must be taken when interpreting empirical results since there may be an upward bias on the education coefficients owing to the positive correlation that is likely to exist between ability (IQ, drive etc.) and education. On the other hand, if we measure the effects of education by the size of the difference in output or wages obtained by individuals of different educational levels, there is a likely tendency to underestimate the benefits of education caused by the existence of positive externalities that arise in the form of the less educated imitating the more educated. This is likely to be common in a peasant environment where agricultural activities are done out-doors and in small visible plots.[9]

The benefits of education may also be underestimated in studies using local rural samples because they neglect the effects of education on migration. Since schooling in rural areas has the effect of increasing migration, and migrants are likely to obtain higher incomes in their target than in the origin area, measuring returns to education exclusively in rural locations probably underestimates its true effects.[10]

Survey and data

The data come from a survey conducted by the author covering 555 rural households in three regions of the Peruvian highlands for the agricultural year 1982-1983. The regions of the survey were selected to comply with three characteristics required by the study. First, they have a varying degree of technological dynamism: the sample includes a modern region (R1, the valley of Yanamarca), a traditional region (R3, the pampa of Sangarara) and an intermediate region (R2, the plateau of Chinchero). Secondly, they share a similar ecological environment. Given the small size of the sample, the results concerning the effects of technology on productivity were likely to be weakened by agro-ecological factors if the entire range of ecological variation found in the highlands was represented in the sample. Hence, the survey was restricted to unirrigated areas with a narrow range of variation in altitude, temperature and levels of rainfall.[11] This is reflected in the existence of similar cropping patterns in all regions, with a high proportion of the cultivated land assigned to potatoes. Thirdly, the agricultural year was considered "normal" by most farmers in all three regions.

Table 1 presents the definitions of the variables used in the regression analysis. The input and output variables refer to the production of potatoes. The education characteristics refer to the head of household. The means and standard deviations of the

TABLE 1. VARIABLE DEFINITIONS

Variables	Definition
1. Output	Kg. of potatoes harvested.
2. Area cultivated	Area cultivated with potatoes in metres.
3. Labour input	Person-days utilized for potato production; male and female, hired and family labour days arc weighted equally.
4. Animal and tractor input	Measured in equivalent animal-days utilized for potato production; the inputs are weighted in terms of the time required to bring an area of land into the same state of readiness for planting.
5. Village dummy	Dummy variable for households from Acolla in region 1.
6. School attainment	Of head of household, in years.
7. 1-5 years of schooling	Dummy variable; 1 if schooling of head of household in this range, 0 otherwise.
8. 4-5 years of schooling	Dummy variable; 1 if schooling of head of household in this range, 0 otherwise.
9. 6+ years of schooling	Dummy variable; 1 if schooling of head of household in this range, 0 otherwise.
10. 4-5 years of rural schooling	Dummy variable; 1 if schooling of head of household in this range in rural schools, 0 otherwise.
11. 6+ years of rural schooling	Dummy variable; 1 if schooling of head of household in this range in rural schools, 0 otherwise.
12. 4-5 years of urban schooling	Dummy variable; 1 if schooling of head of household in this range in urban schools, 0 otherwise.
13. 6+ years of urban schooling	Dummy variable; 1 if schooling of head of household in this range in urban schools, 0 otherwise.
14. Recent contact with extension agent	Dummy variable; 1 if there was any contact in the 3 years previous to the survey, 0 otherwise.
15. Old contact with extension agent	Dummy variable; 1 if there was any contact 3 years before the survey, 0 otherwise.
16. Migration experience	Number of years the head of household has spent away from the village.
17. Migration experience included agricultural activity	Dummy variable; 1 if the head of household has any migration experience that includes agricultural work away from the village.
18. Age	Of head of household, in years.
19. Households in village with recent extension contact	Proportion of households in the village where the household lives that have received extension contacts in the past 3 years.
20. Households in village with old extension contact	Proportion of households in the village where the household lives that have received extension contacts 3 years before the survey.
21. Households in village with 85 per cent of potato land with HYVs	Proportion of households in the village.
22. Uses HYV	Dummy variable; 1 if some of the area cultivated is planted with high-yielding varieties, 0 otherwise.
23. Received formal credit	Dummy variable; 1 if the household received credit from a formal institution for the agricultural campaign in the year previous to the survey, 0 otherwise.

80

variables in each of the three regions of the study are presented in table 2. Here we review them very briefly.[12]

TABLE 2. MEANS AND STANDARD DEVIATIONS OF VARIABLES

		R1		R2		R3	
		Mean	s.d.	Mean	s.d.	Mean	s.d.
1.	Output (kg.)[a]	12 183	21 317	3 072	2 792	1 708	1 520
2.	Area cultivated (metres)[a]	12 618	172031	7 019	4 865	5 199	4 452
3.	Labour input (person-days)[a]	159	215	86	62	99	78
4.	Animal and tractor (equiv. animal-days)	16	48	12	7	1.0	5.8
5.	Village (dummy for Acolla)	0.22	0.42	-	-	-	-
6.	School attainment (years)[b]	6.2	2.7	4.32	2.81	3.7	3.0
7.	1-5 yrs. of school[b]	0.33	0.47	0.36	0.48	0.41	0.49
8.	4-5 yrs. of school[b]	0.19	0.39	0.25	0.43	0.15	0.36
9.	6+ yrs. of school[b]	0.65	0.48	0.43	0.50	0.33	0.47
10.	4-5 yrs. of rural schooling[b]	0.08	0.26	0.09	0.28	0.15	0.36
11.	6+ yrs. of rural schooling[b]	0.29	0.45	0.08	0.27	0.21	0.41
12.	4-5 yrs. of urban schooling[b]	0.11	0.31	0.16	0.37	0	0
13.	6+ yrs. of urban schooling[b]	0.37	0.48	0.35	0.48	0.12	0.33
14.	Recent contact with ext. ag. (0,1)[b]	0.10	0.30	0.29	0.45	0.07	0.25
15.	Old contact with ext. ag. (0,1)[b]	0.24	0.43	0.30	0.46	0.16	0.37
16.	Migration experience (years)[b]	2.90	4.62	2.13	4.12	1.91	3.41
17.	Migration experience inc. agriculture (0,1)[b]	0.13	0.33	0.16	0.37	0.10	0.30
18.	Age[b]	43.8	13.5	43.4	14.9	47.3	12.9
19.	Households in village with recent extension contact (proportion)	0.10	0.12	0.28	0.14	0.06	0.04
20.	Households in village with old extension contact (proportion)	0.24	0.16	0.37	0.05	0.14	0.04
21.	Households in village with 85 per cent of potato land under cultivation with HYVs	0.70	0.17	0.09	0.06	0.01	0.01
22.	Uses HYV (0,1)[a]	0.92	0.27	0.36	0.48	0.03	0.18
23.	Received formal credit (0,1)	0.24	0.43	0.50	0.50	0.22	0.42
	Number of observations	254		151		150	

[a]Referred to potato production.
[b]Referred to household head.

The ratio of average output to average land or to average labour input shows the "gradient of modernity" which characterizes the comparison of the three regions: productivity of land and labour are highest in R1 and lowest in R3. This same gradient is found for the use of high-yielding varieties (HYVs): most households use them in R1, about a third use them in R2 and only 3 per cent use them in R3.[13]

The educational indicators of most interest for policy purposes are formal educational attainment and exposure to non-formal education (extension and practical course-training). However, informal education indicators will also be included in the analysis because their exclusion from the analysis may produce misleading results concerning the effects of the other types of education.

School attainment shows the same gradient as productivity in the sample, being highest in R1 and lowest in R3. The heads of households studied on average 6.2 years in R1, 4.3 in R2 and 3.7 in R3. One of the hypotheses discussed above is that a minimum level of education is required for certain purposes. This effect is easier to test if schooling is measured by discrete rather than by continuous variables. Hence, school attainment will be divided into three categories and handled by means of two dummy variables.[14] The three categories of classification chosen are: (a) never went to school or studied for less than four years (the omitted variable), (b) studied four or five years and (c) studied six years or more. This breakdown was chosen to reflect the institutional structure of the educational system in Peru. In rural villages where a school is available, the minimal educational supply usually found extends to the fourth grade: we have chosen completion of this basic cycle as the first dividing line. Complete primary education in Peru consists of six years of schooling: this has been taken as the second dividing line.

If non-formal education is concerned with the transmission of specific information about technologies and market structures, the value of this type of education is likely to diminish with time as the specific technologies or market situations grow obsolete. Also, the effects of non-formal education as measured by the differential between households will tend to diminish as other households learn the new techniques by imitating the innovators. The above suggests that recent contacts should be more important determinants of productivity differentials than old contacts, as the households that receive the more recent bits of relevant information take advantage of them by increasing their productivity. We use two dummy variables to measure the impact of non-formal education and test this hypothesis. The two variables show whether there has been direct contact in the past three years, only before that period or not at all (variables 10 and 11).[15]

We also test for the existence of indirect effects of extension through imitation. This is done with the use of special variables that assign to each household the village-wide proportion of households that have been contacted by extensionists. Two such variables are considered: one measures the indirect effect of recent extension (less than three years) and the other measures indirect effects of previous extension.[16] A similar variable is used to measure the impact of imitation in the use of HYVs by "technological leaders", being defined as farmers who cultivate most of their potato land (85 per cent) with HYVs.

Informal education occurs in many ways; in this analysis we include two. The first is the farmer's work experience, measured by the age of the head of household. The expectation is that greater age, indicating more work experience, will increase productive efficiency.

The second form of informal education that seems relevant in the Peruvian context is migration experience. Large numbers of people leave the villages for several years to enter external labour markets in contexts different from that of the village. Experience of this sort is likely to affect attitudes and develop certain skills. Some of these may be general skills which may increase productive efficiency in agriculture: any urban job will give the farmer training in the Spanish language, which will facilitate buying inputs, obtaining credits or bargaining at the market place; a former street vendor will have improved his numeracy by dealing with money and this may facilitate his calculations on the use and mix of chemical inputs. Other skills may be more specific, such as the acquisition of technical information about the use of new agricultural inputs obtained by doing agricultural tasks away from the village. Two variables will be used to measure the effects of migration. One is the number of years spent away from the village by the head of household. This experience is slightly more common in R1 than in R2 and it is lowest in R3. The second variable is a dummy with a value of 1 for households where the farmer had migration experience that included work in agriculture. Mean values of these variables by region are shown in table 2.

The final variable to be included in the equation is an indicator of whether the household received credit from a formal institution in the agricultural year of the survey. Where the market for credit is rationed, education can play a role in facilitating access to credit. The more educated farmers are likely to be able to complete application forms and deal with bank officials with less difficulty than uneducated ones. It is therefore possible that an observed correlation between education and productivity is mediated by the role of credit. If this was the only way in which education leads to increases in productivity, the policies that would be called for would not be to expand education, but to expand the funds available and reduce the rationing. Hence, it is of great interest to establish the indirect effects of education (i.e., those that are mediated by other factors such as credit) and the direct effects (i.e., those that persist when the mediating factors are controlled for).

Differences in productivity among farms imply that different outputs are obtained from a given bundle of physical inputs. If we are interested in examining whether certain characteristics of the household, such as its level of education, have an effect on productivity, we can do this by means of production function analysis. We can specify the production function so that it includes on the right-hand side, in addition to measured physical inputs, measures of the characteristics that we hypothesize to be linked with the use of more productive techniques. Thus, it reads

$$Y=f(X,E)$$

where Y is the quantity of output, X is a vector of physical inputs and E is a vector of variables that characterize a particular farm. The functional form is a modified version of the Cobb-Douglas produc-

TABLE 3. PRODUCTION FUNCTION ESTIMATES

	R1				R2				R3			
	1	2	3	4	1	2	3	4	1	2	3	4
Constant	0.26 (0.56)	0.25 (0.53)	0.26 (0.50)	0.24 (0.44)	0.74 (1.35)	1.00 (1.89)	1.22[a] (2.34)	2.76 (1.09)	0.88 (1.63)	0.84 (1.55)	0.77 (1.37)	0.32 (0.56)
2. Area cultivated (in metres)	0.77[b] (10.88)	0.77[b] (10.78)	0.75[b] (10.32)	0.76[b] (10.3)	0.56[b] (5.22)	0.52[b] (5.02)	0.49[b] (4.83)	0.48[b] (4.80)	0.58[b] (7.95)	0.59[b] (7.99)	0.60[b] (7.95)	0.60[b] (8.04)
3. Labour input (in person-days)	0.35[b] (5.27)	0.35[b] (5.22)	0.32[b] (4.79)	0.32[b] (4.86)	0.49[b] (4.37)	0.52[b] (4.69)	0.49[b] (4.57)	0.51[b] (4.72)	0.34[b] (4.85)	0.34[b] (4.65)	0.34[b] (4.66)	0.32[b] (4.35)
4. Animal and tractor (in equivalent animal-days)	0.02 (1.83)	0.02 (1.85)	0.02[a] (2.00)	0.02 (1.91)	0.01 (0.28)	0.01 (0.21)	0.01 (0.34)	0.02 (0.49)	0.01 (0.75)	0.01 (0.86)	0.01 (0.85)	0.01 (0.90)
5. Village (Acolla = 1, other = 0)	-0.21[a] (-2.23)	-0.21[a] (-2.23)	-0.19[a] (-1.99)	-0.06[a] (-0.54)	-	-	-	-	-	-	-	-
8. 4-5 yrs. of schooling (0,1)	0.14 (1.27)	0.15 (1.28)	0.15 (1.27)	0.11 (0.97)	0.13 (1.35)	0.12 (1.23)	0.13 (1.62)	0.17 (1.86)	0.13 (1.15)	0.14 (1.21)	0.14 (1.22)	0.15 (1.31)
9. 6 or more years of schooling (0,1)	0.37[b] (3.52)	0.36[b] (3.45)	0.35[b] (3.28)	0.31[b] (2.87)	0.24[b] (2.48)	0.16 (1.68)	0.16 (1.65)	0.18 (1.89)	0.05 (0.56)	0.07 (0.70)	0.08 (0.80)	0.08 (0.72)
18. Age (years)	-0.1[b] (-2.81)	-0.01[b] (-2.81)	-0.1[b] (2.74)	-0.1[b] (-2.90)	-0.004 (-1.66)	-0.01[a] (-2.17)	-0.004 (1.60)	0.003 (-1.17)	-0.00 (-0.16)	-0.00 (-0.09)	-0.00 (-0.02)	-0.00 (-0.16)
14. Recent contact with ext. agent (0,1)	0.09 (0.84)	0.10 (0.85)	0.08 (0.75)	0.07 (0.58)	0.29[b] (3.42)	0.33[b] (3.93)	0.27[b] (3.25)	0.27[b] (3.14)	0.11 (0.66)	0.13 (0.80)	0.13 (0.76)	0.15 (0.89)
15. Old contact with ext. agent (0,1)	-0.05 (0.60)	-0.05 (-0.62)	-0.05 (-0.54)	-0.10 (-1.15)	-0.00 (-0.05)	0.01 (0.15)	-0.01 (-0.18)	0.01 (0.16)	0.04 (0.37)	0.04 (0.33)	0.04 (0.40)	0.04 (0.39)

	(1)	(2)	(3)	(4)	(5)	(6)	(7)	(8)	(9)	(10)	(11)	(12)
16. Migration experience (yrs.)	–	0.00 (0.37)	0.00 (0.53)	0.00 (0.62)	–	–0.03b (3.36)	0.03b (3.06)	0.03b (3.11)	–	–0.01 (–0.58)	–0.01 (–0.47)	–0.01 (–0.50)
17. Migration experience included agric. activity (0,1)	–	–0.02 (–0.18)	–0.02 (–0.19)	–0.01 (–0.05)	–	–0.22a (–2.21)	–0.21a (–2.14)	0.24a (2.35)	–	0.13 (1.00)	0.11 (0.86)	0.14 (1.05)
23. Received formal credit (0,1)	–	–	0.11 (1.23)	0.09 (0.99)	–	–	0.08 (1.20)	0.11 (1.51)	–	–	–0.6 (–0.58)	–0.06 (–0.54)
22. Uses HYVs (0,1)	–	–	0.26a (1.99)	0.28a (2.16)	–	–	0.20b (2.68)	0.18b (2.44)	–	–	0.07 (0.32)	0.07 (0.30)
19. Households in village with recent extension contact (proportion)	–	–	–	0.30 (0.86)	–	–	–	–1.00 (–0.59)	–	–	–	3.19a (1.98)
20. Households in village with old extension contact (proportion)	–	–	–	0.71a (2.36)	–	–	–	–3.65 (–0.73)	–	–	–	2.89b (2.64)
21. Households in village with 85 per cent of potato land under cultivation with HYVs	–	–	–	–0.32 (–1.19)	–	–	–	0.17 (0.10)	–	–	–	2.33 (0.21)
R square	0.853	0.853	0.857	0.860	0.782	0.800	0.813	0.821	0.717	0.719	0.719	0.736
Adjusted R square	0.848	0.847	0.849	0.851	0.769	0.786	0.797	0.801	0.701	0.699	0.695	0.707

NOTES: Numbers in parentheses are t values.

a Coefficient significant at 0.05 level in two tail test.

b Coefficient significant at 0.01 level in two tail test.

85

tion function. In linear form the equation estimated can be represented as:

$$ln\ Y = ln\ \alpha + \Sigma\ \beta i\ ln\ Xi + \Sigma\ \gamma i\ Ei$$

Let Y represent level of output, $ln\ Y$ the natural logarithm of output, X a vector of physical inputs and E a vector of variables that characterize a particular household. α is an efficiency parameter and βi the elasticity of output with respect to physical input i. The interpretation of the parameter γi depends on whether Ei is a continuous variable or a dummy variable. In the first case, the coefficient can be interpreted as indicating an approximation to the proportionate change in output that results when characteristic Ei (say, length of migration experience) increases by one unit (a year). When Ei is a dummy variable, then the coefficient indicates the approximate proportionate difference between the output produced by a household demonstrating this particular characteristic (say, having had recent contact with the extension services) and one produced by a household not demonstrating this characteristic.

Productivity: basic results

Table 3 shows the least-squares regression results. For each region the variables are entered in four steps, at each step adding new variables to the equation. The physical inputs, schooling, extension and experience variables are entered first. The migration variables are then added to examine whether the common neglect of these variables is likely to affect the coefficients of formal and non-formal education. Thirdly, the variables indicating use of credit and "technological level" are introduced, in order to discuss some of the direct and indirect effects of education on productive efficiency. We can thus investigate whether the main effects of the different types of education on productivity occur indirectly, through the greater access to credit and the greater propensity to adopt, or whether it has direct effects on productivity when use of credit and technological level are controlled for. Education influences the adoption of modern technology and facilitates access to credit; hence, we can expect that the inclusion of these variables in the third step will rob education of some of its indirect effects on output. This implies that equation 2 can be regarded as a reduced form equation, combining direct and indirect effects of education, and the coefficients estimated at that stage may be preferred for some effects. Separating the direct and indirect effects, however, can give us important insights into the processes through which education and the supply of new inputs and of credit interact and lead to output growth. Finally, in the fourth step, we introduce the variables measuring indirect effects of extension and learning the use of new technologies by imitation.

86

Physical inputs

The coefficients for land and labour are positive, highly significant and stable across different specifications of the production function in all these regions. The coefficient for animal and tractor inputs is positive and stable in all regions, but it is significantly different from zero at the 0.05 level only in R1. The elasticities for the physical inputs (from equation 3) add up to 1.09 in R1, 0.99 in R2 and 0.95 in R3, implying that essentially constant returns to scale exist in the production of potatoes for the three regions.[17]

Formal education

The estimated effects of the educational variables are summarized in table 4. We look first at the impact of formal education (variables 8 and 9) on output. Both variables are positive for all regions. However, the estimated effects of schooling are seen to be larger in the more modern region and to be weakest in the traditional region. Only in R1 does one find a schooling variable significantly different from zero at the 0.01 level. For this region the regression results suggest that the completion of primary school has a strong positive effect on agricultural productivity, increasing potato output

TABLE 4. SUMMARY OF PRODUCTION FUNCTION REGRESSION RESULTS

	R1				R2				R3			
Equations	1	2	3	4	1	2	3	4	1	2	3	4
From table 3												
4-5 years of schooling ..	0	0	0	0	0	0	+	+	0	0	0	0
6+ years of schooling ..	+++	+++	+++	+++	++	+	+	+	0	0	0	0
Recent extension	0	0	0	0	+++	+++	+++	+++	0	0	0	0
Old extension	0	0	0	0	0	0	0	0	0	0	0	0
Age.....................	—	—	—	—	-	–	-	0	0	0	0	
Migration experience ...		0	0	0	+++	+++	+++			0	0	0
Migration to agriculture		0	0	0	-	–	-			0	0	0
Indirect recent extension			0				0					++
Indirect old extension ..			++				0					+++
Received formal credit			0	0			0	0			0	0
Uses HYV			++	++			+++	++			0	0
From table 5												
1-5 yrs of schooling					0	0	0	0	++	++	++	++
6+ yrs. of schooling....					0	0	0	0	+	+	+	+

NOTES:
+   Positive and significant at 0.10 level.
++   Positive and significant at 0.05 level.
+++   Positive and significant at 0.01 level.
-   Negative and significant at 0.10 level.
–   Negative and significant at 0.05 level.
—   Negative and significant at 0.01 level.
0   Coefficient not significant.

by approximately one third, whereas incomplete primary education seems to have no effect on output.

In R2, equation 1 suggests that complete primary education is important, but this variable loses significance when migration is included in the production function (more about this below). Equations 3 and 4 show that complete and incomplete primary schooling have t values which closely approach levels conventionally considered satisfactory for statistical significance.[18] In this region the effects of complete or incomplete primary education on output are similar, and they imply an increase of about 15 per cent in output as compared to farmers with less than 4 years of education.

Table 3 shows that in R3 there is no significant difference between different education levels. However, since we have seen the threshold of "impacting schooling" fall as we move from a modern into a more traditional region, could it be the case that as we move into a still more traditional region the threshold would fall even further? To test this hypothesis we ran the same regressions shown in table 3, replacing the variable used to measure incomplete primary education. In the original equations, "incomplete primary" begins with 4 years of schooling. We redefined the variable to start with one year of schooling.[19] The results for regions 2 and 3 are shown in table 5 and the estimated effects of the education variables are summarized in the second block of table 4.[20] Table 5 shows that in R3 schooling does have an effect, but only when one compares peasants with schooling with those with no schooling at all. The effect of completing primary education does not add to that of having "some education". By contrast, in R2 there is not only no effect of incomplete primary education but the effect of complete primary education is much weaker than that found with the previous specification. This suggests that in R2 "a couple" of years of schooling does not help and may even harm output.[21]

TABLE 5. PRODUCTION FUNCTION COEFFICIENTS FOR FORMAL EDUCATION, USING FARMERS WITH ZERO YEARS OF SCHOOLING AS THE BASE GROUP[a]

	R2				R3			
	1	*2*	*3*	*4*	*1*	*2*	*3*	*4*
1-5 years of schooling (0,1)	-0.3	-0.3	-0.00	0.00	0.24[b]	0.24[b]	0.25[b]	0.24[b]
	(-0.29)	(-0.28)	(-0.04)	(0.91)	(2.39)	(2.37)	(2.45)	(2.40)
6+ years of schooling (0,1)	0.15	0.07	0.08	0.09	0.20	0.21	0.24	0.21
	(1.31)	(0.69)	(0.71)	(0.81)	(1.66)	(1.72)	(1.87)	(1.72)
R square	0.78	0.80	0.81	0.82	0.73	0.72	0.73	0.74
Adjusted R square	0.77	0.78	0.79	0.80	0.71	0.71	0.70	0.72

NOTE: Numbers in parentheses are t values. Equations 1-4 include all variables included in equations 1-4 respectively in table 3.

[a]We could not run the regression for R1 because we have only four observations where the head of household had no education.

[b]Coefficient significant at 0.05 level in two tail test.

In summary, the analysis suggests two patterns with respect to formal education. The first is that there seems to be an effect associated with formal education in the production of potatoes for all regions in our sample, but the larger and stronger effect occurs in the modern region. This finding is fully consistent with the Schultz hypothesis. Schooling has a greater impact where conditions are dynamic and there is a greater need for economic adjustment. In traditional regions, where the economic and technological environment changes slowly, there are fewer tasks for education to fulfil, and schooling has weaker effects on productivity. None of our regions is completely stagnant, however, and that is probably what accounts for the positive effect found in all regions.

Secondly, there seems to exist in the three regions a level of schooling that represents a threshold at which formal education begins to have an effect. However, the level of this threshold differs across regions, increasing with the complexity of the technology found in each region. It is lowest in R3, where "some" schooling has an effect, increases in R2, where 4 years are required to obtain an effect, and is largest in R1, where only complete primary education shows an effect. Adoption of the simplest modern inputs is only starting in R3, and it is in R1 where one finds more modern inputs and practices being used and in more complex combinations. There is good reason to expect the educational threshold to be different where the tasks imposed upon education are different. The pattern found in the Peruvian highlands suggests that there is a threshold regarding the amount of schooling needed to have an impact on productivity, and that the level of this threshold depends on the degree of modernity, that is, the complexity of the technological and market problems that need to be solved. The greater their complexity, the larger the minimum level of education required to obtain an impact on productivity. This suggests that, while the generalization of literacy in the traditional areas may act as a catalyst speeding traditional regions into the first stages of technical change, further technological development will require higher levels of formal education.

Migration is widespread in all regions. It is usually the young who migrate; more than 60 per cent of the offspring who leave the parental home do so through migration. In all regions, migration is more common among the better educated, but as with total migration, the propensity to migrate among youngsters with complete primary education is stronger in the traditional region (64 per cent), decreases in the intermediate region (57 per cent) and is lowest in the modern region (34 per cent).

Part of the interregional differences in education levels are due to differences in the rates of migration of the educated and differences in the supply of schooling. It should be noted, however, that part of the difference is also due to the demand for schooling. School attendance depends partly on the existence of local schools but this is not the sole factor. In villages without a school, some

89

children commute to the school in the neighbouring village. For instance, in Sacas, in R1, the local school was founded in 1965, but less than 5 per cent of the farmers aged more than 40 are illiterate, and almost half completed primary school in the neighbouring school (two hours away by foot). Just as the lack of a local school does not imply a necessary "educational ceiling", the existence of a secondary school does not guarantee school attendance. This is illustrated in R3, where a group of rich farmers obtained the foundation of a primary state school in the 1920s. Farmers in Pomacanchi have had the possibility of sending their sons to this school for the past half century, yet one fourth of heads of household never went to school and over two thirds never completed primary school.

Expanding the availability and quality of schools in rural areas will not be sufficient to raise the education levels of the farmers in the long run. The achievement of this objective will also require increasing the incentives for parents to send their children to school and keep them there, and reducing the outmigration of the educated children. The right incentives are more likely to be present if agriculture becomes more dynamic in the medium term.

Non-formal education: direct effects

We argued above that if extension services transmit specific information about technologies or market structures, the impact of extension contacts—as measured by a productivity differential—is likely to diminish with the passing of time as the specific technologies become obsolete, or the differential is lost by other households imitating those that had the direct contact. We would therefore expect recent contacts to show a greater effect than old contacts. This is what the coefficients for the extension variables suggest (table 3). The table shows, however, that the direct effects of extension are significantly different from zero only in R2. In this region, other things being equal, output is increased by a quarter to a third in those farms that received extension contacts.

Many factors may help explain why non-formal education has an impact in some regions and not in others. One concerns the quality of the extension service (as an institution) and the quality and commitment of the individual extensionists. It is likely that PRO-DERM, the institution providing most of the extension in R2, being a non-state, experimental, better-paying institution, would get higher marks on these two counts.

However, the crucial explanation is likely to lie in the relevance of the services being offered. The impact of extension depends on the value of the information that is being transmitted. At the time of the survey, the Peruvian extension service used a similar message for all regions in the highlands, despite the great differences that exist among regions in the use of modern inputs. The message concentrated on the use of a sophisticated technological package which included the use of a high density of fertilization and pesticides together with the introduction of high-yielding varieties of potato and a greater use of seed per hectare.

We have shown elsewhere that, in traditional regions of the Andes, adoption of new inputs occurs in a sequence (Cotlear, 1986a, chap. VI). Peasants reach the use of the frontier package of technology after proceeding through a succession of slow stages. Hence, the package promoted by the extension services was too complex to be appropriate for the needs of R3, where farmers were only starting to get acquainted with the use of low doses of chemical fertilizers. On the other hand, in R1 most farmers are already using the modern package and the extensionists had in their message few elements that could improve the use of this technology under local conditions. By contrast, in R2 there was already some use of chemical inputs, but the use of HYVs was still unknown. Here, the message was appropriate for the needs of the farmers, and this shows clearly in the value of the coefficients measuring the impact of extension on productivity.

Non-formal education: indirect effects

In R1 recent extension shows no indirect effects, and only the coefficient for the indirect effects of old extension is significantly different from zero, with a regression coefficient of 0.71. The interpretation of this variable is that a 10 per cent increase in "old" extension coverage in the farmer's village is associated with a 7 per cent increase in the farmer's potato output, other factors being the same, including the farmer's own direct extension exposure. The implication here would seem to be that a farmer can acquire technical information relevant to the production of potatoes indirectly from other farmers who have been in direct contact with extension agents, but that this indirect transmission occurs with a certain lag.

In R2 both variables measuring indirect effects of extension are not significantly different from zero. In R3 they are both positive and significant; however, the value of the coefficients there seems too large to be reflecting the real impact of extension, especially since the effect of extension on productivity should occur through a wider use of modern technologies and this has not occurred in R3. We must conclude that, at least for this region, this variable is measuring something other than what we have tried to measure.[22]

Informal education

Age, being a proxy for experience, is expected to have a positive impact on output. Table 3, however, shows that the coefficient has a negative sign in all equations for the three regions. One can also observe that the coefficient is insignificant in R3, is larger (in absolute value) in R2 (and is significant in this region in equation 2) and is most negative and significant in R1, that is, the negative effect of age on productivity increases with "modernity". This probably reflects a "cohort effect", by which the old tend to stick to the older less productive techniques they started off with. "Age" is then acting here as a proxy for the "vintage" of the techniques in use. Since "old" techniques are obsolete in R1, where technology has been going through a stage of change, but have not been much improved upon in R3, where agricultural technology has been comparatively less active, we find "age" to be significant in the modern region but not in the traditional one. The reluctance to change among the old is likely to reflect their greater risk-aversion, true even when formal education is taken into account.

An alternative explanation would be to suggest that age has a negative effect because farmers become weaker for physical work as they become older. This effect is unlikely to be of importance, because the farmer's own labour constitutes only a fraction of the total labour involved, and this fraction is likely to become smaller as the children grow up, and later as more wage-workers are hired.

We suggested above that a migration experience could provide the peasant with general skills influencing productivity. Migration to work in agricultural activities could develop specific skills. There is an even greater expectation that this sort of experience will have a positive effect on productivity.

Table 3 shows that in R2 both variables are significant. The coefficient for the number of years of migration is 0.03, suggesting that, other things being equal, output will increase by about 3 per cent for each year the peasant has spent away from the village. The mean number of years spent away by returnees is 4.8, hence the coefficient suggests that a returnee with average experience will have an output almost 15 per cent larger than non-returnees.

Surprisingly, the dummy for migration experience in agriculture has a negative sign. The coefficient for this variable shows the additional effect that an agricultural experience has on top of the migration experience variable. The relative values of the coefficients of variables 12 and 13 suggest that for long periods of migration there will be a slightly positive effect, but for short periods there may be a net negative effect. The negative coefficient is probably not due to a negative effect of learning on productivity (I found no evidence that people were unsuccessfully trying to apply inappropriate agricultural techniques learned away from the village). Instead, it probably reflects a process of self-selection: wages obtainable by migrating to work in agricultural activities are lower than those obtainable in the more selective urban labour markets, and so migration of external agricultural labour markets constitutes a process that may self-select peasants who have lower productivity to start with. This finding is also a reminder that the positive coefficient of migration must be taken with some care because it may partly reflect some above-average abilities which led to migration in the first place.

In R2, when the variables for migration experience are introduced, the coefficients of the schooling variables are reduced. The coefficient pointing to the effects of complete primary schooling loses a third of its value and is no longer significant. The same effect occurs in R1 but in a much slighter way. Many of the peasants studied while in migration, and the most educated are more prone to migration, hence there is a correlation between schooling and migration experience. However, when both variables are introduced in the R2 equation, only migration experience remains significant. This suggests that it is the migration experience, and not schooling, that causes the differences in output in this region.

It is an important point, generally overlooked in the literature, that the exclusion of relevant categories of informal education may, as in the case of our sample, produce estimates of the effects of formal education that overestimate its true effect.

Technology and credit

The effects of education on output are obtained partly by increasing the efficiency in the use of a particular technology, but they also occur indirectly by elevating the technological level utilized in the farm. Two indirect ways in which this may occur are through the selection of more productive technology and through allowing greater access to credit, which in turn allows the adoption of modern inputs. Consider the effects on the regression coefficients of explicitly including variables that control for adoption of modern technology and use of credit.

The use of high-yielding varieties (variable 17) is significant in R1 and R2. In both regions it shows that the shift to this new technology can have substantial effects on output. The few households that are already using HYVs in R3 seem to be still in the phase of learning the use of this new technology since in this region the variable for HYVs is positive but not significant.

Use of formal credit does not have a coefficient different from zero in any of the regions. The main role of credit is to give access to inputs, and we would expect it to be a major determinant, say, of the adoption of HYVs. Once the inputs are utilized in production, however, it is these and not credit that play a role in increasing productivity, and in this sense the results obtained are plausible.

When these variables are introduced, controlling for some of the "indirect effects" of education, we notice that in R1 the coefficient on formal education falls by one point, and that in R2 the coefficient on non-formal education (variable 10) falls by six points. This is

93

consistent with the argument that part of the impact of education on productivity can be traced to the indirect effects it has through gaining better access to the credit markets and through adoption of modern technology. The fact that the coefficients of education remain positive and significant once these effects are controlled for suggests that the direct effects are themselves important.

Conclusions

We have shown in this chapter that education can be seen to be an important factor in raising productivity among small farmers. The effects of formal, non-formal and informal education were explored, and we found that each of these types of education can, in specific contexts, increase the productivity of the farm.

The effects of education on productivity are obtained through two complementary paths. First, education accelerates adoption of new inputs and farming practices. Rogers defines the adoption process as "the mental process an individual passes from first hearing about an innovation to final adoption" (Rogers, 1962, p. 17). This definition stresses the fact that adoption is not a single action referring to the moment of introduction of a new technology into the farmer's production process, but rather it is a process that takes time. The required time lag to final adoption can be conceptually divided into two stages: the discovery stage, from the availability of the new technology to awareness of its technical characteristics, and the evaluation stage, from awareness to use.[23] Education has a role in reducing the time required to complete both stages.

The time lag involved in the discovery stage will depend on the peasant's "information field", and this is increased by all three types of education. Formal education facilitates the capacity to search for information and to order and systematize this information. Agricultural extension programmes are specifically designed to take this type of information to the farmer, explaining the technical details and the likely consequences of the use of the new technologies. Some forms of informal education are equally likely to put the farmer in contact with the effects of the use of new technology.

The evaluation stage usually includes the assessment of two aspects. One is whether the new technology will be appropriate to the farmer's technical and economic conditions of production, for example, to his own soils, his use of bullock traction, his availability of land and labour, or his access to finance or markets. The second assessment is whether the technology will be profitable under those conditions. This assessment is often rendered particularly difficult by the existence of uncertainty in production, for example, net incomes were higher last year with the new technology, but will that be the case under different weather conditions? Perhaps average incomes are higher over the years but are the probabilities of total failure in any year larger with the new technology? Especially important in the early stages of modernization, innovation will imply further involvement in the markets for inputs and outputs and this will add uncertainty from market fluctuations to the already uncertain natural environment of the peasant. Furthermore, innovation will often imply not only a change of inputs, but also an increase in the total expenditure required for production. Under these conditions, even if the average profitability is increased and the probabilities of failure reduced, the harm caused by failure will be greater.

Many variables must be taken into consideration when assessing the new technologies. Imposing order on the existing evidence and understanding the results is a difficult process, and here education plays an important role. Schooling facilitates the process in several ways. Increased numerical skills are of importance. A greater capacity for abstraction will make it easier for an educated farmer to uncover causal relations between technology and outputs which—because of long lags between application and results and weather-related randomness influencing the results—may remain obscure to a less educated farmer. Well-designed extension programmes also help the farmer through this process by demonstrating the technologies under conditions that are similar to the farmer's own, by pointing out the causality between the use of the new inputs and specific results and by facilitating the calculations of profitability. Also crucial in this phase are the non-cognitive roles of education, which can make the farmer more receptive to new ideas, more self-confident and, consequently, more willing to innovate.

In addition to education's role in the identification of superior technologies, education itself is a crucial complementary input in the technological package. The superiority of the new technology over the traditionally used ones may require the presence of high levels of education. The productivity levels obtained with the new technology have been seen to depend on the farmer's education.

This study has confirmed a crucial result suggested previously in the literature: the effects of schooling are stronger in modern regions where technology is changing in a more dynamic fashion and where market fluctuations have a wider impact in the local economy than in traditional regions where technology is stagnant or changes very slowly and where farmers are isolated from the market. Our results thus confirm the Schultz hypothesis that the value of education consists in enhancing the peasant's "ability to deal with disequilibrium". While this finding has been reported before in the literature, previous results were obtained by comparing data from modern and traditional regions which may differ in several characteristics apart from the degree of modernity (such as cropping patterns, tenure system, availability of irrigation) and which could mediate in the relationship between education and productivity. We have been able to confirm this hypothesis by comparing regions which were selected as similar in those crucial factors but different in their degree of modernity, as defined above.

Also, as to schooling, the results show the existence of a threshold-effect, by which formal education begins to have an effect on output only after a certain number of years of schooling have been obtained. The existence of a threshold has been reported before but we have found no effort in the literature to explain its level (see, for example, Chaudry, 1979). Far from there being a general threshold, the number of years necessary for an effect to appear seems to increase with the complexity of the technologies involved. This suggests that, while basic levels of education may be effective in speeding traditional regions into the first stages of technological modernization, further technological development will require higher levels of formal education.

With respect to non-formal education, we examined the direct and indirect effects of extension, that is, on those directly contacted by extension services and on those who imitate them. The first hypothesis with respect to the direct effects of non-formal education on productivity was simply that there is a positive effect. This positive effect exists only in the intermediate region in our sample. We suggested several reasons for this finding. One concerned the quality of the extension agency in the intermediate region. The other concerned the adequacy of the message transmitted by extensionists. While the message transmitted is similar in the three regions, it seems to be appropriate only in the intermediate region, being too advanced for the traditional region and not including any important innovations for the technological levels already achieved in the modern region.

If non-formal education transmits specific information on new technologies, its effects should become obsolete as new technologies appear. Also, the differential between those who receive the information directly and those who do not should fade away as imitation occurs. The hypothesis is that the effects of recent contacts on output should be larger than the effects of old extension. Implied in this hypothesis is the related one that imitation takes time. Our empirical results are consistent with the first hypothesis, in that, for each region, the value of the coefficient of recent extension is larger than the one of old extension. However, it is only in the intermediate region and only for the coefficient of recent extension that any of the coefficients are statistically significant. The second hypothesis is sustained by the data in the modern region. Here, imitation does appear to have an effect, but only with a lag, since it is only the indirect effects of old extension that appear to affect output.

Finally, the effects of two forms of informal education on output were examined, that of age (as a proxy for experience) and that of migration experience. With respect to age, the expectation was of a positive effect on output, but negative coefficients were found in the three regions, the effect being more pronounced the more modern the area. These findings were interpreted as reflecting a "cohort effect", according to which older peasants tend to stick to older, less productive technologies. This could be due to the existence of greater risk-aversion or conservatism among the old even when formal education is taken into account.

Migration experience shows important effects for productivity in the intermediate region. Several points were noted with respect to this kind of informal education. First, it was shown that when this experience was not included in the regression analysis, the effects of formal education tend to be strongly overestimated. Most previous studies that examine the effects of education on rural productivity have neglected to control their schooling coefficients for the effects of this form of informal education.[24] An implication of this finding is that, since formal education and migration tend to be strongly correlated, some of the coefficients reported in the previous literature may be overestimated since they may be picking up the effects of migration. Secondly, we found that migration experience from other rural areas has a smaller effect on productivity than urban experiences. This suggests that the main gain from this kind of informal education is not the transmission of information, but rather its broader effects in the formation of competences.

NOTES

[1] Most of the results discussed here were presented in the author's doctoral dissertation; some of them were previously published in a discussion paper (Cotlear 1986b). The author wishes to acknowledge comments received from John Knight, Joy de Beyer, Peter Moock and Dennis de Tray.

[2] The relative importance of these effects is still poorly understood: see, for instance, the debate between the "anthropological" and the "economic" views in Wharton (1969).

[3] World Bank, *World Development Report, 1980* (Washington, D.C.), p. 47.

[4] A survey describing the effects of schooling on adoption is provided in Feder, Just and Zilberman (1985).

[5] The original argument was presented in Schultz (1964); it has been further refined and developed in Schultz (1975). The quotation is from the latter article.

[6] This description of the possible interpretation of the correlation is taken from Jamison and Moock (1984), p. 68.

[7] A strong version of the screening hypothesis asserts that education merely identifies students with particular attributes, acquired either at birth or by virtue of family background, but does not itself produce or in any way improve those attributes. Since there is little point in self-screening, this version implies that education has no effect on earnings when it comes to the self-employed.

[8] Jamison and Moock (1984) did a study specifically designed to provide a test between these two hypotheses among small farmers. They controlled for "ability" with the use of variables measuring family background. Their findings support the claim that, under conditions of self-employment such as the ones described, if a correlation is found, it is likely to be due to the productive effect of education.

[9] When the benefit of education is measured in the way indicated, then if imitation reduces the gap by x, it underestimates the true benefit obtained by at least $2x$.

[10] The effects of schooling on migration and the urban/rural income gaps in Peru are discussed in Cotlear (1982).

[11] For a fuller description of the methodology utilized, see Cotlear (1986a), chap. III and appendix 1.

[12] For a fuller description of the economic anatomy of the households in the three regions, see Cotlear (1986a), chap. IV.

[13] The village of Acolla in R1 is at a slightly lower altitude than the other villages and was slightly drier than the others during the year of the survey. For these reasons, the households in Acolla may have a lower agricultural productivity than those of the other villages and we include a dummy variable for it.

[14] In the initial stage of the analysis, we also experimented with the use of a continuous variable for schooling. The t coefficients for this variable were found to be generally lower than for the dummy variables.

[15] These variables do not overlap. In the case of households with recent and old extension contacts, only the former have been considered.

[16] Similar variables were used by Jamison and Moock (1984).

[17] In R1, the village dummy for Acolla is, as was expected, negative.

[18] Both coefficients are different from zero at the 0.06 level in a two tail test, or at the 0.03 level in a (possibly more appropriate) one tail test.

[19] By doing this, we redefine the "base group" with respect to whom the impact of education is being calculated: the original base group includes all farmers with less than 4 years of schooling, the new base group includes only those with no schooling at all.

[20] Unfortunately, by doing this we were left with scarcely any observations in the base group in R1, and it was not possible to run the new regressions for this region.

[21] A similar pattern was found in a study of Kenyan farmers; Moock (1981) argues that ". . . an *a posteriori* justification would need to show that those who begin school but drop out before earning even the first credential are dull from the start, or that they become demoralized or, conversely, that they develop a self-importance that blinds them to their technical incompetence" (p. 732).

[22] Possibly this is due to the fact that there are only 4 villages in R3 (5 in R2 and 9 in R1) and hence these variables could be correlated with many other characteristics of the villages.

[23] The two stages are not fully independent one from the other, and there may exist some overlap; in this sense, the distinction is more conceptual than empirical in nature.

[24] An early exception is Moock (1981), which does examine the effects of migration experience but finds it to have no impact on productivity.

REFERENCES

Bowman, M. J. (1976). Through education to earnings?. *Proceedings of the National Academy of Education,* vol. 3, pp. 221-292.

Chaudry, D. P. (1979). *Education, Innovations and Agricultural Development.* International Labour Organisation, Vikas.

Coombs, P. and Manzoor Ahmed (1974). *Attacking Rural Poverty: How Non-Formal Education Can Help.* Baltimore: The Johns Hopkins University Press.

Cotlear, D. (1982). Empleo urbano y migraciones internas en Peru. Lima: Pointifical Catholic University, Centre for Social, Economic, Political and Anthropological Research.

————— (1986a). Technological and institutional change among the Peruvian peasantry. Ph.D. dissertation. Oxford: Oxford University.

————— (1986b). Farmer education and farm efficiency in Peru: the role of schooling, extension services and migration. Discussion paper, Education and Training Series, Education and Training Department, Report No. EDT49. Washington, D.C.: World Bank.

Feder, G., R. E. Just and D. Zilberman (1985). Adoption of agricultural innovations in developing countries: a survey. *Economic Development and Cultural Change,* vol. 33, pp. 255-298.

Figueroa, A. (1986). Productividad y educación en la agricultura campesina de América Latina. Rio de Janeiro: Programme of Joint Studies on Latin American Economic Integration.

Jamison, D. T. and L. J. Lau (1982). *Farmer Education and Farm Efficiency.* Baltimore: The Johns Hopkins University Press.

Jamison, D. T. and P. R. Moock (1984). Farmer education and farm efficiency in Nepal: the role of schooling, extension services and cognitive skills. *World Development,* vol. 12, pp. 67-86.

Lockheed, M. E., D. T. Jamison and L. J. Lau (1980). Farmer education and farm efficiency: a survey. *Economic Development and Cultural Change,* vol. 29, pp. 37-76.

Moock, P. R. (1981). Education and technical efficiency in small farm production. *Economic Development and Cultural Change,* vol. 29, pp. 723-739.

Rogers, E. (1962). *Diffusion of Innovations.* New York: Free Press of Glencoe.

Schultz, T. W. (1964). *Transforming Traditional Agriculture.* New Haven: Yale University Press.

————— (1975). The value of the ability to deal with disequilibria. *Journal of Economic Literature,* vol. 13, pp. 872-876.

Welch, F. (1970). Education in production. *Journal of Political Economy.*

Wharton, C. R., ed. (1969). *Subsistence Agriculture and Economic Development.* Chicago: Aldine.

5

IMPROVING THE QUALITY OF EDUCATION IN DEVELOPING COUNTRIES

*John Oxenham**
with Jocelyn DeJong and Steven Treagust

CONTENTS

Introduction

In the years following 1945, developing and industrialized countries alike expanded their schools and universities at historically unprecedented rates. This commitment to quantitative expansion highlighted the question: what kind and quality of systematic instruction should be provided and at what cost? On this point, the richer industrialized countries were more fortunate: having gradually established their systems of both private and public provision to already generous degrees, having relatively slow-growing populations and being better off for resources, they did not need to make too drastic a choice between quantity and quality. By contrast, many developing countries not only have had to construct their educational systems from very small bases but have also had to pursue the task in the face of both much scarcer resources and faster-growing populations. Since expanding an educational system and raising its quality both cost money, trade-offs have been necessary in the past and the current international economic climate threatens to enforce even more.

Despite the relatively vast investments in schooling in the

*Fellow in Education and Development/Academic Adviser, Institute of Development Studies, University of Sussex.

developing countries, its overall quality continues to give rise to widespread disappointment. Although notable progress has been made in quantitative terms, improving quality has proved a more elusive goal. Many developing countries do have schools and universities of excellent quality, but the quality of the average school or university department is unsatisfactory. For example, according to the studies of the International Association for the Evaluation of Educational Achievement (IEA), educational attainments requiring one year of schooling in an industrialized country tend to require three or four years of schooling in the average school of the developing countries examined. Children in India spent more time in school compared with their counterparts in the industrialized countries, but achieved only 48 per cent as much in reading and about 50 per cent in science (IEA, 1976a, pp. 60, 100, 120; IEA, 1976b, p. 280).

The misgivings mentioned above have to do with the quality of the cognitive results of education. This educational perspective has an economic reinforcement:

"[Our findings in Brazil] indicate that 'deepening' schooling by increasing quality has a higher social rate of return than 'broadening' schooling by increasing quantity . . . the conventional wisdom about schooling investments in developing countries . . . may cause substantial over-investment of resources in schooling and the wrong composition of what investments are undertaken" (Behrman and Birdsall 1983, p. 929).

There may be attitudinal as well as cognitive reasons why improving educational quality may be economically productive. Attitudes acquired in school may contribute to "educated unemployment", where the more education a person has the more likely she or he is to remain without waged or salaried employment for extended periods. Similarly, more educated people, unlike the overwhelming majority of the unschooled, are either unable or unwilling to use their education to create their own employment, that is, they are not the "prime movers of development", as Harbison and Myers (1964) suggested. Furthermore, when the educated do secure waged or salaried jobs, many of them are alleged not to give their employers proper satisfaction: their education seems not to have prepared them to do a job well. However justified or exaggerated these complaints are, they are long-standing and seem not to diminish with time.

The purpose of this paper is to look at the quality of education in developing countries. It will focus on what goes into education, on the assumption that what goes in significantly determines what comes out. Further, taking the present squeezes on educational expenditure as a strict constraint, it will attempt to assess whether there might be ways in which leverage may be exerted to attain higher quality in the inputs without necessarily entailing higher expenditure. Table 1 suggests that raising quality usually requires raising expendi-

TABLE 1. ESTIMATED PUBLIC EXPENDITURES ON EDUCATION, PER INHABITANT,
IN MAJOR REGIONS OF THE WORLD, 1985
(*In United States dollars*)

Africa (excluding Arab States)...........................	20
Asia (excluding Arab States)...........................	42
Latin America and the Caribbean......................	67
Northern America	1 101
Europe (including USSR)	294
Developing countries	27
Developed countries....................................	515
World total...	147

Source: United Nations Educational, Scientific and Cultural Organization, *Statistical Yearbook 1987* (Paris), table 2.12.

tures. However, the working hypothesis here is that opportunities do exist for improving the quality of education without additional resources, provided sufficient thought is given to identifying and implementing them.

Education will be restricted here to the kinds of teaching and learning which are practised in schools and kindred institutions. The reason for this restriction is a simple recognition of fact. In most countries, the government budgets for scholastic institutions heavily outweigh the allocations for other forms of education and training. The same is likely to be true of household budgets in countries where school and university systems are well developed, even though forms of artisanal apprenticeship in the informal sectors of the economy may persist. Education has come to be almost synonymous with the school and will be so treated here.

Quality in education will have two connotations: one broad, the other narrow. In the broader sense it embraces entire programmes, such as a cycle of primary schooling. Here, the more effectively an educational programme enables its learners to achieve its and/or their learning objectives and the more widely and deeply it enables its learners to identify and enhance their abilities, in terms of awareness, knowledge, understanding and behaviour, the better its quality. In the narrower sense it refers to the components of education, both human and material: the quality of a component is generally reflected in the extent to which it contributes to the attainment of the learning objectives of either an educational programme or a particular set of learners.

The scope of this survey is necessarily limited. A sweep over all 120 or so developing countries is not feasible, nor is a set of regional summaries on Africa, Asia and Latin America. Instead, seven large countries will be used as the main bases for discussion. They are listed in table 2, along with their populations and a few basic indicators relevant to the provision of education. One large industrialized country—Japan—will be used as a comparator. Japan has been selected because it was a "late developer" which quite deliber-

ately used its schools and universities to aid its drive for modernization and socio-economic development. Now, in terms of both
educational and economic attainments, Japan ranks among the
leaders of the world. The selected countries are drawn from the three
main regions of developing countries. Even though not "representative" in a technical sense, their relatively large populations mean that
anything said about them reflects the situations of large numbers of
people.

The educational systems of all eight countries are constructed
along common lines. They have primary and secondary cycles, with
minor variations between them, amounting in all to 11 or 12 years of
education. Then comes the tertiary, or higher, stage, which offers a
range of education—from short vocational or professional courses at
institutions of low prestige to university degree courses that can take
up to six or seven years. In all eight countries there are great
variations in quality and prestige among the schools and universities.
All have structures of administrative and professional support, with
the common purpose of ensuring and maintaining the good operation
of their educational institutions.

As can be seen from table 2, all eight countries have near
universal primary school enrolment, reflecting an important and
widely held objective of the Governments of the developing countries. On the other hand, there are wide variations in secondary and
higher enrolments, as well as in the proportions of national income
and of public expenditure that are appropriated for educational
expenditure. These differences should be borne in mind as cautions
against attempting to generalize about developing countries.

The quality of inputs

The quality of inputs is examined under four headings: learners,
teachers, materials and support systems.

LEARNERS

Since schools exist to teach learners, it may seem odd to list the
latter as the first component of quality. The step can be justified by a
quote from an international study:

> "Differences in achievement among schools within coun-
> tries were related mainly to the qualities of the students entering
> the school: factors such as teaching methods or equipment
> played only a minor part" (IEA, 1976a, p. 120).

What an educational programme can achieve with its learners is
crucially dependent on the learners themselves. This observation is
particularly important for programmes that have standard objectives
for all their learners, such as cycles of primary or general secondary

TABLE 2. BASIC STATISTICS FOR THE SEVEN SELECTED DEVELOPING COUNTRIES AND JAPAN

Region	Country	Population (millions) 1985	Population growth rate 1973-1984	GNP per capita 1985	GNP per capita 1965-1985	Enrolment rates, 1984 P	Enrolment rates, 1984 S	Enrolment rates, 1984 H	Educational expenditures as a percentage of GNP, 1983	Educational expenditures as a percentage of Government expenditures, 1983
Africa	Nigeria............	100	2.8	800	2.2	92	29	3	2.2	9.3
	Zaire	31	3.0	170	-2.1	98	57	1	..	..
Asia	China	1 040	1.4	310	4.8	118	37	1	2.8	8.1
	India	765	2.3	270	1.7	90	34	9	3.2 (1982)	..
	Rep. of Korea ...	41	1.5	2 150	6.6	99	91	26	5.0	24.2
Latin America	Brazil	136	2.3	1 640	4.3	103	35	11	3.3	18.4
	Mexico............	79	2.9	2 080	2.7	116	55	15	2.8	6.4
Industrialized	Japan............	121	0.9	11 300	4.7	100	95	30	5.7 (1982)	19.1 (1982)

Note: P = primary, S = secondary, H = higher or tertiary.

Sources: United Nations Educational, Scientific and Cultural Organization, Statistical Yearbook 1986 (Paris), table 4.1; World Bank, World Development Report, 1986 (Washington, D.C.), table 25; ibid., 1987, tables 1, 27, and 31.

education. Where learners can be selected to fit the objectives of a programme, attaining the objectives is probably less difficult than where a programme is intended for universal use and has to accept all comers. But the quality of a learner is not unidimensional. On the contrary, it has itself a number of elements.

We begin with the effect of poverty on the quality of learners. Both the direct and the opportunity costs of education can deter the poor from learning. In Botswana and Kenya the immediate leaps in primary school enrolments following the abolition of primary school fees tend to confirm that the direct costs of primary schooling, however token, do deter poor people from sending their children to school. As to the opportunity costs, Brooke and Oxenham (1980) found that the propensity to send children to school corresponded inversely with the use made of children in family businesses in rural Mexico, while Harriss (1986) found that even the noonday meal scheme in Tamil Nadu, India, failed to attract the children of the poorest families away from assisting with the family income. Similarly reflecting opportunity costs is the custom in some parts of China of dividing the school year into the "very busy farming season", the "quite busy farming season" and the "not so busy farming season" (Hayhoe, 1984).

Poverty often affects the quality of learning through infrequent attendance and premature withdrawal. In India, only 25 per cent of the pupils entering the first grade of primary school manage to complete the full eight-year course without repeating a year or, worse, dropping out altogether (Naik, 1980). In Brazil, a study traced 1,000 primary school students from 1972 to 1979 and found that only 18 per cent of them reached even the third year of a six-year course (IIEP, 1984). Mexico similarly showed a high drop-out rate in the late 1970s: 43 per cent of its primary school entrants and 37 per cent of its secondary school entrants did not complete their courses (British Council, 1981). In China, rural schools reported attendance rates for those enrolled of only 60 per cent (Hayhoe, 1984). A recent examination of the schools in Madagascar may well be symptomatic of the majority of the poorer developing countries. It revealed that the total retention rate in primary schools was only 35 per cent for boys and a somewhat better 49 per cent for girls (Khan and Berstecher, 1988). That is, fewer than half the children recorded as managing to enrol in a primary school completed their primary education. These studies confirm that poor attendance and desertion from school not only continue to occur at high rates but are correlated with family income and the family's need for its children's labour.

Poverty also affects the physical ability to learn through its effect on health and nutrition. A sick child cannot concentrate, nor can a hungry one or one who has suffered brain damage from chronic malnutrition. Children who suffer these misfortunes most commonly

106

come from the families of the poor (see Medeiros, 1985, for Brazil; Onokerhoraye, 1984, for Nigeria; and Heyneman and Jamison, 1980, for Uganda).

Among the poor there is often the perception that education does not matter or might even be injurious. Such a view is readily understandable in large parts of most of the countries selected here, for much of their societies had long operated without literacy and school education and had no obvious use for them. They also operated with expectations of relatively swift returns to learning and with modes of training related to very clear and precise objectives and functions. The view might be characterized as instrumental and not readily adaptable to a mode that requires a minimum of six years of learning matter the application of which is obscure, and that depends heavily on an ability to defer gratification almost indefinitely. The implication is that, where the goals of learning are clear, the rewards tangible and worthwhile and the link between the learning and the reward reliable, both motivation and perseverance will be enhanced, and so too should the quality of learning. Such an inference is well supported by Unger's report (1985) on Chinese urban vocational schools. The Chinese experience contradicted the generally lamentable history of vocational schooling and confirmed Foster's (1965) thesis of the "vocational school fallacy". Unger showed that, when vocational schools were able to guarantee their graduates placements in the occupations for which they had undertaken their learning, the schools (a) were not treated as second-class or dead ends; (b) had no shortage of good candidates; (c) were not under-utilized; (d) did not suffer the disciplinary disturbances experienced by other schools; and (e) produced graduates who seemed by and large to satisfy the objectives for which the schools were set up. The implication is that if all educational institutions were similarly linked to clear, desired and rewarding destinations, their enrolments, workings, retention rates and learning would all benefit. Somerset's experience of the vocational guidance system introduced in the late 1960s and early 1970s for Kenyan secondary schools tends to bear this out (Somerset, 1982).

Three serious constraints to realizing such linkages have to be recognized. One is the sheer magnitude of the task: it seems infeasible to provide every single primary, secondary and tertiary institution with the kind of linkage that was devised for China's vocational schools. On the other hand, selective and experimental beginnings with particular sets of schools do not seem out of the question. The second constraint lies in the nature of general education: how might specific linkages be constructed for what is an unspecific course of learning? What seems to be implied is a particularly sensitive system of guidance based upon a comprehensive, alert and continually updated system of social and economic information. This leads to the third constraint: linkages of the nature envisaged cannot easily be

107

constructed by a single ministry or department. Rather, they require joint policies, continuous co-operation and interaction at each level the scheme will operate—a formidable requirement.

Social attitudes are relevant as well as economic motivation: the school often represents a channel of social mobility. For those who want their children to move out of their native community in search of something better, pursuing education remains worthwhile so long as their children's success at it keeps mobility within reach. This desire for mobility is such that it has tended to operate, at least in the early stages, in favour of only males. Almost everywhere, the enrolments of females have lagged behind, for economic reasons or because social mobility has not been thought to concern them. Only as education has become the norm for everyone have the enrolments of females drawn level with those of males.

Islamic societies have long been noted for the slow narrowing of the disparity between male and female enrolments. In northern Nigeria—and doubtless other Islamic societies—the school was at first deemed a hostile institution for everybody. Introduced by Christians and Westerners, it appeared an engine for proselytization and the destruction not only of the Moslem religion, but of the ancient feudal order as well. Only after the end of British colonial rule, when the school system could be controlled by Moslems themselves, was there a gradual change of attitude (Thornley, 1987). Such social indifference, ambivalence or denigration can, of course, undermine the motivation and perseverance of learners.

As education becomes more widespread in a pre-literate population, it necessarily draws in more learners from pre-literate communities and households. It has to function with less than ideal social support and to accept that the ensuing quality of many of its learners could well disable them from achieving their own, as well as its, objectives. Educational expansion also draws in a wider spread of traits and abilities and makes groups of learners more heterogeneous. Coupled with large classes and inadequacies in both teachers and teaching materials, this heterogeneity increases the difficulties of achieving educational objectives.

Parents and communities can often ensure the success of an educational institution. Accountability is perhaps best exemplified in Japan, where parents have the right to monitor and question the quality of teachers, even in the State schools. In the other selected countries, high-cost private schools, which pay salaries above the average and are financed by parents who are themselves well educated and closely interested in their children's education, do display accountability to the parents. Those private schools that are poorly financed and draw their pupils from families of relatively low educational levels and insufficient social confidence can be much less accountable. The teachers in State schools, especially if patterns of frequent transfer are prevalent, are perhaps least accountable to parents. They are employed by the State, look to the State for recognition and advancement and tend to have little to do with the families of their pupils.

Although little by way of systematic evidence is available, there is a widespread presumption that, where teachers can be called to account by parents and the teachers and parents are on roughly equal terms, the quality of teaching and learning is improved. Where adult literacy rates, particularly among women, are low, and teachers can look down on the uneducated public, achieving the "equal terms" would be problematic. None the less, devices for devolving continuing responsibilities to parents might gradually create the confidence on which to construct a more solid relationship with the school. One example could be responsibility for encouraging high and regular attendance rates and reducing drop-out rates—a responsibility that few schools or teachers undertake voluntarily. An advantage of such an approach is, of course, enhanced by the probability that it would not add to the State's financial costs, even though it might consume some of the time and patience of teachers.

TEACHERS

To the lay-person, the quality of teachers would seem an obviously crucial determinant of the quality of education. A primary indicator of a teacher's quality might reasonably be thought to be professional qualifications. Supplementing that would be experience and length of service. In fact, neither indicator has proved entirely reliable, as numerous studies have found (e.g., Coleman and others, 1966; IEA, 1976a; Jencks and others, 1972 and 1979; Khan and Berstecher, 1988; Peaker, 1971). On the other hand, there seems to be fair evidence that these indicators are weightier in poor countries than in rich ones (Comber and Keeves, 1973; Heyneman and Loxley, 1983; Husen, 1979). Indeed, Heyneman and Loxley put it more strongly:

". . . school and teacher quality appear to be the predominant influence on student learning around the world; and the poorer the nation in economic terms, the more powerful this school effect appears to be" (1983, p. 1184).

That view was supported by Behrman and Birdsall (1983) who found that using teachers' qualifications as a proxy for school quality in Brazil significantly influenced the correlation between the education and the earnings of school graduates. Similarly, Khan and Berstecher (1988) calculated that the number of teachers with the highest qualifications correlated significantly with both the gross wastage ratio and the total retention ratio in Madagascar. A caveat is in order, Khan and Berstecher nevertheless warned:

". . . should [the Government of Madagascar] put their resources into formal teacher training in order to fight educational

109

wastage? We do not think so. Many other factors, human and material, are at play, and formal certificates may be less important in making an effective teacher than experience, familiarity with the community, personal commitment and other personal characteristics" (1988, p. 12).

Their caution in the case of a developing country is echoed in the conclusions of Rutter and his colleagues (1979) and Mortimore and his colleagues (1988) in the case of an industrialized country, the United Kingdom, that the quality of teachers and teaching was not adequately reflected by qualifications and experience. Be that as it may, it remains useful, at least as a starting-point, to ask how well qualified the teaching forces of the selected countries are.

In Brazil, 35 per cent of schoolteachers lacked the minimum qualifications (Medeiros, 1985). In its north-east region, a third of the teachers had fewer than four years of primary schooling themselves (Fuller, 1986b). In Zaire, the teachers with six or fewer years of primary schooling numbered more than half the cadre, while the proportion of qualified teachers reached only 3.3 per cent in 1972-1973 (Abemba, 1985). In 1976, northern Nigeria had only 9 per cent of its teachers certified (Bray, 1981). While Chuncai does not estimate proportions of qualified or unqualified teachers for China, he does assert that the "key to improvement of educational quality lies in the improvement of teachers' qualifications" (1985, p. 704). In short, many developing countries seem to be trying to run their education with teachers of inadequate quality.

What are the obstacles to improving the quality of teachers? On the face of it, the unwillingness of Governments to try is not one of them: all the selected countries have set up considerable systems of teacher training and have launched numerous projects to upgrade the training offered; all have sought outside help in raising the expertise and effectiveness of their teacher trainers. Even so, it is possible that a revised approach to teacher training could raise the quality without increasing costs. The suggestion arises from the experience of the United Republic of Tanzania when it became necessary to train large numbers of primary teachers in a hurry to meet its target of universal primary education. Because its usual training colleges could not cope with the extra load, the Ministry of Education reversed the training cycle. It put the new recruits into the schools to teach under the supervision of experienced colleagues and brought them to the colleges for intensive short bouts of training, when the ordinary trainees were on vacation or out on teaching practice. Later assessments indicated that the "crash trained" teachers were more effective in the classrooms than their conventionally trained contemporaries. What is more, their training proved considerably cheaper than the usual (Adams, 1987). Although there were a great many problems with the crash scheme, the apparent scope for simultaneously enhancing quality and reducing costs deserves careful scrutiny.

One of the more intractable obstacles to improved teaching appears to be the difficulty of attracting and retaining people in the teaching profession. This has its roots in the remuneration, conditions of service and social status of teaching. In Japan, teaching is clearly a valued profession—teachers enjoy security from their first employment, they earn reasonable salaries, they are respected socially—and is able to attract people of good calibre. Moreover, it is well organized through a powerful trades union, "Nikkyoso", and can defend itself from what it sees as attacks on its standards (Cummings, 1980). The picture in the selected developing countries is not as pleasant. In Brazil, 42 per cent of the teachers in 1984 received not merely less than the official minimum wage (approximately $US 410 per month) but even than the national per capita income of $US 136 per month. Teachers also suffer from insecurity of employment (IIEP, 1984) and they have no strong union to defend their interests. Nor have their counterparts in Mexico, where many teachers are reported to be leaving the profession because of low pay (British Council, 1981). Naik (1980) and Abemba (1985) report similar situations for India and Zaire. Teachers in Nigeria earn more than similarly qualified people in the manufacturing industry, but still feel that their status in the public sector is undervalued. Indeed, among the selected developing countries, only in the Republic of Korea has the Government attempted to make teaching attractive. It exempts those who go to teachers' colleges from fees and later exempts them from military service, if on graduation they teach in State primary schools (UNESCO, 1983).

There is little doubt that the conditions of economic crisis since the late 1970s have worsened the position of teachers. Casual empiricism suggests, too, that a number of teachers are resorting to part-time work outside the school in order to maintain or enhance their earnings. While such practices need not necessarily damage their teaching, the extent to which it might do so is worth monitoring. In so far as raising the quality of teachers requires better pay and conditions, improved quality may well have to await an improvement in the economic and fiscal situation of a country.

In some cases, teaching is also handicapped by the inadequate numbers and maldistribution of teachers. Table 3 shows that the supply of teachers for primary schools has failed to keep pace with the expansion of enrolments in three of the selected countries. Although they seem to be the poorer countries, it is well to note that China, despite being among the poorer ones, appears to have managed to keep the recruitment of teachers ahead of enrolments. The fact suggests that official determination to realize policy might be as significant a factor as resources. Where enrolments were allowed to outstrip teachers, the effect was to require teachers to manage larger classes (see table 4). The average figures mask wide variations within a country: some high-cost, well-endowed schools might offer classes of only 20 pupils or so, and so also might a few remote and not easily accessible schools in small villages, but many schools in the poorer neighbourhoods of towns or in large villages try to provide space for 60 or more children in a classroom.

A number of studies, most recently that of Khan and Berstecher (1988), suggest that pupil-teacher ratios have little effect on the outcomes of education. The uncertainty is perhaps most easily captured in the following two quotes:

> "No relation was found between achievement and class size in five of the subjects. In the sixth (Literature) it was found that 14-year-old students in larger classes had higher achievements than those in smaller classes" (IEA, 1976b, p. 231).

> "There appears to be moderate confirmation of the hypothesis that more generous system-wide staffing is associated with higher average level of achievement, *over the wide range of achievement exhibited by all IEA nations taken together*. However, in the narrower range exhibited by the developed countries, the associations are generally weaker" (IEA, 1976a, p. 218; italics in original).

The uncertainty is underlined by Fuller's finding (1986b) that only 5 out of 21 analyses tended to confirm the hypothesis that the larger the class size, the lower the quality of education. It is possible that, the higher the quality of the teacher, the weaker the deleterious effects of excessive pupil-teacher ratios. It would follow that, where teachers are poorly qualified, the larger the pupil-teacher ratio, the lower would be the quality of education.

On the question of maldistribution, two forces are at work. Teachers who are recognized to be committed and effective are almost systematically creamed off for the better schools, which are mainly in the better-off neighbourhoods of towns, and are promoted. The creaming is engineered by the school system's administrators, often under pressure from influential parents anxious for their own children, or, where they are allowed, by private schools able to offer more attractive terms. The second force comes from the teachers themselves. In the interests of their families and children, they prefer posts in schools where the facilities for health, education, communications and general welfare are good, and will actively seek to get themselves transferred to such places. The upshot is that the better teachers tend to concentrate in the already more fortunate areas, while the less successful and the less experienced new entrants are distributed to the poorer and more rural schools.

A consequence of both the weak holding power of the teaching profession and the preference for particular areas and schools is the high turnover of teachers within schools and the ensuing lack of

TABLE 3. COMPARISON OF GROWTH IN PRIMARY ENROLMENTS AND GROWTH IN
NUMBERS OF PRIMARY TEACHERS, 1950-1985

Country (1)	Growth in primary enrolments, 1950-1985[a] (2)	Growth in primary teachers, 1950-1985[b] (3)	(2)–(3)[c] (4)
Nigeria	15.61[d]	9.47[d]	+6.14
Zaire..................	2.25[e]	2.03[e]	+0.22
China	2.51[f]	3.37[f]	−0.86
India.................	4.97[g]	2.34	+2.63
Republic of Korea ..	1.82	2.70	−0.88
Brazil	6.76	8.77	−2.01
Mexico	5.67	6.82	−1.15
Japan	0.99	1.51	−0.52

Source: United Nations Educational, Scientific and Cultural Organization,
Educational Statistical Yearbooks, 1970-1987 (Paris).
[a] Quotient from dividing 1985 enrolments by 1950 enrolments.
[b] Quotient from dividing 1985 numbers by those reported for 1950.
[c] i. A plus sign (+) indicates that pupil enrolments have outpaced the
recruitment of new teachers (both qualified and unqualified);
ii. A minus sign (−) indicates that the recruitment of new teachers (qualified and
unqualified) has kept ahead of the increases in pupil enrolments.
[d] Quotient from dividing 1983 enrolments by 1950 enrolments.
[e] Quotient from dividing 1983 numbers by 1965 numbers.
[f] Quotient from dividing 1985 numbers by 1955 numbers.
[g] Quotient from dividing 1984 numbers by 1950 numbers.

TABLE 4. DETERIORATION IN PRIMARY PUPIL-TEACHER RATIOS, 1950 AND 1985

	Primary pupil-teacher ratios	
	1950	1985
Nigeria	25	40[a]
Zaire.................................	37[b]	42[a]
India.................................	27	42

Source: United Nations Educational, Scientific and Cultural Organization,
Educational Statistical Yearbooks, 1970-1985 (Paris).
[a] Figure for 1983.
[b] Figure for 1965.

continuity in the educational development of many pupils. The
quality of education can safely be presumed to suffer. Wolff (1971)
showed that in Brazil, turnover among teachers was associated with
both desertion from school and lower academic achievements among
the pupils who persevered.

Pre-service training, in-service training and on-the-job counsel-
ling have all been implemented to one degree or another by the
selected developing countries. As in the developed countries, they
have not proved capable of equalizing the performances of teachers
or of stimulating adequate initiatives in improvement or innovation.
An approach to creating the conditions for innovation and improvement, as well as for their wider dissemination, is to concentrate
resources into a small number of special facilities or departments

known as "centres of excellence". The hope is to form a critical mass of qualified and dynamic personnel, with sufficient material support, who will develop high standards of quality for their colleagues elsewhere to emulate. Such a "multiplier effect" through the example of peers might well be expected to furnish a more effective stimulus than the more ordinary routines of training. China, both before and after the Cultural Revolution, established "key point" schools, while India, having had some experience during the 1960s, is proposing something similar in its present round of reforms. Unfortunately, because it has never been possible to equip the ordinary schools as generously as the centres of excellence, it is not clear whether the latter do indeed generate multiplier effects for the rest of the system or whether they come to constitute one more means whereby the better-off and more influential families are enabled to keep their children relatively privileged.

MATERIALS

Although the studies of the World Bank (1978), Heyneman and Jamison (1980), Loxley (1983) and Fuller (1986b) do not relate directly to the countries selected for this paper, they support the common-sense view that the quality of textbooks and similar supports for learning would have some effect on the quality of education. The impact of these aids appears to be more powerful or at least identifiable in the developing countries than in the industrialized countries. The first consideration concerning the provision of educational materials is the proportion of the budget they should consume, compared with what they actually do. No information appears to be available to the United Nations Educational, Scientific and Cultural Organization (UNESCO) for three of the developing countries selected (see table 5). If the comparator country, Japan, is taken as a guide, it would seem that a relatively small percentage of expenditure suffices to furnish the schools of a system with teaching materials. Indeed, Neumann and Cunningham (World Bank, 1982) argue, on the basis of the Mexican programme of providing free textbooks to all schools, that as low a proportion as 2 to 4 per cent of an educational budget is all that has to be allocated to textbooks to ensure proper coverage. If that is the case, table 5 suggests that it is Mexico itself that has had to reduce its allocations for teaching materials from earlier, higher levels, while India appears to be not far below the desirable minimum and China to be even excessively generous. In other words, if India, China and the Republic of Korea are typical of developing countries, the situation concerning textbooks could be read as reasonable. Certainly, the fact that all the developing countries selected have established special organizations to revise the curricula, texts and other support materials of their schools suggests that this aspect of quality is well cared for.

TABLE 5. ALLOCATIONS FOR TEACHING MATERIALS, AS PERCENTAGE OF NATIONAL EDUCATIONAL BUDGETS

Nigeria	..
Zaire	..
China	10.6
India	1.3
Republic of Korea	2.5
Brazil	..
Mexico	0.7
Japan	6.5

Source: United Nations Educational, Scientific and Cultural Organization, Statistical Yearbook 1987 (Paris), table 4.2.

On the other hand, casual empiricism in a number of countries raises doubts about the accuracy of the statistics. The classes that have to make do with one text shared among several pupils or even one for an entire class in Brazil, India, Mexico, Nigeria and Zaire suggest that what is budgeted for texts may not actually be used for them and that what is disbursed may be distributed to relatively few and favoured schools. There is also the consideration, reinforced by the figures in table 1, that 2 per cent of a small budget of $20 per inhabitant may not afford what 2 per cent of a budget of $515 can. Further, countries such as China, India and Mexico, with large populations, much of their own raw materials and well-developed publishing systems, may well be able to produce texts and other materials cheaply for themselves, whereas other countries may need to rely more on relatively more expensive imports. The implication is that, although the importance of teaching materials is well recognized and although efforts to produce and distribute them have been by no means negligible, their actual provision has not yet been adequate and, if Mexico is a guide, may even be worsening.

Apart from teaching materials, there are items such as actual school buildings, school desks, blackboards, chalk and writing materials, which all affect, in one way or another, educational quality. Comprehensive surveys have been located only for India: a 1985 report from the Government stated that, in rural areas, 9 per cent of the primary schools did not even have a school building, 40 per cent of all schools lacked blackboards and 70 per cent had no library facilities whatever. A decade earlier, the IEA studies cited above had suggested that investment in physical equipment and learning materials would affect the achievement of Indian children three to four times more than a similar investment in the developed countries (IEA, quoted in World Bank, 1979). Doubtless, much the same kind of observation would apply to Nigeria, where urban schools run double shifts for their pupils, because of shortages of classrooms and supplies. If the rate of progress reflected in India and Nigeria is typical of other developing countries, optimism for the improvement of quality has to be guarded.

Just as one should not automatically equate higher expenditure per student with higher quality of education, so too the mere existence of educational "inputs" does not ensure that they are effectively used. This is the role of support systems of supervision, advice and administration. They are intended to see that no school is left without what it requires to function properly, to maintain national standards of teaching and learning, to minimize variability among schools and to monitor the well-being and progress of the entire system. In Japan, such support is taken seriously and is tightly regulated. Consequently, there is relatively little variation in the standards among schools (Cummings, 1980, IEA, 1976b). The Ministry of Education provides guidelines for curricula, courses and credit requirements at all levels and screens all texts for the primary and secondary levels. These directives are further promoted by prefectural and municipal educational boards, which administer personnel matters, choose texts and advise educational institutions generally.

It is arguable that, as with other components, support systems play a role even more critical in the developing countries than in a country such as Japan. Unfortunately, none of the cases selected here can boast such an articulated administrative support network. In India, the National Council of Educational Research and Training contributes substantially to the quality of schooling by providing centralized standards and materials for preparing curricula, producing textbooks and reforming examinations. In general, however, the quality of administrative support for education is weak and variable, just as it tends to be in other federal countries where the central Government has only residual responsibility for education, in particular at the first and second levels; Brazil, Nigeria and, to a lesser extent, Mexico are cases in point. Typically, federal Governments retain control over higher education and devolve responsibilities for primary and secondary education to States, municipalities and even private bodies. The cost of such decentralization is variable quality. Such variations are particularly striking in India (see India, 1985). However, it has to be said that centralization may not be an infallible remedy, as Zaire found when it nationalized its schools in 1974. Three years later the Government returned them to the hands of the religious organizations that had set them up during the colonial period. The gaps in administrative support remain glaring, however. For instance, many teachers still have to rely on curriculum guidelines from the pre-independence period of the 1950s (Chinapay and Dau, 1981). In China, a similar variability in the quality of rural schools results from the principle of "the people run, the State assists". Although the Ministry of Education supplies standard

116

textbooks for primary and secondary schools, marked disparities exist in the provision of other materials and facilities (Hayhoe, 1984).

The quality of support through supervision and advice still appears to be deficient in most of the selected developing countries, despite long-standing attempts, with and without external assistance, at improving the administration and the inspectorate. Systematic accounts cannot be located, so that the impressions offered here rely on casual empiricism. In many countries, teachers still regard their district offices as banes rather than helps and their school inspectors as professional fault-finders rather than sympathetic counsellors. For their part, the administrators and inspectors complain of being overburdened with paperwork and undersupported with transport and travel allowances. It is difficult to avoid the suspicion that the malaise infecting the teaching profession also infects its intended supports: the roots may lie in feelings of being undervalued and underpaid and in a consequent lack of commitment to the work at hand.

There may be scope for improving the quality of education without increasing costs through the better management of resources. Psacharopoulos, in a study of schools in Colombia and the United Republic of Tanzania, suggests that considerable scope exists in the public sector:

". . . in Colombia the operating cost of private schools is on average 42% lower than that of the INEM and conventional public schools. Therefore, although private schools spend substantially less per student, they have been effective in raising academic achievement relative to public schools. In Tanzania also, the operating cost of private schools is significantly lower than that of public schools, although private schools have been more efficient in transforming limited resources to learning outcomes" (1987, p. 66).

While there is controversy about how Psacharopoulos reached his conclusions, there is a need to see precisely what scope there might actually be for higher productivity in education through better management.

Management involves personnel as well as finance and materials. Systematic research has confirmed that the quality of a school is substantially dependent on the quality of leadership and personnel management provided by the head teacher and senior colleagues (see, for example, Rutter and others, 1979; Mortimore and others, 1988; Malvankar, 1987). By extension, it can be inferred that the quality of leadership provided by head teachers is substantially dependent on the quality of support they receive from their colleagues operating the administrative, supervisory and training systems. Since virtually all head teachers and administrators are drawn from the general corps of teachers, a first implication is that, within the corps, the distribution of capabilities to lead, manage, administer and support is uneven.

117

Some teachers are better able to manage than others. The selection, training, induction and monitoring of head teachers might be reviewed to ascertain whether they draw fully on the qualities of leadership available in the corps of teachers. It is quite possible that customs of seniority or excessive reliance on paper qualifications, rather than on aspects of performance, prevent the proper and full utilization of the talent available.

The centralized examination is an element of the support system used for various purposes: to monitor what the schools are teaching and the pupils learning; to encourage comparable standards among schools; to discriminate among pupils, selecting those who are to advance and those who are to be excluded from further educational opportunity; and to discriminate among schools, pointing out those with apparently ineffectual teachers and those that do well by their students. The influence that springs from these uses is powerful and widely thought to be baleful (see, for example, Dore, 1976). Yet, where the centralized examination is replaced by assessment left in the hands of the teachers and schools, quality tends to decline (see, for example, Brooke and Oxenham, 1980, for Mexico; JASPA, 1980, for Liberia; and, for a case in Ghana where easy examinations undermine quality, Boakye and Oxenham, 1982).

The possibility that the centralized examination can in fact promote good education and raise its quality has been well demonstrated in Kenya (Somerset, 1982). The effort took almost a decade and involved a great deal more than simply designing better exam papers. It went as far as analysing every question in every paper and explaining why certain approaches and answers were acceptable, while others were not, and making sure that every school had a copy of the explanation. In effect, the examination and its aftermath were used as opportunities for intensively training the teachers and not merely for assessing the pupils. Few other countries or even consortia of countries, for example, the West African Examinations Council and the Caribbean Examinations Council, can match this. A review of examinations in eight African countries by the Jobs and Skills Programme for Africa (JASPA, 1982), for example, found that the range of intellectual skills tested was narrow and the questions rarely seemed to take account of the wider objectives of education, much less the development objectives of the Government.

The quality of process

All the components considered so far find their final expression in the quality of the interactions between teachers and pupils, how the one instructs, how the other learns and puts that learning to use. We term it the quality of process. Its grist is the content of the curriculum. Whether this is close to or remote from the daily or even future lives of teachers and learners has a heavy bearing on how the two parties will treat it. The well-known accounts of students in tropical countries having to learn about the climate, geography and history of cold northern countries, just because the latter held the former in thrall, are happily becoming fewer. Reassessment and revision of the curricula have been central to the educational reforms of all the countries considered here, so that, although few might claim complete satisfaction, what pupils learn in school is now rather more readily associated with the realities of their lives or those of their wider societies.

The search for an appropriate medium of instruction has increased the teaching of vernacular languages, even though a common national language—Bahasa Indonesia, Bahasa Melayu, English, French, Hindi, Portuguese, Spanish, Swahili—has to be learned as well, eventually. This has helped narrow the gulf often experienced between the culture of the students' homes and that of the school. In the case of the Republic of Korea, the shift in the curriculum to emphasize the language and history of the Republic of Korea gave impetus to the entire educational system and widened educational opportunities. None the less, the language factor does affect the interaction between teachers and pupils, and the necessity for switching to a national language in secondary and higher education may well hinder the learning of some students.

The simple differences of language between persons are aggravated by their often connoting differences of culture and social class. Bernstein (1977) has noted how such differences affect relationships in schools in the United Kingdom. Brooke and Oxenham (1980) observed much the same phenomena in Mexico between mestizo teachers and Tarascan pupils, while Nunn's (1987) observations of transactions between Quechua-speaking pupils and Spanish-speaking teachers in Ayacucho, Peru, echoed them. Avalos (1986) suggests that the phenomena are widespread throughout Latin America and that teacher training does little to prepare teachers for the social and cultural realities of their students. On the contrary, all these authors intimate that, if anything, schooling and teacher training can serve to alienate some of the teachers from the "lower" social classes in their communities of origin and make it harder for them to teach in the very schools from which they themselves have sprung.

Teaching methods are another ingredient of the learning process and will have some bearing on its quality and outcomes. Despite the widespread advocacy of approaches that challenge children to be more active in their school learning, reliance on repetition, memorization and text-bound learning—where texts are available—still characterizes much of the classroom activity in the developing countries selected (see Avalos, 1986, for much of Latin America; Malvankar, 1987, for India; Brooke and Oxenham, 1980, for Mexico). The compelling cause of this apparent stubbornness is perhaps the education system itself, since the outcomes of such learning do seem to satisfy the criteria used for assessment. The centralized examination can influence teaching and learning. If the assessment were to reward the kind of teaching that stimulates rather than inculcates, teachers would presumably respond rationally. Here again is an area where improvement could be achieved at little or no extra cost.

In most educational systems, learning is latently comparative and competitive and leads to a spectrum of success and failure. This can cause the demoralization of the less successful and erode the quality of their education, even as it succeeds well enough with the academically more able students. The issue is, of course, not confined to the developing countries; it is much debated in the schools of Japan, where the "examination hell" is merciless to the less successful. Similarly, in China, the policy of streaming students according to their intellectual ability is reported to make the "slow" students feel they are doomed:

> "What merits our attention is the present situation in the slow classes. Students often give themselves up as hopeless and drift along" (Hayhoe, 1984, p. 55).

However, the alternative may be worse. In the light of European experiences, many developing countries heeded the encouragement of UNESCO in the late 1960s to introduce automatic promotion from class to class, irrespective of actual attainment in a particular class. The pedagogical arguments were reinforced by the practical considerations of the resource costs of repetition in terms both of extra years in school and of repeaters excluding potential pupils. Nigeria, for example, adopted automatic promotion but, like many others, reverted to repeating, because of the alleged unmanageability of classes where the attainments of the pupils could not be taken for granted (Bray, 1981). Tedesco (1983) has argued that automatic promotion tends simply to increase the number of failures at the end of primary school, thus delaying, but not solving, the problem of ineffective learning. If widely differing abilities and learning speeds are not recognized, the quality of education suffers because teachers are unable to cope; if the differences are recognized, quality suffers because the less able and slower are discouraged. As far as can be ascertained, none of the selected developing countries has solved the dilemma—nor for that matter has any industrialized country.

Quality as a function of priority

The introduction to this paper linked the quality of education with the resources that are devoted to it. A trade-off often has to be made between providing educational opportunities more widely but at a relatively low level of quality and making it more effective but for relatively fewer people. Here we consider the trade-off between levels of education: should the expansion of the secondary and tertiary levels await the achievement of good-quality universal primary schooling or should resources be concentrated on producing high-level manpower in the form of university graduates at the cost of restricting primary education? It is possible to contrast two approaches to the dilemma. On the one hand, there are the cases of Japan and the Republic of Korea; on the other, there are those of Brazil, Mexico, India and Nigeria.

The educational development of Japan and the Republic of Korea had in common an emphasis on attaining universal primary education at a good level of quality, before they embarked on large-scale expansions of the secondary and tertiary levels. Japan abolished fees for primary schooling in 1980 and, while legislating for compulsory education, took active steps against desertion in the nineteenth century (Koizumi and Amano, 1967). The effect was to form a trainable total work-force, while keeping the flow of more highly schooled people roughly in line with the growth of the kinds of employment that needed them. Further, when the two upper levels were expanded, it was not at the expense of primary education. As can be seen from tables 6 and 7, there is little variation in the unit costs of students in the three levels: the distribution of expenditure corresponds with that of enrolments.

India provides a convenient contrast. On attaining political independence in 1947, its Government committed the country to attaining universal primary education by 1960. As that date grew near, the target was deferred two decades, to 1980. Even today, although the gross enrolment ratios suggest that the target has almost been met, the non-enrolment of a considerable number of girls and the continuing high rates of drop-out mean that India still falls short of its aspiration. Yet, a comparatively high proportion of the relevant age group (9 per cent) are enrolled in tertiary education (see table 2). This apparent bias in favour of the higher level is reflected in table 8. Although the unit cost of a university student declined in real terms over the quarter century, while that of a primary student inched upwards, in 1975 the resources that bought a single university place represented the forgone opportunity to buy 66 primary places. India has in effect chosen to give more education at a higher price to a few who have already had more than average education, rather than work for sound education for all. The effect has been to have a less trainable total work-force, and a flow of highly skilled people notoriously larger than the numbers of jobs available. There has been another regrettable effect: the declining cost of a university student has been reflected in the declining quality of the average university graduate. That all quality has not suffered is only too palpably reflected in the brain drain of excellent Indians to where their talents can be better utilized and rewarded.

That India is by no means alone is shown in table 9. What stands out from the figures offered there is that, despite the lack of effective

TABLE 6. COMPARATIVE DISTRIBUTION OF ENROLMENTS AND EXPENDITURE BY LEVEL OF EDUCATION

Country	Level	Enrolment (As percentage of total)	Expenditure (As percentage of total)	Ratio
Nigeria, 1984 ...	1	79.0	17.2	0.2
	2	20.0	39.8	2.0
	3	1.2	25.0	21.7
Zaire, 1980	1	77.0	47.1	0.6
	2	22.0	27.5	1.3
	3	0.5	—	—
China, 1985	1	72.0	28.6	0.4
	2	27.0	33.2	1.2
	3	1.0	21.8	22.9
India, 1984	1	68.0	44.6	0.7
	2	28.0	30.3	1.1
	3	4.9	18.7	3.8
Brazil, 1984	1	85.0	48.1	0.6
	2	10.0	6.9	0.7
	3	4.9	20.8	4.2
Mexico, 1985 ...	1	66.0	27.2	0.4
	2	29.0	15.9	0.5
	3	5.3	29.2	5.5
Republic of Korea, 1985 ..	1	44.0	46.7	1.1
	2	43.0	36.7	0.9
	3	13.1	10.9	0.8
Japan, 1980	1	50.0	38.2	0.8
	2	40.0	34.6	0.9
	3	10.1	11.1	1.1

Source: United Nations Educational, Scientific and Cultural Organization, *Statistical Yearbooks, 1965-1987* (Paris).

universality and the low quality in primary education in the developing countries, the secondary and tertiary sectors have been financed to grow at very fast rates. Indeed, the most expensive and necessarily the most selective sector has grown the fastest. During the 1980s, the period of the most severe financial stringency, in all three developing regions, primary education has expanded at less than the population growth rate, which in turn was less than the birth rate. The implication is that the primary enrolment rate is in the process of decline and the target of universal primary education is receding. By contrast, the rates for growth in the secondary and tertiary sectors, though certainly reduced, continue relatively rapidly. In many developing countries, primary education does not appear to enjoy the priority it was accorded by Japan and the Republic of Korea. Tables 6 and 7 illustrate how expenditures relate to enrolments and what a

122

TABLE 7. PRIMARY AND SECONDARY UNIT COSTS ABSORBED BY ONE TERTIARY UNIT COST

Country	1950	1955	1960	1965	1970	1975	1980	1985
A. *Primary unit costs absorbed by one tertiary unit cost*								
Nigeria	—	—	—	110.2	—	120.8	133.3	—
Zaire	—	—	—	—	—	—	—	—
China	—	—	—	—	—	—	—	57.3
India	6.5	5.6	21.4	46.4	31.5	4.3	5.1	—
Brazil	14.1	—	46.9	222.2	235.3	9.0	6.9	7.5
Mexico	1.7	—	—	11.6	8.1	6.0	10.9	13.4
Republic of Korea	—	15.0	12.0	2.8	1.8	3.4	1.6	0.8
Japan	—	6.2	7.4	2.4	1.8	1.2	1.4	—
B. *Secondary unit costs absorbed by one tertiary unit cost*								
Nigeria	—	—	—	7.50	5.80	5.70	13.60	—
Zaire	—	—	—	—	—	5.60	2.00	—
China	—	—	—	—	—	—	—	3.0
India	4	3.50	12.30	5.10	5.00	1.30	1.60	—
Brazil	4	—	3.70	7.60	4.60	2.40	1.30	1.20
Mexico	15	—	2.10	2.10	3.30	2.80	1.50	1.30
Republic of Korea	—	0.40	—	0.70	0.50	0.70	0.90	0.80
Japan	—	1.30	1.40	1.00	1.10	1.10	1.10	—

Source: United Nations Educational, Scientific and Cultural Organization, *Statistical Yearbooks, 1965-1987* (Paris).

TABLE 8. COMPARATIVE UNIT COSTS OF PRIMARY AND UNIVERSITY EDUCATION
IN INDIA, 1950-1976

	Primary	University	Ratio of university to primary costs
	(Cost in rupees at constant 1970-1971 prices)		
1950-1951	41.9	4 011.7	95.7
1960-1961	50.1	4 581.1	91.4
1975-1976	55.2	3 664.5	66.4
Growth rate (percentage), 1950-1976 ..	1.1	−0.3	

Source: Tilak (1988).

TABLE 9. GROWTH IN ENROLMENTS: AVERAGE ANNUAL RATES OF GROWTH

	Levels of education		
	Primary	Secondary	Tertiary
1970-1980 Africa[a]	8.4	14.6	14.2
Asia[a]	3.1	6.0	7.2
Latin America ..	3.4	8.1	11.5
1980-1985 Africa[a]	2.4	9.5	8.3
Asia[a]	0.8	2.4	5.9
Latin America ..	1.7	3.9	5.9

Source: United Nations Educational, Scientific and Cultural Organization, Statistical Yearbook, 1987 (Paris), table 2.2.
[a]Excluding Arab States.

secondary and a tertiary place cost in terms of primary places. They reflect in varying degrees the greater resources absorbed by secondary and tertiary education. It is probable that better quality would be possible in the primary schools, and hence in the work-force as a whole, if lower priority and fewer resources were given to the secondary and tertiary institutions.

Points of leverage

Our review of the main factors that affect the quality of education has hinted at ways in which quality might be improved without additional resources, even though additional effort might be called for. A brief review might be helpful, taken not in the order of appearance in the paper, but rather in the order of the potential for leverage.

In the first place is the suggestion by Psacharopoulos, stemming from his study of schools in Colombia and the United Republic of Tanzania, that more deliberate and efficient management of resources and costs can raise quality without raising costs. The fact that the private schools in these two countries are cheaper than the State schools makes an investigation all the more challenging.

Secondly, there is good evidence that better leadership from

124

head teachers and their senior colleagues can by itself raise the quality of performance among both teachers and students.

Thirdly, there is good evidence that patterns of assessment and examination do influence teaching and learning, and that they can be used with greater deliberation to steer teachers to the closer observance of the higher objectives of education.

Fourthly, there are possibilities of training teachers both more effectively and more cheaply.

In addition, there may be ways to make the goals of learning clearer, the rewards more tangible and the link between learning and reward more reliable, so that both students and teachers apply themselves more effectively.

Further, reorganizing teaching so as to de-emphasize failure versus success and to emphasize instead achievement and progress by all learners at their own paces may enhance the general motivation to learn.

Finally, there is evidence that, where schools and teachers are, on the one hand, directly accountable to the parents of their pupils, but, on the other, enjoy sufficient professional autonomy, the quality of education is enhanced.

REFERENCES

Abemba, B. (1985). Zaire: system of education. In *The International Encyclopaedia of Education,* T. Husen and N. Postlethwaite, eds. Oxford: Pergamon Press.

Adams, J. (1987). Planning and implementation: education and health in Tanzania. Glasgow: Paisley College of Technology, Ph.D. thesis (unpublished).

Avalos, B. (1986). Teaching children of the poor: an ethnographic study in Latin America. Ottawa: International Development Research Centre. IDRC Monograph No. 253e.

Behrman, Jere and Nancy Birdsall (1983). The quality of schooling: quantity alone may be misleading. *American Economic Review,* vol. 73, No. 5, pp. 928-946.

Bernstein, B. (1977). *Class, Codes and Control,* vols. 1-3. London: Routledge and Kegan Paul.

Boakye, K. and J. Oxenham (1982). Qualifications and the quality of education in Ghanaian rural middle schools. Brighton: Institute of Development Studies Research Reports, Education Report No. 6.

Bray, Mark (1981). *Universal Primary Education in Nigeria.* London: Routledge and Kegan Paul.

British Council (1981). *Mexico: Education Profile.* London.

Brooke, Nigel and John Oxenham (1980). Qualifications and the quality of education in Mexican rural primary schools. Brighton: Institute of Development Studies Research Reports, Education Report No. 4.

Chinapay, V. and H. Dau (1981). *Swedish Missions and Education in the Republic of Zaire.* Stockholm: University of Stockholm, Institute of International Education.

Chuncai, D. (1985). China, People's Republic of: system of education. In *The International Encyclopaedia of Education* . . .

Coleman, J. S. and others (1966). Equality of educational opportunity. Washington, D.C.: Department of Health, Education and Welfare.

Comber, L. C. and J. P. Keeves (1973). *Science Education in Nineteen Countries: An*

Empirical Study. International Studies in Evaluation. London: International Association for the Evaluation of Educational Achievement (IEA).

Cummings, W. K. (1980). *Education and Equality in Japan*. Princeton: Princeton University Press.

Dore, R. (1976). Education, qualification and development. In *The Diploma Disease*. London: George Allen and Unwin Ltd.

Foster, P. (1965). The vocational school fallacy. In *Education and Economic Development*, C. A. Anderson and M. J. Bowman, eds. Chicago: Aldine Publishing Co.

Fuller, B. (1986a). Quality in education. *Comparative Education Review*, vol. 30, No. 4, pp. 491-507.

———— (1986b). Raising school quality in developing countries: what investments boost learning? World Bank Discussion Paper No. 2. Washington, D.C.: World Bank.

Harbison, F. and C. A. Myers (1964). *Education, Manpower and Economic Growth*. New York: McGraw Hill.

Harriss, B. (1986). Meals and noon meals in south India: food and nutrition policy in the rural food economy of Tamil Nadu State. Development Studies Occasional Papers. Norwich: University of East Anglia, School of Development Studies.

Hayhoe, R. (1984). *Contemporary Chinese Education*. London: Croom Helm.

Heyneman, S. P. and D. Jamison (1980). Student learning in Uganda: textbook availability and other factors. *Comparative Education Review*, vol. 24, No. 2 (part 1, June), pp. 206-220.

Heyneman, S. P. and W. Loxley (1983). The effect of primary school quality on academic achievement across twenty-nine high- and low-income countries. *American Journal of Sociology*, vol. 88, No. 6, pp. 1162-1194.

Husen, Torsten (1979). Teacher education in developing countries: patterns and structures. In *A Spotlight on Educational Problems*, H. Dahl, Anders Lysne and Per Rand, eds. Oslo: Universitets forlarget.

IEA (International Association for the Evaluation of Educational Achievement) (1976a). *The IEA Six Subject Survey: An Empirical Study of Education in Twenty-one Countries*. By David A. Walker. Stockholm: Almqvist and Wiksell.

———— (1976b). *The National Case Study: An Empirical Comparative Study of Twenty-one Educational Systems*. By A. H. Passow. Stockholm: Almqvist and Wiksell.

IIEP (International Institute for Educational Planning) (1984). Quelques réflexions sur la question de la valeur de l'éducation dans l'ensemble des valeurs de la société. By Claudio Neiva. IIEP cahier No. 70. Paris.

India, Ministry of Education (1985). *Challenge of Education: A Policy Perspective*. New Delhi.

JASPA (Jobs and Skills Programme for Africa) (1980). *School Leavers, Unemployment and Manpower Development in Liberia*. Addis Ababa: International Labour Organisation.

———— (1982). *Paper Qualification Syndrome and Unemployment of School Leavers: A Comparative Sub-regional Study*. Addis Ababa: International Labour Organisation.

Jencks, C. S. and others (1972). *Inequality: A Reassessment of the Effect of Family and Schooling in America*. New York: Basic Books.

Jencks, C. S. and others (1979). *Who Gets Ahead? The Determinants of Economic Success in America*. New York: Basic Books.

Khan, Q. U. and D. Berstecher (1988). The problems of repetition and drop out in basic education in Madagascar. *Notes, Comments No. 180*. Paris: United Nations Educational, Scientific and Cultural Organization—United Nations Children's Fund—World Food Programme Co-operative Programme.

Koizumi, K. and I. Amano (1967). The process of eradicating wastage in primary education: Japan's experience. *Research Bulletin of the National Institute for Educational Research*, No. 8. Tokyo.

126

Loxley, W. (1983). The impact of primary school quality on learning in Egypt. *International Journal of Educational Development,* vol. 3, No. 1, pp. 33-46.

Malvankar, Alka (1987). A study in the sociology of education: some high schools in Goa. Delhi: University of Delhi, Ph.D. thesis (unpublished).

Medeiros, E. B. (1985). Brazil: system of education. In *The International Encyclopaedia of Education* . . .

Mortimore, P. and others (1988). *School Matters: The Junior Years.* London: Open Books.

Naik, J. P. (1980). Reflection of the future development of education: an assessment of educational reform in India and lessons for the future. Paris: United Nations Educational, Scientific and Cultural Organization.

Nunn, A. (1987). An evaluation of the Peruvian educational reforms 1972-1985. Sussex: University of Sussex, Ph.D. thesis (unpublished).

Onokerhoraye, A. G. (1984). *Social Services in Nigeria.* London: Kegan Paul International.

Peaker, G. F. (1971). *The Plowden Children Four Years Later.* London: National Foundation for Educational Research.

Psacharopoulos, G. (1987). Public versus private schools in developing countries: evidence from Colombia and Tanzania. *International Journal of Educational Development,* vol. 7, No. 1, pp. 59-68.

Rutter, M. and others (1979). *Fifteen Thousand Hours: Secondary Schools and Their Effects on Children.* London: Open Books.

Somerset, H. C. A. (1982). *Examination Reform: The Kenya Experience.* A report prepared for the World Bank.

Tedesco, J. C. (1983). Pedagogical model and school failures. *CEPAL Review,* No. 21. United Nations publication, Sales No. E.83.II.G.5, pp. 132-146.

Thornley, J. C. (1987). Politics and technocracy in organising an education system: the development of primary schools in northern Nigeria 1960-1970. Sussex: University of Sussex, Ph.D. thesis (unpublished).

Tilak, J. B. G. (1988). Costs of education in India. *International Journal of Educational Development,* vol. 8, No. 1.

UNESCO (United Nations Educational, Scientific and Cultural Organization)—Government of the Republic of Korea (1983). *Education in Korea—A Third World Success Story.* By J. E. Jayasuriya. Seoul.

Unger, J. (1985). *Education Under Mao: Class and Competition in Canton Schools 1960-1980.* New York: Columbia University Press.

Wolff, L. (1971). The use of information for improvement of educational planning in Rio Grande Do Sul, Brazil. Cambridge: Harvard University, Ed.D. thesis (unpublished).

World Bank (1978). *Textbooks and Achievement: What We Know.* By S. P. Heyneman, J. P. Farrell and M. A. Sepulveda-Stuardo. World Bank Staff Working Paper No. 298. Washington, D.C.

———— (1979). *Investment in Indian Education: Uneconomic?* By S. Heyneman. World Bank Staff Working Paper No. 327. Washington, D.C.

———— (1982). *Mexico's Free Textbooks: Nationalism and the Urgency to Educate.* By P. H. Neumann and M. A. Cunningham. World Bank Staff Working Paper No. 541. Washington, D.C.

6

HUMAN RESOURCES DEVELOPMENT AND INDUSTRIALIZATION, WITH SPECIAL REFERENCE TO SUB-SAHARAN AFRICA

Sanjaya Lall*

CONTENTS

Introduction

Human resources development is rightly regarded as a critical ingredient of economic development. The causation appears to run both ways. It is necessary for human resources to grow if development is to proceed in the productive sectors. The productive sectors, in turn, have to grow and diversify in order to permit more opportunities for human resources to develop, and to employ the enhanced flow of skills and talents that are produced. Many factors contribute to a phenomenon as complex and multifaceted as human resources development. Formal education is a major determinant, but there are others: on-the-job learning, training, research, induction of foreign skills and knowledge and so on. The precise contribution of formal education, and, within it, different levels of education, as opposed to other methods of learning and training, is not well understood. It is likely that the rule of the various factors varies by country and level of development. What is not in doubt is the significance of human resources to economic development.

What is true of economic development in general is true of industrial development in particular. In fact, most observers would regard industrialization as more dependent on human resources advancement than the growth of primary or service sectors. Modern industry, and some modern service activities, utilize advanced forms of scientific knowledge in methods of production. To a large extent

---

*Lecturer in Development Economics, Oxford University, Institute of Economics and Statistics.

this knowledge is embodied in plant and equipment. However, not entirely: to select the right equipment, to operate it efficiently, to improve it over time, all require a variety of technical and other skills which have to be acquired in developing countries. Formal education is one important means of acquiring those skills (see McMahon, 1987), but the learning of industrial skills is a broad-based process in which training, experience, foreign technology transfer and deliberate search and research are of great importance.

This paper explores the nature and pattern of human resources development, which is necessary for efficient industrialization. To illustrate the argument, it draws on the experience of one of the most industrially backward regions of the developing world—sub-Saharan Africa. Despite substantial efforts at industrial development during the past three decades, the results in sub-Saharan Africa have been disappointing. Several reasons are advanced for this. External circumstances have not been propitious, and foreign resources for industrial operation and investment have diminished alarmingly over time. Domestic demand has diminished correspondingly in several countries. In some, droughts, political turmoil and other such events have eaten into the dwindling resource supplies. At the same time, industrialization has been promoted behind barriers of high protection against imports. This has often permitted considerable inefficiency. Governments have tended to take the lead role in industrialization, but parastatal enterprises have often lacked management and technical skills. Several African countries started with unrealistically high wages and artificially cheap supplies of imported capital goods and components. This biased facilities towards undue capital-intensity and perpetuated dependence on imports.

All these factors certainly contributed to the poor performance of industry in sub-Saharan Africa, but they are not unique to the region. Other parts of the developing world also faced adverse terms of trade and interventionist, inward-looking policies. Yet, by and large, their experience of industrial development was better than that of sub-Saharan Africa. It will be argued here that the main factor distinguishing sub-Saharan Africa from the rest of the third world (in industrialization, but perhaps also other aspects of development) is the relatively small initial stock of human resources of the former and its relatively slow growth over time. The region is thus an ideal case study of the significance of human resources development for industrialization.

If human resources development is critical to efficient industrialization, its importance is certainly underplayed in many current debates on industrialization. Many developing country Governments still subscribe to the dated growth-model characterization of development. Here, higher physical investment is translated into higher GNP by given (and presumably efficient) technical relationships between input and output. Thus, growth depends only on the rate of investment, and failure to grow derives only from shortfalls in (imported) resources available for investment or for capacity utilization. The primacy of physical investment in industrialization still rules in many African countries, and leads them to argue that revival in industrial growth only requires renewed inflows of foreign resources.

A different approach, currently fashionable in the literature on development strategy, is that the essence of industrial development is to "get prices right". Physical investment is important, but only if guided into proper uses by market prices that reflect true opportunity costs and long-term comparative advantage in a broad international setting. Moreover, even "good" investments may perform inefficiently if they operate with wrong price signals: import barriers, price controls, inflated wages and so on. Government-created market failures are, in this view, the major cause of inefficiency or stagnation. If prices are set right, on the other hand, economic factors will respond (presumably spontaneously, it being assumed that other forms of market failure are absent) in a relatively short period to ensure that greater efficiency results. This is characterized as the neo-classical view.

There is some literature debating these propositions (see a succinct recent article by Pack and Westphal, 1986), and it is not intended to review it here. The relevant point is that both approaches, while containing some valid elements—physical investment is obviously necessary for growth and prices do matter—tend to ignore, among other factors, the central role of human resources. The fixed coefficient planning approach assumes either that human resources are irrelevant or that they are available in the right amount and quality to match physical investments. The neo-classical view does focus on the human element, but primarily on its motivation and response to market signals in achieving efficient resource allocation. It assumes that the requisite skills and capabilities are present or will be called forth by price signals. Problems in the acquisition of these capabilities, dynamic and external effects associated with "learning", are largely ignored.

Needless to say, both approaches may be invalid in developing countries. There are differences between individual countries, but in general terms the underdevelopment of human resources is a characteristic—and a cause—of economic backwardness. Moreover, human resources cannot be developed quickly, nor do they spring forth simply in response to profit signals. Depending on which skills are being considered, a mixture of formal schooling, advanced education, post-university training, on-the-job training, and experience is needed to generate specific requirements. The implications for industrial strategy are more complex, difficult and gradual than suggested by the planning or neo-classical approaches.

The following section sets out a simplified classification of the

131

human resources needed for successful industrial development and describes how each may arise. The third section analyses the African industrial experience, describing the failures as well as the successes, and highlighting the significance of human resources. The final section includes policy recommendations for the development of the capabilities needed for industrialization.

Human resources for industrialization

NATURE AND SIGNIFICANCE OF INDUSTRIAL CAPABILITIES

Industrial development requires a broad array of capabilities, both directly in the setting up and operation of manufacturing facilities and indirectly in supporting services, infrastructure and administration. This paper deals only with the capabilities needed directly by manufacturing enterprises.

The installation, efficient operation, expansion and upgrading of manufacturing facilities are among the most complex and demanding tasks in modern economic life. The demands vary by activity and specialization, but in essence they can be broken down into three basic categories:

Entrepreneurial capabilities;

Managerial and organizational capabilities;

Technological capabilities.

In this simplified scheme, entrepreneurial capabilities refer to the skills needed to identify suitable investment opportunities, muster the financial, technical and other resources to mount a project and implement the project at an appropriate scale and with an appropriate market orientation. Managerial and organizational capabilities refer to the skills needed to handle the non-technical aspects of an industry once the initial entrepreneurial functions have been fulfilled. Technological capabilities refer to the various specialized technical skills needed in all phases of the investment, operation and subsequent expansion of an industry.

The lines between these sets of capabilities cannot be drawn very sharply. Nevertheless, the schematization is useful in focusing attention on the different kinds of human resources development required. This paper concentrates on the third kind, technological capabilities, but the others are also briefly reviewed. The critical point to note is that each of these capabilities has to be learned and developed. Each has its own pace, sequence and determinants, but none is born fully-fledged in a developing country, ready to take on the task of modern industrialization.

Entrepreneurial capabilities are usually conceived of as resulting from innate psychological traits, conditioned by communal, social and family factors, rather than skills acquired from a "learning"

132

process. Indeed, this is true to some extent: in any given setting, a number of people display an entrepreneurial drive in the sense that they are motivated to seek out profitable opportunities or take risks. Thus, the profusion and vibrancy of informal sector activity in developing countries, including sub-Saharan Africa, shows that the entrepreneurial spirit is fairly universal. What capabilities are then to be "learned" for modern industry?

These are capabilities that are not simply the product of an innate drive to seize profitable opportunities or take risks. Given such a drive, the ability to set up a modern industrial venture requires special knowledge of the relevant technology, financial systems, marketing and organizations (of the appropriate scale and complexity). Even if the entrepreneur himself does not possess all this knowledge, he must be able to tap it relatively readily, from his community, friends, official agencies, specialized consultants and so on. The fostering of industrial entrepreneurship is a process that encompasses not just the individual investor, but his entire environment. There are, in other words, indivisibilities, externalities and unpredictable dynamic effects involved in creating entrepreneurial capabilities. Once launched, the process snowballs.

This is why in several societies some communities enter into a virtual circle of entrepreneurial development while others languish. The latter do not build their drive into the capabilities needed for modern industry. Thus, while Africans display considerable entrepreneurial spirit at the informal level, their educational and cultural background and historical exposure to industrial activity have not provided an adequate learning ground for entrepreneurial development in modern manufacturing (see the following section). Experience suggests that there is a sort of sequence in entrepreneurial development: from peasant agriculture to monetized agriculture, to simple trade and informal manufacturing, to more organized commercial activity (retailing and property), to small-scale modern industry, to traditional large-scale industry and, finally, to large-scale industry using modern technologies. The sequence may not be linear, and may be foreshortened in special cases, but it cannot be short-circuited or bypassed. There is an increasing degree of complexity in entrepreneurial activity along the scale which indicates the need to learn new skills, consolidate the knowledge of each stage and build upon experience and new knowledge. In developing countries, it also requires changes in socio-cultural attitudes.

One reason why the systematic learning of entrepreneurial capabilities has received relatively little attention is the image of the pathbreaking, unique "Schumpeterian entrepreneur", who shatters existing moulds and establishes vast industrial empires, as the only true entrepreneur. Such a figure probably is born, not made, and the learning process described here is probably irrelevant. But the Schumpeterian entrepreneur accounts for a relatively small part of industrial activity (Baumol, 1986). Much of industry is set up by more "routine" entrepreneurs, the managers of large enterprises, who are trained for the job by specific educational programmes and by learning on the job.

Managerial capabilities are increasingly cultivated by formal education in the developed countries, though in many places premium is still attached to experience and individual flair. Managerial skills overlap with routine entrepreneurial skills, as well as technological skills (many analysts lump them all together), but it is useful to keep them separate. Managerial skills can be further broken down into financial, accounting, marketing, personnel, strategic planning and other categories, each with its own discipline and related training.

Apart from the learning of specific managerial skills, efficient industrial operation also requires the setting up of particular organizational structures appropriate to the size, spread, complexity and rate of growth of each enterprise's activities. The management of the growth of an organization, which behaves rather like a living organism (in Penrose's terms) is itself a major skill.

Technological capabilities are among the most difficult skills to acquire in the process of industrialization. They are also among the most critical, since the efficiency with which technologies are implemented and adapted determines the success of any industrial operation. Moreover, no technology remains constant, and any technology in place has to be continuously upgraded to reduce costs or introduce new products. And no technology should be an island unto itself. The process of industrial development necessarily requires that industrial technologies spread between enterprises, industries and across sectors. All these requirements are based on a range of technological functions, some of which can be brought in or imported by an enterprise, but many of which necessarily have to be performed by the enterprise itself.

Simplifying greatly, the technological capabilities needed by a manufacturer fall into three broad categories (for a more detailed exposition, see Lall, 1987): investment capabilities, production engineering capabilities and linkages capabilities. Each contains several different technological functions, of differing degrees of complexity, as reviewed below.

Investment capabilities are related to the initial setting up of a project and to its subsequent expansion. Included in this category are such preparatory activities as project identification and evaluation; feasibility studies; specification of products, scale, technology; identification of sources of technology and negotiation on technology transfer; project scheduling and site preparation. The actual implementation of the project then includes: basic and detailed engineering; identification of equipment suppliers; civil construction; installation and testing of plant; start-up and initial training of operatives.

Investment capabilities are critical to the choice of feasible projects, technology and equipment, and the process design: once these basic parameters are embodied in a plant, it is costly to alter them substantially later. In other words, wrong choices can saddle the investor with high capital and/or operating costs; in extreme cases, they can create "white elephants" (inherently unviable facilities), which too often litter the industrial landscape of developing countries.

Investment capabilities not only affect the selection of projects and technologies, they also determine how well and speedily projects are implemented, how well they are adapted to local conditions and materials and how much of the knowledge of the basic production process is passed on to and retained in the enterprise. These factors, again, influence the capital cost of the investment and subsequent operational costs. More importantly, perhaps, they affect the extent to which the developing country can undertake major adaptations, expansions and improvements on its own.

Most investment capabilities can be imported by developing countries from developed country consultants, engineering firms, capital goods manufacturers and so on. Does it then make economic sense to develop such capabilities internally? Certainly, some very specialized skills, which are expensive to learn and may only be deployed rarely (process design of sophisticated petrochemicals, for instance), may not be worth learning. But a number of more general investment skills (detailed engineering, some basic design, equipment selection or manufacture, civil construction, commissioning etc.) may well be worth acquiring, for several reasons. First, several critical project choices are best made by the country itself. Secondly, the cost of local engineering and design tends to be far lower than that of international consultants. Thirdly, the "unbundling" of a technology package can further reduce its cost and raise its appropriateness; a complete package, such as a turnkey plant, is the most expensive way to implement an investment. Fourthly, local learning of investment skills enables expansions, adaptations or improvements to be undertaken efficiently. Finally, investment capabilities can to some extent be transferred across activities, generating external benefits.

By this reasoning, the lack of investment capabilities can lead a developing country to select wrong projects, get the wrong technology, pay high prices for what it buys, implement projects slowly or inefficiently, gain little or no understanding of the technologies it operates and so fail to make subsequent improvements, and be dependent on expensive foreign expertise for later expansion. The higher costs (capital and operating) entailed by this, the inappropriate technologies and industrial white elephants that are so often found in developing countries, are testimony to underdeveloped investment capabilities.

Production engineering capabilities determine how efficiently a

135

plant is operated over time, and also the extent to which its productivity is raised, new products introduced and new process technologies tapped. It is generally assumed that a technology, once in place, is easy to master (i.e., to reach "best practice" norms of quality, operating efficiency, maintenance, by-product utilization, inventory control, downtime and so on). Unfortunately, this is untrue. Many industrial technologies cannot be properly mastered without considerable technological effort and experience. The same plant in two different countries will show enormous differences in cost, productivity and quality, simply because of differences in the quality and quantity of the production engineering effort provided.

Furthermore, technological efforts do not cease once a given level of efficiency is achieved. A competitive enterprise will constantly seek to improve on its initial norms of cost. Product ranges and raw materials will change as external conditions evolve. Capital equipment will be changed, to work faster or last longer. Where imports are difficult, processes will be adapted and simple spares or components will be made in-house. Costs and productivity will be closely monitored in each part of the plant. Inventory control and work scheduling will be improved and so on.

All this occurs within a given technology. But industrial technologies are themselves subject to constant change, and a dynamic enterprise will seek out those improvements that are relevant to its operations and implement them. This may be based on buying new foreign technologies, developing them by independent research and development or some combination of brought-in and own efforts.

It is evident that successful production engineering requires a broad range of technological capabilities and takes several forms. The precise requirements vary with the scale, complexity and nature of the activity, but only the enterprise that can mount the pervasive and unremitting effort described here will be efficient and successful by world standards. This does not necessarily mean that it will undertake all technological work itself—advanced R and D into new technologies may well be left to developed country firms, and its results purchased on licence. It does mean that it will have the ability to select the new technology and graft it cost-efficiently onto its production facilities. The success of the newly industrializing countries in so many industries has been due precisely to their production engineering capabilities, drawing liberally on foreign know-how, embodied in equipment, disembodied in licencing or imitated by "reverse engineering".

The lack of production engineering capabilities concomitantly entails various costs and inefficiencies. The effects can range from simply high production costs to poor quality of output, idle capacity (owing to machinery breakdown, poor scheduling), wastage, rigid product range, obsolescence in technology and so on. The process of maturation of "infant industries"—the core of successful industrialization by developing countries—depends critically on the development of production capabilities (Bell and others, 1984).

Linkage capabilities determine to what extent and how efficiently an enterprise's technical knowledge is diffused to other enterprises in the economy. In part, such diffusion occurs naturally—by imitation, turnover of personnel, personal contacts and so on. In part, it requires the setting up of extra-market linkages between vertically related enterprises (buyers and sellers of producer goods). Extra-market linkages involve the transmission of information, designs, skills, equipment, training etc. and are critical to the functioning of industry in developed and developing countries (Lall, 1980).

Vertical linkages are nevertheless of particular significance to developing countries, since they lead to a deepening of the industrial structure, the spread of technology, the growth of small subcontractors and the diffusion of skills. They also lead to the establishment of various types of industrial services (consultancy and technical), which specialize in particular tasks and act as reservoirs and transmitters of technical knowledge.

Linkages can also exist horizontally, between competing firms. Large firms can license their technology to smaller ones, or sell technical services to them. They can set up turnkey plants for each other, or set up co-operative research facilities, or collaborate in industry-wide quality control centres. Horizontal linkages help the realization of scale economies in certain industrial functions. They also help all firms in an industry to move towards common norms of efficiency and "best practice". Persistent and wide disparities in operating efficiency between firms within an industry, a common feature in many developing countries, are a sign of poor horizontal linkages.

The creation of linkages of either type requires the development of specific capabilities. On the receiving side, they require enterprises to have the technological capabilities noted above to set up and efficiently operate an industrial plant. On the imparting side, they require departments that can locate, screen and help set up potential suppliers; technicians who can transmit production engineering know-how over a broad range; personnel to provide technical drawing, blueprints and designs ("codified" knowledge); and also financial and training personnel to impart relevant assistance. Capital goods manufacturers should be able to help their customers to select, modify, install and operate their equipment. More advanced firms should be able to offer turnkey facilities to customers. Mature enterprises can offer these internationally, with financial support.

Linkage capabilities may not appear difficult to acquire. In fact, however, they are fairly demanding, and only the more advanced newly industrializing countries have been able to set up "deep" industrial structures with widespread linkages. In lesser developed countries, industries remain enclave operations over long periods. Vertical and horizontal linkages remain minimal; the small-scale sector remains divorced from formal manufacturing, retaining the original dualistic structure of industry; few servicing and consultancy enterprises are formed; and gaps between efficient and inefficient enterprises remain large.

This concludes our review of the nature and significance of the industrial capabilities necessary for efficient industrialization. Industrialization can proceed without the entire array of capabilities. Indeed, developing countries must start without most of these capabilities. However, their ability to learn the necessary skills quickly determines the success of their industrial effort: the growing up and maturing of their "infant industries". The tremendous dynamism and export success shown by the newly industrializing countries demonstrates how far such maturation can proceed: a vital ingredient in the process has been the building-up of industrial capabilities (Bell and others, 1984). Let us now consider how the capabilities arise.

DETERMINANTS OF INDUSTRIAL CAPABILITIES

The development of industrial capabilities depends on a complex interaction of historical and cultural factors, formal education, industrial experience itself, government policies, institutions and exogenous events which affect the rate of economic growth. The interactions are not well understood; indeed, this entire area is an underdeveloped one for economic analysis (see Fransman, 1986, for a good survey). A few comments based on recent research are, nevertheless, in order.

The acquisition of industrial capabilities is essentially a product of two forces on which various factors impinge: formal training and learning on the job. Formal training occurs in the education system as well as in courses organized by industry. Learning on the job is, to a small extent, automatic learning by doing (the acquisition of skills simply by repetition); most of it occurs by conscious technological search, experimentation and development directed at solving specific problems. The problems addressed may be relatively minor—production lay-out, quality control, substitution of raw material, extending the life of a machine—or they may be major—expensive, long-term R and D to produce new technologies.

It is impossible to say which element of learning is more important. The weight of each varies with circumstance, and its significance to industry depends on the nature of the activity. Simple manufacturing relies on capabilities acquired by apprenticeship and experience. More complex activity requires some formal technical training and on-the-job learning. Within this, the solving of more

138

difficult problems calls for more technical research and experimentation, the precise discipline and scale of activity depending upon the industry and problem in question.

The role of historical and cultural factors, formal education and institutions (for training, science and technology, technology transfer etc.) is obvious enough. What needs emphasis is the interaction between industrial experience, government policies and exogenous events.

The mere fact of production does not ensure that appropriate capabilities will be generated. The widespread incidence of "infant industries" that never grow up shows this clearly. Experience has to be matched, on the one hand, by the requisite "receptacles" for technological capability acquisition—trained manpower—and, on the other, by the right incentives, direction and conditions for such acquisition. Some of these incentives and conditions are internal to the enterprise, and thus derive from good management, salary and other incentives and adequate flows of information vertically and horizontally. Some are external to the enterprise, and these depend critically on government policies and exogenous events.

Government policies on trade and industry directly affect the direction and content of the technological activity undertaken. They determine how much competition, and of what sort, a manufacturing enterprise faces, how large a market it serves, how much foreign technology it has access to, who owns it and how it manages its employees. All these affect the process of capability development. In addition, government policies on macro-economic management, primary exports and infrastructure affect industry indirectly. The rate of growth of the economy, foreign exchange availability and infrastructural facilities affect the growth of manufacturing and so condition its learning potential.

Recent research (see Dahlman and others, 1987; and Lall, 1987) suggests that inward-looking trade régimes, with the web of internal regulations that inevitably accompanies them (World Bank, 1987), do generate a lot of technological activity. However, in contrast to more outward-oriented régimes, with greater reliance on market forces, they tend to distort the activity in directions that do not lead to sustained increases in productivity or international competitiveness. In India, for instance, a large stock of technical manpower with prolonged and extensive experience in industrial activity has developed considerable mastery of manufacturing technology. Yet, most Indian industry is uncompetitive, undynamic and saddled with obsolete technologies. On the other hand, the Republic of Korea, with a shorter history of industrialization, has developed competitive advantages in an impressive range of industries. In large part, its outward-looking strategy has promoted healthy and specialized technological learning (Pack and Westphal, 1986), while its access to imported capital goods and technologies has enabled it to keep far more up to date than India.

The impact of exogenous shocks is similar to that of misguided macro-policies: low, uneven or negative growth and constrained foreign exchange. These prevent industries from growing, sometimes even from operating, and so curtail the learning base. Even existing capabilities are frittered away in "making do" with scarce resources and falling real earnings.

The worst possible combination of circumstances for technological learning is probably that of a country with a low initial stock of capabilities, an inadequate growth of the education system, inward-looking and interventionist industrial strategy and slow or no growth caused by unwise macro-policies and/or exogenous shocks. This, unfortunately, was the typical scenario for most sub-Saharan African countries. Many Governments exacerbated it by placing an inexperienced public sector at the spearhead of the industrial effort; far from solving problems of scarce industrial capability, this stretched existing resources thinner and attenuated the process of building up capabilities (see the following section).

There is no simple recipe for stimulating the development of industrial capabilities. Massive investment in education by itself is not enough. Neither is experience with industry. Outward-looking strategies *per se* will fail if the stock of capabilities is insufficient to respond to the competitive stimulus provided. Moreover, outward orientation does not mean free trade. The acquisition of the more difficult capabilities calls for infant industry protection (Westphal, 1982). As the experience of the Republic of Korea shows, a stiff dose of selective protection can coexist very happily with aggressive export activity. Too much protection, however, is counter-productive.

The complexity of determinants means that many developing countries fail to hit the right balance in their policies. Some capabilities cannot be directly created by policy in any case, and most are acquired slowly and falteringly. This unpredictable, and partly ungovernable, course of capability acquisition perhaps leads policy makers to neglect it, or take it for granted. We believe this is unwarranted. Policy matters will be taken up in the final section of this paper; we now consider the African industrialization experience.

Industrialization in sub-Saharan Africa

BACKGROUND

As a region, sub-Saharan Africa is among the least industrialized in the developing world. The contribution of manufacturing to GDP of sub-Saharan Africa as a whole was 7.3 per cent in 1984, compared to 15 per cent for low-income economies and 25 per cent for middle and upper middle economies (excluding oil exporters).[1] Since 1973, this share had declined for two groups (low-income countries, from 9.3 to 7.1 per cent, and middle-income oil importers, from 21.7 to 16.7 per cent), while it had risen for one group (middle-income oil exporters, from 2.8 to 5.6 per cent). It was thus the rise in oil revenues that sustained Africa's recent industrial effort. Other sources of revenue (from other primary commodities or foreign aid) failed to support sustained industrialization, while manufacturing itself generated insufficient resources to sustain growth, or even modest levels of capacity utilization.

Total manufacturing value-added (MVA) for sub-Saharan Africa amounted to $12.4 billion in 1983, just under that of the Philippines, 42 per cent of India's, 58 per cent of the Republic of Korea's or 18 per cent of Brazil's. One country, Nigeria, accounted for 28 per cent of the region's total, followed by Zimbabwe (11 per cent) and Côte d'Ivoire (7 per cent). Of the 39 countries in the region, only five had MVA per capita of over $100 in 1983, and only nine of over $50; at the other extreme, 10 had MVA per capita of below $10, which indicates a rudimentary level of industrialization. By comparison, Brazil and the Republic of Korea had MVA per capita of about $530, the Philippines of $235 and India, with its huge population, of $41.

There are, however, a few countries in sub-Saharan Africa that stand out. Zimbabwe is relatively highly industrialized, with a diverse manufacturing sector making a variety of consumer, intermediate and capital goods, many of which are sold abroad. Mauritius, a small island, has a dynamic industrial base developed to serve export markets for garments and knitwear; it is the only successful export-oriented manufacturer in sub-Saharan Africa. Côte d'Ivoire and Kenya have fairly diverse industries, some of which export consumer goods and some petrochemicals regionally. Gabon has a relatively large petroleum-based industry. Nigerian industry is large in absolute terms, and also fairly diverse, but is not well-developed in terms of its efficiency or operation.

STRUCTURAL CHARACTERISTICS

Apart from these exceptions, African industry reflects its early stage of development in several features. First, it is heavily biased towards traditional, low-technology activities such as food processing, tobacco and textiles. Intermediate goods are relatively underdeveloped, except for oil-based chemicals, while capital goods (and mechanical engineering activities more broadly) are significant by their virtual absence (Zimbabwe being the major exception). This means, secondly, that most African industry remains highly import-dependent, with local linkages remaining tenuous over the past three decades. Apart from the agricultural or mining resource-processing activities, manufacturing remains predominantly an enclave sector.

141

The dynamic "deepening" effects on the economy that developing countries look for from industry have been largely lacking. Not only have linkages stayed firmly with suppliers of imported capital goods, components and services, but also the high import dependence has raised costs of operation, imparted considerable inflexibility and led to significant under-utilization of capacity when foreign exchange resources have dwindled.

Thirdly, partly as a consequence of the above, African industry displays extreme dualism, with little sign that the traditional informal sector is establishing links with modern, formal industry. The informal sector is entirely African. The formal sector is predominantly non-African (either multinational or owned by local non-African communities); the only inroads made into this have been by public ownership. As yet, there is little emergence of private African entrepreneurship in modern industry. Fourthly, the small-scale and informal sectors are characterized by three features: modern, small-scale industry is tiny, much smaller than its counterpart in other developing regions; the informal sector is very active, but shows little evidence of the upgrading of size, technology, products etc. which would denote structural transformation towards industrial development; and the sector as a whole has not proved a training ground for the entrepreneurial and technical skills needed for modern industry. Schemes to promote African small-scale industry have had only modest success. However, the informal sector has survived economic vicissitudes much better than the modern sector, and is at this stage the "natural" comparative advantage of indigenous African industry.

Fifthly, many Governments have, as noted, promoted public enterprises as the main African thrust into industrial development. In attempting to create skills and capabilities by fiat, Governments have often set up extremely inefficient entities, which are now proving major drains on national resources.

Sixthly, the performance of sub-Saharan Africa in the field of manufactured exports has been much poorer than that of other developing regions. During the period 1972-1983, the share of sub-Saharan Africa in non-petroleum manufactured exports in total non-Organisation for Economic Co-operation and Development exports declined from 3.9 to 1.9 per cent. The region missed out on the boom in exports from the developing world of both labour-intensive products (textiles, garments, footwear, electronics) and non-traditional manufactures of all sorts. Its direct foreign exchange earnings were far below its foreign exchange needs. Unlike some other import-dependent countries, the countries in sub-Saharan Africa were unable to add value to their components efficiently enough to generate self-sustaining growth in manufacturing.

Finally, nearly all African industries faced extremely small domestic markets, only partly compensated by the larger regional market. This deprived many activities of necessary scale economies and further raised operating and capital costs. Regional co-operation has helped to some extent, but some agreements have collapsed (East Africa) and others have been vitiated by political problems, shortages of foreign exchange and the unco-ordinated nature of industrial expansion, with each country setting up similar facilities.

The result of all these features has been that the industrial structures that have been set up in sub-Saharan Africa have been weak, disjointed from their economies and fairly inefficient by world standards. Manufacturing has not been dynamic, in terms of either raising productivity or entering world markets; it has not deepened its structure or struck up local linkages; it has not generated beneficial externalities for the rest of the economy. Exogenous events reduced the physical expansion of industry or its capacity utilization, but they essentially overlay deeper structural deficiencies in efficiency and dynamism.

Many developing countries have encountered similar problems in the early stages of their industrialization. However, most of them have overcome them to some extent—it is the pervasiveness and degree of difficulties faced by African industry that makes it different from industry in other regions. But there are exceptions even within sub-Saharan Africa—Zimbabwe, Mauritius, Kenya and Côte d'Ivoire are obvious ones. Though they face various problems of their own, they are at a higher level of development, diversity or competence than the other countries and offer important lessons for the rest of the region.

Let us turn then to drawing out some of these lessons. What are the reasons for the generally poor state of African industry?

REASONS FOR POOR PERFORMANCE

A number of factors have interacted to produce the conditions we observe today in the region's industry. The explanations advanced, however, have tended to be partial and unsatisfactory. They can be grouped under two broad headings: those blaming exogenous shocks and those blaming misguided trade and industrial policies.

African Governments themselves appear to blame exogenous shocks as the main culprit for their poor industrial performance. They see the problem as one mainly of slowing or negative investment in industry and low capacity utilization—here declining foreign exchange availability has clearly played a major role. They tend, by the same token, to ignore or minimize other structural problems such as high costs, low productivity, lack of export success and low or stagnant local linkages.

Some foreign analysts, as typified by the World Bank, tend to focus on high costs and poor export performance, and trace their causes to inward-looking trade policies, overvalued exchange rates,

143

overblown public sectors, high wages, price controls and the like. Their view is that incentives for efficient resource allocation and operation have been distorted by government intervention. Thus, "getting prices right" would, within a short period, solve the structural problems: African industry would not only become trimmer and more efficient, it would also become export-oriented to the extent that it would emulate that of the Republic of Korea or Taiwan, Province of China.

As with the previous explanation, there is an element of truth in this reasoning. Highly protected, import-substituting policies have permitted plants to be set up which, for scale or technological reasons, were inherently unviable. They have permitted even potential export markets. African public enterprises have not been efficient, being given "deep pockets" to finance continuous losses (Nellis, 1986). High wages and cheap capital goods imports have fostered an excessively capital-intensive performance. This general line of argument is too well established in the literature (see World Bank, 1987) to merit repetition here.

What this approach does not satisfactorily deal with is the fact that several countries outside Africa have shown much greater industrial deepening, linkages and productivity, despite having adopted similar trade and industrial policies. China and India are obvious examples of inward-looking, public-sector-led, interventionist countries which have established impressive industrial bases. While these are not as dynamic or competitive as the newly industrializing countries in South-East Asia, there is little doubt that their industrial achievements are far more impressive than Africa's. Several medium-sized countries in Latin America, pursuing import-substitution policies, have also built up reasonable manufacturing sectors.

More interestingly, the industrial leaders within Africa itself show strikingly more competence in setting up and operating industry than other countries in the region, and this despite rather similar policies of imports substitution, public enterprise promotion, price controls, investment licensing and the like. Zimbabwe's capital goods industry was built up essentially during the period when it was economically isolated and forced to become inward-looking. Its iron and steel complex (ZISCO, the only integrated plant in sub-Saharan Africa that is efficient) has always been a public enterprise. Its private industrial investments have been tightly regulated, directed and price-controlled since 1965. Côte d'Ivoire raised the share of public enterprises in capital employed in manufacturing to 51 per cent. Its industry, while dominating the regional Francophone market, is inward-looking in the world context. Similarly, Kenya, the industrial leader in East Africa, has an inward-oriented manufacturing sector with various controls on prices, ownership and so on. Yet these countries have reasonable rates of capacity utilization; their facilities

144

seem better operated and more competitive than many other African countries; and local linkages are somewhat better established. In part, this is explained by better macro-economic management, especially of the export sector; in part, it is due to more developed industrial capabilities.

The missing element in the other analysis of African industry is, therefore, the consideration of industrial capabilities. It is this factor that is critical in explaining both why African industry in general lags behind that of other regions, and why some countries in sub-Saharan Africa have progressed well beyond others. Africa started with a tiny indigenous base of all types of industrial capabilities. Over time, although it added to them, the growth of physical investment far exceeded the growth of relevant human resources. Exogenous shocks and inward-looking, interventionist policies also detracted from the process of developing the capabilities base. But in the final analysis it was the constricted supply of capabilities that distinguished African industry from that of the other developing regions.

The African countries that could overcome, to a greater or lesser extent, the shortage of indigenous capabilities by drawing upon foreign ones were those that were relatively successful in industrial development. There are three main ways of tapping foreign capabilities: having a foreign settler population that moves into industry; having direct foreign investment in manufacturing; and using aid or export earnings to hire foreign consultants or individual experts. All African countries drew to some extent on one or more of these sources, but all were not equally capable of exploiting them. Zimbabwe and Kenya were fortunate in starting with large, entrepreneurial settler populations (Uganda and the United Republic of Tanzania had such resources but for political or ideological reasons emasculated them). Côte d'Ivoire could draw liberally on French expatriates and foreign investors. Other countries did start with some foreign investments, but then restricted them severely, or failed to attract continuing investments (because of macro-economic difficulties), or forced the pace of indigenization too rapidly. Yet others were too poor or remote, or ideologically hostile, to attract significant foreign capabilities in any form: these ended up with rudimentary industries, extremely inefficient and ultimately a drain on national resources.

The tapping of foreign industrial capabilities is a useful starting point and a supplement to the building of local human resources. In the long term, however, it cannot substitute for local capabilities. Several reasons may be advanced for this.

Non-African settler populations cannot now be expanded, nor, for socio-political reasons, can their role in the economy be enlarged. If anything, there is an unfortunate tendency to reduce their economic scope.

Foreign investors do not find much of the region attractive, partly because of remoteness and low incomes and partly because of the lack of local capabilities. Most countries, thus, cannot realistically hope to use foreign investors as the driving force in industrial development. Even those countries that can attract more foreign direct investment may not attract enough to base broad industrial development on it. In any case, the upgrading of foreign-owned industry into more complex, high-value-added activity requires a more advanced local skill base, better infrastructure and various supporting services—all necessities of local capabilities. Finally, foreign investments are truly beneficial when they strike extensive local linkages and employ nationals in top positions: again, local capabilities have to be developed enough to cope.

The use of expatriate experts is useful where there are no other solutions, but unless their skills are transferred to the local population, this is an unsatisfactory way to operate industry. Expatriates are expensive; they are not conducive to local linkages or externalities; they are by definition temporary. Unless they are consciously used as short-term "tutors" of local counterparts, they saddle operations with high cost and a longer-term inability to cope. Sub-Saharan Africa is replete with horror stories of wasted technical assistance and unsuccessful transfer of skills from expatriates.

In sum, while foreign capabilities have helped launch many of the better-operated industries that exist in sub-Saharan Africa, long-term industrial efficiency and diversification must rely on the development of local capabilities. These capabilities must draw liberally on foreign skills and knowledge, but they must possess an independent core of skills that enable industry to be properly set up, operated, expanded, improved and deepened, in line with resource endowments and market size.

Before coming to the policy implications of this analysis, it may be useful to illustrate some of the costs of industrializing without adequate capabilities. The evidence is necessarily anecdotal and patchy, but it helps to explain why African industry is where it is today.

SOME CONSEQUENCES OF INADEQUATE INDUSTRIAL CAPABILITIES

In an earlier section, the significance of various types of industrial capabilities to the industrialization process was noted. The absence of those capabilities does not mean that industries cannot be set up. Clearly, a Government with the necessary financial resources or foreign assistance can always buy a physical plant and have an industrial facility set up. Without the relevant skills and experience, however, there is a grave danger that the project chosen may be uneconomical, it may be "packaged" incorrectly or expensively, it may be poorly managed and organized, or it may suffer technical inadequacies which prevent it from ever achieving efficient operation.

As noted earlier, the indigenous entrepreneurial capabilities in sub-Saharan Africa had been concentrated in small-scale and informal activities. Even here, they had not extended to modern manufacturing, except to some extent in Ghana and Nigeria. In comparison to the capabilities displayed by non-African entrepreneurs in the same settings, it would appear that African capabilities were at an earlier stage of development. Government efforts to promote the pace of entrepreneurial learning had borne some fruit, but mainly outside the manufacturing sector. Within the manufacturing industry, three main lines of policy to encourage African entrepreneurship can be distinguished:

(a) Setting up of parastatals or public enterprises;

(b) Dilution of foreign equity to nationals;

(c) Promotion of modern small-scale industries.

The consequences of the inadequate skill base for industrial entrepreneurship meant that each of these initiatives ran into problems. Public enterprises have several problems in most regions of the world traceable to their lack of autonomy and loose market or financial discipline. In sub-Saharan Africa, their problems were exacerbated by poor project selection and organization, and the general lack of knowledge of the complexities of setting up and running modern industry. The only cases where public enterprises operated successfully were those in which sufficient skills had been transferred to an experienced managerial and work force. Similarly, the dilution of equity worked well when experienced managers and technicians were retained, or expatriates inducted. Small-scale industry promotion programmes suffered high failure rates. In Kenya, their success increased greatly when non-African partners were allowed.

Similarly, shortages of managerial capabilities appear to have had deleterious effects on operating efficiency in enterprises with no access to trained managers. By contrast, the two most industrialized countries in sub-Saharan Africa, Zimbabwe and Côte d'Ivoire, drew liberally on non-African managers. Thus, in 1984, 72 per cent of professional employees in Zimbabwean industry were of European origin and a further 4 per cent of Asian origin. In Côte d'Ivoire, 68 per cent of all managers (including directors) were foreign. Even small-scale enterprises in Côte d'Ivoire employed substantial numbers of expatriate managers and technicians.

The growth of African managerial capabilities has, however, progressed faster than entrepreneurships. Perhaps the skills of management are easier to learn through formal education, or the administrative skills that Africans have acquired translate more easily into business management. Whatever the reasons, there are

147

encouraging signs of capability development. There is a long way to go, however, before the amount of industry already established can be made to function efficiently with African managers.

The consequences of shortages of technological capabilities can be illustrated for each of the major categories. The paucity of investment capabilities has led to the commonly observed fact that project costs in Africa tend to be much higher than in other developing regions. This is only partly traceable to higher infrastructural costs: deficient skills bear a significant part of the blame. Thus, investment costs per ton of steel in Nigeria are three to four times higher than in, say, India. The poor choice of projects, wrong siting, the selection of wrong technologies, the inability to bargain with technology suppliers, and heavy reliance on expensive foreign engineers and consultants are all common features of the African industrial scene; all are traceable to this sort of deficiency.

The shortage of production engineering capabilities has even more serious consequences. In comparison with other developing regions, most African countries display low levels of mastery of technology in place, and a comparative inability to adapt processes and products to local conditions or changing environments. The exceptions that are observed in a few relatively advanced countries only support this generalization. The shortage of mechanical engineering capabilities is particularly significant: it results in the poor maintenance of equipment, the inability to "stretch" its applications or manufacture simple spares and components, and the underdevelopment of local subcontracting of simple machining and similar tasks. It leads to long down times (when equipment is idle), expensive repairs and an undue reliance on foreign experts for repairs, improvements, troubleshooting and so on. Even in relatively simple industries, the poor setting of machines, misalignment, inability to achieve rated speeds and other such consequences of inadequate production engineering skills lead to high costs, poor quality of output, wastage of materials or energy and general lack of competitiveness. In more complex industries, the costs to operational efficiency are much greater.

A comparison of the textile industry in Kenya, Zimbabwe, the United Republic of Tanzania and Somalia may be a good illustration of the effects of differing levels of technological capability (Pack, 1987; Mlawa, 1983; and various World Bank and UNIDO industry reports). Of these four countries, Somalia's public sector plant has the most modern technology in place in terms of the vintage of equipment (about 10 years old), capable of producing high-quality textiles of international standards. The United Republic of Tanzania, with three parastatal textile mills, has equipment some 15 years old. Kenya and Zimbabwe have older facilities, ranging from 20 to 30 years, all in private hands; Zimbabwe's facilities are somewhat more outdated than Kenya's.

If production engineering capabilities had been equally distributed, Somalia would have been the most efficient producer, followed by the United Republic of Tanzania, Kenya and Zimbabwe, in descending order. In fact, the actual order of efficiency and competitiveness is just the reverse. Zimbabwe gets the highest total factor productivity out of its facilities, and is able to export some textiles to Europe. Kenya is a little behind, and would be competitive with a slightly better performance. Both show clear signs of technological learning and increasing mastery of technology in place. By contrast, the United Republic of Tanzania and Somalia show little technological mastery. Productivity has declined over time, even after all exogenous constraints are taken into account. Output is of poor and uneven quality. Equipment is badly set up and maintained. Costs are high, and the mills are unprofitable even in protected markets. The Somali facility is practically bankrupt.

The differences in technological capabilities between these countries have arisen in broadly similar policy settings. The patterns of ownership and the impact of exogenous shocks have differed, but this by itself does not account for the vast differences in operating efficiency. The differences must therefore be accounted for by the initial stock of technological skills, the successful induction of new (foreign) skills and the development of capabilities locally. The Somali and Tanzanian mills are run with little or no experienced, qualified technical manpower (each mill has one textile engineer, with limited experience); training is minimal; quality control is practically absent; there is no supporting network of technical services or spare-parts manufacturing. Kenya has drawn heavily on the "Indian connection": the local Asian community has recruited experienced textile engineers from India to run its facilities and train locals. Zimbabwe has done the same with its "European connection", and for a longer period. Both now have a sufficient local technological base to manage most production engineering demands effectively.

Finally, the absence of linkage capabilities has drastically reduced the growth of industry in sub-Saharan Africa. As noted, dualism is still marked in most African industrial sectors, with a large "missing middle" between tiny informal and large-scale formal enterprises. Dependence on imports for a number of parts and services, which are elsewhere subcontracted, is still high. There are few linkages between manufacturing and universities. The consultancy sector is underdeveloped. There is relatively little transfer of knowledge between large manufacturing establishments, with wide disparity in their efficiency. Certainly, policies biased towards large-scale industry and the public sector have contributed to the shallowness of African industry. The lack of linkage capabilities has, however, played an important role.

To summarize, sub-Saharan Africa started with a tiny base of industrial capabilities. It added to this base over the past two or three decades, but not sufficiently to sustain the pace of industrialization undertaken. Exogenous shocks and unwise macro-policies slowed growth and deprived industry of the growth and foreign exchange needed to promote capability development. Trade and industrial policies biased the learning that did take place into channels that were not conducive to competitive efficiency. Many of the structural problems of African industry are traceable to these deficiencies. The countries that did better were precisely the ones that could induct and deploy "ready-made" industrial capabilities from non-African communities or investors.

The critical role of industrial capabilities was not realized, or was underplayed, by African Governments and by aid donors and international institutions. While it was widely acknowledged that Africa had a "skills gap", the precise nature of the "capabilities gap" and its possible effects on industrial development were not analysed. Even today, most remedies proposed inside Africa and outside it ignore this difficult and pervasive problem. Yet, it is increasingly obvious that policies that take industrial capabilities for granted have little chance of success when those capabilities do not exist.

Policy implications

Existing policy recommendations on African industry tend to embrace either the "physical investment" or the "get prices right" view of industrial development, discussed at the beginning of this paper. Both are based on partial truths. Both physical investment (including the rehabilitation of existing capital stock) and correct price signals will be necessary to resolve the long-term problems of African industry. However, by themselves they will be rapidly vitiated by the shortage of industrial capabilities: such capabilities will not be summoned forth by price signals or created by physical investment. Specific policy measures must be addressed to the process of "learning" itself. There are no magic solutions to the problem of capability acquisition—it is necessarily a slow process, drawing on many sources of knowledge and practical experience—but certainly correct policies can help it along and speed it up.

Correct policies must include broad measures which govern the trade and industrial setting in which learning takes place, and also specific policies aimed at capability development directly. Let me start with a general view of what a relatively healthy structure of African industry would look like.

The comparative advantage of most African countries lies in products that use relatively simple production technologies, enjoy natural protection because of transport costs and rely largely on domestic materials. Much of the existing industry in Africa does not conform to this pattern. Some countries, however, have gone beyond their potential for economic industrialization by setting up intrinsi-

150

cally unviable activities and building capacity that exceeds domestic market needs, export prospects and the ability to operate facilities efficiently. The structural needs and characteristics of most African countries suggest that the ideal industrial configuration should be along the following lines.

The small-scale and informal sectors should remain areas of strength and be encouraged to grow, upgrade productivity and enter export markets. Past policies to promote the small-scale sector have not been particularly successful, and should be reformulated to focus on upgrading industrial capabilities. Policy biases against small enterprises should be removed and incentives introduced to grow larger, attract people with modern skills (including non-Africans), establish linkages with large-scale industry, and export. Measures that protect small units from competition with large ones and discourage growth should be avoided. Market forces should determine which activities are viable, enabling small enterprises to exploit competitive advantages where there are economies of small-scale production. Metalworking and engineering are particularly promising areas for small-scale industry to build vital industrial skills and reduce dependence on imported spare parts, components and services.

In medium-term and large-scale industry, two kinds of inefficient capacity need to be eliminated to reduce the drain on national resources: unviable "white elephants" and activities that surpass the existing capability to operate competitively. Available industrial capabilities should be concentrated in subsectors where: (*a*) technical requirements are low and change slowly; (*b*) adequate technical and managerial skills exist and can be readily transmitted; (*c*) productivity can be raised rapidly with minimal infusion of capital and know-how; (*d*) local resource availability provides an advantage in exporting; (*e*) scale economies are fully exploited within the limits of the domestic market; (*f*) production for the domestic market can survive with only moderate protection; and (*g*) import dependence is low.

These considerations imply a trimmer industrial sector, specializing in resource-based activities and those where transport costs give local processing a comparative advantage. Obvious examples of such industries with low or moderate engineering and skill requirements would be agro-based industries, textiles, paper, wood, cement, simple metal products and, perhaps, some chemicals.

Exceptions to this ideal would include Nigeria, whose large, resource-endowed economy could take on many heavier industries (although the availability of industrial capabilities remains a pertinent constraint), and Zimbabwe, whose advanced capabilities could digest more skill-intensive, complex technologies. At the other extreme, some remote, resource-poor countries such as Chad and Burkina Faso are unlikely to establish viable industries, except for a few basic food-processing activities.

The macro-economic and trade policy reforms needed for

industrial producers and investors to make decisions on the basis of relatively undistorted prices are well known. The critical instruments are internationally realistic exchange and interest rates, non-inflationary monetary policies, removal of price controls and labour market rigidities, elimination of artificial restraints to internal investment and competition, and fair economic prices for agricultural commodities and infrastructural services. The adverse effects of wrong price signals and excessive controls in these areas on investment decisions, technology choice, skill acquisition and international competitiveness are well established.

Some reforms produce immediate effects: shifting to a market-determined system of foreign exchange allocation, for example, can enable efficient industries to raise capacity utilization and productivity quickly (if they can obtain the necessary finance). Some operate over the medium term: small-scale producers can expand as prices improve, uneconomic enterprises close and former export markets are regained. Other responses take much longer: raising technical efficiency, improving factor allocation, accelerating technological learning and establishing new export markets.

Small-scale producers should benefit relative to large-scale firms as policy reforms remove biases that favour the latter, for example, through import restrictions or low interest rates. But inadequate demand may constrain growth, especially under contractionary macro-economic policies. Since most small enterprises are located in rural areas where the expenditure elasticity of demand for their products is high, policies to promote broad-based agricultural development are important to stimulate the growth of the small-scale sector.

Since the success of policy reforms depends on efficient supply response from industry, different elements may have to be implemented at different rates to enable the desired response to take place. For instance, if the shift in resources between product lines and industries depends on industrial capabilities that must build up over time, then the pace at which potentially viable industries are exposed to international competition must also be gradual. A problem of balance may arise between providing the competitive spur by changing the incentive structure and ensuring that economic agents are able to respond appropriately.

Needless to say, macro-policies must also address infrastructural deficiencies. "White elephants" must be phased out if they remain inherently unviable; other industries must be brought to appropriate scales of production needed to realize economies of scale.

Let us come now to policies on industrial capability development. It has been argued above that capability learning draws on a variety of formal and informal sources, that is, the education system, learning on the job and learning by conscious search and experimentation. Given this diffused nature of learning, and the lack of

152

economic knowledge of the latter two components, our discussion must remain tentative and suggestive. What follows is intended only to highlight some of the main features of the "learning" process.

First, concerning formal education and training, a great deal of informal and small-scale manufacturing activity, which will continue to predominate in terms of industrial activity in sub-Saharan Africa, requires little formal education or technical training. However, as the industrial structure develops and relies more on modern technology, the need for such education and training in management, technology, marketing etc. increases. The need is both general—literacy, awareness of modern ideas and receptivity to change—and specific—particular types of technical skills, particular scientific disciplines, specific managerial skills and so on. General educational needs are relatively easy to anticipate; specific ones may not be.

This is not the place for a discussion of educational strategies in sub-Saharan Africa. The need for certain types of managerial and engineering skills (e.g., mechanical, metalworking, chemical) may be so broad that Governments may be justified in supporting their creation regardless of the projected pattern of industrial development. Some other skills may be specific to the resource base of the country (textile engineering for countries with cotton, or food technologies for those with a large agricultural base), and may safely be created as industry expands. Yet others may be based on emerging future needs (e.g., electronic or electrical engineering), but these should be accorded lower priority until their need becomes more obvious. However, there may be a general case for training technicians in larger numbers than anticipated for large-scale industry needs, in order to create a pool of manpower that can go into small-scale entrepreneurial activity, or meet unexpected bottlenecks.

Secondly, formal education and training should serve as a basis for internal training by industry, on the job, in special training facilities, by foreign technology or equipment suppliers or in some combination of these. On-the-job training requires experienced tutors and trainers. Many industrial skills are "tacit" in the sense that they cannot be conveyed through books or formal instruction, but are best imparted by "showing how" and hands-on experience. In sub-Saharan Africa, there is a strong case for inducting foreign technicians to act as tutors in established plants, but the induction should last for at least three to five years to ensure that their skills are fully transferred. To lower the cost of this strategy, African countries should consider drawing upon the pool of technical manpower in the newly industrializing countries. Firms should be provided with fiscal incentives to train labour intensively; they may be subject to special training levies or provided with subsidies. The Government should try to deal with the problem of securing adequate returns to private investments in training. This is probably a bigger problem in sub-

Saharan Africa than in most other developing regions because of the extreme scarcity of skills.

Special training facilities for the specific technological needs of each industry could be set up by the Government or, in larger and better organized industries, by the firms themselves. It is always desirable to have some industry participation in training facilities, to ensure that changing needs are adequately met and manufacturers themselves contribute tutors.

Thirdly, firms could be encouraged to engage in more technological activity themselves. A more competitive environment and a larger supply of trained manpower will facilitate this, but other measures can also be adopted. Salary and incentive structures should be geared to encouraging productivity-enhancing innovations and the promotion of technically capable personnel. They should be helped to acquire information on technological changes, sources of technology, equipment suppliers, consultancy organizations and so on. Technical personnel should be facilitated in making contacts with counterparts overseas in similar plants, equipment makers and export buyers. The larger and more sophisticated enterprises should be encouraged, by fiscal incentives, to set up research and development units. Production engineering functions should be carefully developed and subjected to close monitoring and evaluation: enterprises should be advised by technical assistance units on how to develop these functions and organizations.

Fourthly, Governments should attempt to utilize the existing science infrastructure (universities, research centres) for the production needs of industry. Laboratories should seek to work on a contract basis for manufacturing enterprises. The adaptation of imported technologies to the peculiar needs of the local environment should be a priority. The dangers of setting up "ivory tower" research institutes divorced from industry should be avoided, by involving industry in the financing and management of such institutes. These considerations will be relevant to only a few of the most advanced countries in sub-Saharan Africa, but it is important that they launch their efforts on the right path.

Fifthly, consultancy organizations of various types are an important repository of technical knowledge and vehicle for technology transfer. Governments should foster the growth of consultants, especially in the private sector. At this stage of sub-Saharan Africa's development, consultants should confine themselves to relatively easy technological activities (project supervision, trouble-shooting, layout, civil construction etc.) rather than advanced design and engineering. However, given the chance to work with foreign consultants, they should be able to improve their competence rapidly and extend their sphere of activity. Enterprises should be encouraged to seek technical consultancy help domestically, as far as possible.

Consultants themselves should be given the facility to employ expatriates.

Sixthly, special attention should be given to the improvement of standards and quality control. A national bureau of standards can help to improve manufacturing practices, and special training for quality control (together with provision of equipment) can raise the levels of industrial competence. Again, quality control centres sponsored by industry associations themselves can play a critical role; in the Republic of Korea, for instance, many industries were able to break into export markets on this basis.

Seventhly, the small-scale metalworking industry is one of the breeding grounds for general technological skills and deserves special promotion efforts. The reasons for this have been given earlier.

While the general provision of technical and managerial skills, promotion of quality control and consultants, and removal of biases against small-scale industry will help, an eighth policy should be concerned with specific measures to promote linkages between and within industries. Large manufacturers could be encouraged to strike up subcontracting relationships with small firms, by providing training in local procurement and technology transfer skills, and by giving temporary incentives for local purchases. Industry associations could help in the process by exhorting members to sponsor local suppliers, or encourage employees to set up as independent suppliers. Technical assistance could be provided to subcontractors to overcome specific problems.

The process of developing industrial capabilities is self-reinforcing, with different elements interacting to support each other. The general industrial environment affects its content and direction: a competitive, outward-looking régime is likely to call forth an appropriate set of technological responses. The rate and continuity of economic growth affects the speed of development: sustained rapid growth enables new technologies to be deployed and enables faster learning to occur. It also permits firms to take long-term risks and invest in the gradual build-up of local capabilities. An assured supply of foreign exchange, similarly, allows a more rapid and smooth acquisition of technologies from abroad. These broader economic considerations, while not part of an industrial restructuring programme as such, should be kept in mind when reviewing the feasibility of industrial development in sub-Saharan Africa.

To conclude, let us introduce a dose of realism. The disparity of national resources and human endowments within sub-Saharan Africa will continue to determine the pace of industrial development of different countries, whatever the policies adopted. The cumulative nature of learning dictates that the better-off countries will continue to industrialize more efficiently and rapidly than others. A few countries may be able to compress the "learning curve" by attracting or buying substantial foreign capabilities, both to fill gaps and to teach local personnel. Others may not be able to afford this, and will have to rely mainly on building up indigenous skills. Some countries will be able to draw on local non-African communities to a greater extent than others. Many countries have a tiny base of non-African skills, and will have to rely almost entirely on indigenous sources. The speed with which indigenous capabilities can be built up will also depend on the resources that can be devoted to relevant education and training. Formal education is only part of the process—the rest occurs in manufacturing enterprises themselves. Good management, learning from experience, acquiring new information abroad, and innovating by experimentation are all necessary ingredients of capability development. All take time.

While there can be no "quick fixes" to Africa's structural problems, the pursuit of correct strategies can at least ensure that industrial development in all countries is healthier than it has been in the past. If it is generally accepted that the process of restructuring and future development will be slow in most countries, then African Governments and others concerned with African development can adopt more realistic attitudes and expectations. African industrialization cannot be promoted only by pouring in resources for physical investment. It cannot be speeded up only by "getting prices right", nor indeed by concentrating only on building up human capital. Much of Africa will continue to industrialize slowly. A few countries may do better, but none is, for the time being, likely to achieve the kind of industrial development achieved by the newly industrializing countries of East Asia, whatever the policies pursued; the base of industrial capabilities is simply too constricted.

NOTE

[1] Figures for sub-Saharan Africa are calculated from the *Handbook of Industrial Statistics 1986* of the United Nations Industrial Development Organization and the World Bank's data bank. Other figures are from the *World Development Report, 1986* (Washington, D.C., World Bank), table 3; see S. Lall, assisted by G. Kayira (1987).

REFERENCES

Baumol, W. J. (1986). Entrepreneurship and the long-run productivity record. New York: New York University, C. V. Starr Center for Applied Economics, Research Report No. 86-OU.
Bell, M., B. Ross-Larson and L. E. Westphal (1987). Assessing the performance of infant industries. *Journal of Development Economics,* vol. 16, pp. 101-128.
Dahlman, C., B. Ross-Larson and L. E. Westphal (1987). Managing technological development: lessons from the newly industrializing countries. *World Development,* No. 15, pp. 759-775.
Fransman, M. (1986). *Technology and Economic Development.* Brighton: Wheatsheaf.

Lall, S. (1980). Vertical inter-firm linkages in LDCs: an empirical study. *Oxford Bulletin of Economics and Statistics,* vol. 42, pp. 203-226.

———— (1987). *Learning to Industrialize: The Acquisition of Technological Capabilities by India.* London: Macmillan.

———— , assisted by G. Kayira (1987). Long-term perspectives on sub-Saharan Africa: industry. Washington, D.C.: World Bank, Special Office for African Affairs.

McMahon, W. W. (1987). Education and industrialization. Washington, D.C.: World Bank, World Development Report background paper.

Mlawa, H. M. (1983). The acquisition of technology, technological capability and technical change: a study of the textile industry in Tanzania. Sussex: University of Sussex, Ph.D. dissertation.

Nellis, J. (1986). Public enterprise in sub-Saharan Africa. Washington, D.C.: World Bank, Discussion Paper No. 1.

Pack, H. (1987). *Productivity, Technology and Industrial Development.* New York: Oxford University Press.

Pack, H. and L. E. Westphal (1986). Industrial strategy and technical change: theory versus reality. *Journal of Development Economics,* vol. 18, pp. 87-129.

Teitel, S. (1984). Technology creation in semi-industrial economies. *Journal of Development Economics,* vol. 16, pp. 34-61.

Westphal, L. E. (1982). Fostering technological mastery by means of selective infant-industry protection. In *Trade, Stability and Equity in Latin America,* M. Syrquin and S. Teitel, eds. New York: Academic Press, pp. 255-279.

World Bank (1987). *World Development Report, 1987.* Washington, D.C.

7

INVESTING IN HUMAN RESOURCES: HEALTH, NUTRITION AND DEVELOPMENT FOR THE 1990s

Giovanni Andrea Cornia*

CONTENTS

Background and scope

After nearly three decades of substantial, if uneven, improvements, health and nutritional conditions deteriorated sharply in the 1980s in the majority of the developing countries of Africa and Latin America. These countries were affected by adverse climatic conditions, by the most severe economic decline since the Great Depression, and stringent, often uncaring, adjustment programmes. South and East Asian countries were, on the whole, able to maintain satisfactory rates of growth and to continue social progress. For some of them, such as India and Indonesia, where in the 1970s living conditions stagnated or improved only marginally, the 1980s have brought an acceleration in the rate of reduction of mortality and malnutrition.

Restrictive and inequitable fiscal policies have often contributed to the decline of health and nutritional standards. Reductions in tax revenue, typical of recessionary periods, and fiscal austerity, invariably part of any adjustment package, have seriously curtailed government resources for health and nutrition. A comprehensive analysis of the latest available evidence for 57 developing countries shows that real health expenditure per capita declined between 1979 and 1983/84 in 47 per cent of the African, 61 per cent of the Latin American, 43 per cent of the Middle Eastern and 33 per cent of the Asian countries (Pinstrup-Andersen and others, 1987). Although it

*Senior Programme Officer, United Nation's Children's Fund, International Child Development Centre, Florence, Italy.

was not possible to analyse the distribution of the cuts by level of expenditure, suggestive evidence indicates that primary health care might have suffered disproportionately. No global estimates of government expenditure on food subsidies and feeding programmes are available. However, over the 1980-1985 period, real government per capita expenditure on food subsidies declined, in most cases substantially, in 8 out of the 10 countries for which comparable data could be obtained (*ibid*).

The prospects for growth and social development remain highly uncertain for most developing countries. Even discounting the negative influence of highly unstable currency, financial and equity markets, recent forecasts indicate that by 1990 GDP per capita in Latin America will have barely recovered its 1980 level, while real resource use per capita will remain well below that level in view of the large debt servicing obligations faced by the region (ECLAC, 1986). Despite important and painful efforts at domestic policy reform, adverse trends in commodity prices, trade volume and capital flows are expected to severely restrict growth in Africa south of the Sahara. As an indication of the tragedy faced by this continent, GDP per capita in 1990 and 1995 is projected, even under a high-growth scenario, to be lower for low-income African countries than in 1973 and 1980 (World Bank, 1986a). Although still positive for the aggregate, current and future growth prospects have recently deteriorated in a number of Asian countries dependent on commodity exports and/or affected by growing debt servicing obligations (such as in Burma, Indonesia, Malaysia and Sri Lanka), or by natural disasters (such as in Bangladesh and India).

Admittedly, the situation does not favour an optimistic assessment of the prospects for future improvements in the health and nutritional status of the poor, and of the positive contribution to overall development that social programmes could make over the next decade. Yet, this paper contains the following arguments:

(*a*) Developments that have occurred over the past 10-15 years in the areas of social mobilization and community participation, technological breakthrough, mass communication and information, and targeting of interventions on the poor have led to the formulation and adoption on a limited scale of new project/policy approaches holding the potential for rapid and widespread improvements in health and nutrition even in the context of an adverse economic environment;

(*b*) Most of these new approaches have shown positive impact and have probably moderated the human cost of the economic decline of the 1980s;

(*c*) These new health and nutrition approaches are cost-effective and, hence, replicable at the national level over the next 10-15 years. With the exception of low-income countries, for which additional community and government resources, and international

160

aid, will have to be mobilized, existing resources should be sufficient to finance the expansion of low-cost basic services. To achieve this, a significant restructuring of existing government and aid budgets is required;

(*d*)   There is evidence of the positive impact of low-cost health, water supply and nutrition interventions on economic performance and relative income distribution. These programmes—with rates of return often larger than those for infrastructural and other investments—show their impact both in the short run, in the form of increased labour productivity, reduced work loss and substantial resource savings, and in the long run, in the form of improvement in the quality of the labour force, further resource savings and reduced population growth;

(*e*)   Despite class interests and bureaucratic inertia, on the whole, the political economy of the new approach seems to rest on relatively solid ground. There are indications that a few Governments are expanding the delivery of a few basic services on a national scale;

(*f*)   The international community, and the United Nations system in particular, can play an important role to support progress in this area.

Trends in health and nutritional status

Over the past 30-35 years, health and nutritional status have improved rapidly and substantially in most developing countries. However, two distinct phases can be identified. The first, from the early 1950s to 1980, is characterized by a broad decrease in rates of mortality and malnutrition. During the second phase, from 1980 to the present, such rates declined less rapidly or even increased in a large number of countries of Africa and Latin America, but declined at historical rates, or faster, in several Asian countries.

THE 1950-1980 PERIOD

Table 1 illustrates changes in health status on the basis of the infant mortality rate (IMR) data estimated by the Population Division of the United Nations Secretariat. While not well suited to describe short- to medium-term fluctuations in IMR, these data are generally considered to provide an accurate picture of long-term trends. IMR declined at a record, or near-record, pace throughout the 1950s, 1960s and 1970s. The improvement was particularly rapid in a few Asian and Caribbean countries such as China, Jamaica, Malaysia and Sri Lanka where several of the low-cost programmes described in the following pages were implemented on a national scale. In these countries the rate of progress was unprecedented by

TABLE 1. INFANT MORTALITY RATE BY SELECTED YEARS[a]
AND REGIONS

	1950-1955	1955-1960	1960-1965	1965-1970	1970-1975	1975-1980	1980-1985
Africa	191	180	169	158	142	124	112
Latin America	125	112	100	91	80	70	62
South Asia	180	163	148	135	125	115	103
East Asia[b]	182	167	112	76	57	39	36
Arab countries	181	164	146	125	107	88	78
Developing countries ..	180	165	137	117	104	96	88

Source: United Nations (1986).
[a]Averages over the five-year period considered.
[b]Includes China, Democratic People's Republic of Korea, Hong Kong, Japan, Mongolia and Republic of Korea.

any standard, often three or more times as large as that achieved in western Europe at a comparable stage of mortality transition.

However, three qualifications are in order. First, the regional averages presented in table 1 conceal a wide variety of experiences, some very successful, others not at all. In China, for instance, IMR declined between 1950-1955 and 1975-1980 at an average rate of about six points a year. In Bangladesh the rate of decline was only 1.7 points. Secondly, these gains are modest if seen in relation to the improvements that could have been possible on the basis of existing knowledge of primary health care and basic nutrition and of available resources. In a few extreme cases, health conditions stagnated altogether, for instance in rural India where IMR remained at about 136 over the entire 1970-1978 period. Thirdly, the rate of improvement in IMR started faltering in the 1970s. On a yearly basis, IMR declined by an average of four and five points in the 1960s. In the 1970s the decline was two to three points a year. This slow-down occurred much earlier than predicted and at a time when the prevailing levels of mortality in most developing countries were still high.

Changes in nutritional status are, on average, far more difficult to document because information is incomplete and definitions problematic. Large anthropometric surveys are not available in any significant number prior to 1975, while clinic-based data collected for nutritional surveillance purposes are even more rare. For those years, the extent of undernutrition is thus estimated indirectly on the basis of trends in food production and availability, dietary energy supply (DES) and level and distribution of household incomes and food consumption. The World Health Organization (WHO, 1987b) has compiled and standardized results from more than 50 national surveys on child nutritional status carried out since 1975. These anthropometric data, and those produced by the Food and Agriculture Organization of the United Nations (World Food Surveys), the United Nations Children's Fund and other institutions have been compiled in the *First Report on the World Nutrition Situation* (United

Nations, Administrative Committee on Co-ordination (ACC) Sub-Committee on Nutrition, 1987).

According to this review, the global prevalence of low weight for age in pre-school children declined from about 33 per cent in 1975/76 to 26 per cent in 1981/82. Although from widely different levels, such decline seems to have been shared by all regions, the actual number of underweight children increased in South Asia, Africa south of the Sahara and South-East Asia, because the rate of decline in the prevalence of malnutrition has been slower than the rate of growth in the child population. The number of underweight children remained broadly constant in South and Central America.

TABLE 2. MALNUTRITION BY SELECTED YEARS AND REGIONS

	Prevalence of malnutrition (%) among people			Number of malnourished people (mn)		
	1969-1971	1979-1981	1983-1985	1969-1971	1979-1981	1983-1985
Sub-Saharan Africa	24	22	26	60	80	100
South Asia	21	18	17	155	170	170
South-East Asia	18	10	8	40	25	25
Central America	17	12	11	12	12	12
South America	11	9	9	24	24	30
Near East/North Africa	15	6	5	20	9	7
China	..	..	..	..	..	..
Developing countries (excl. China)	..	..	..	311	320	344

Source: United Nations, ACC Sub-Committee on Nutrition (1987).

Indirect and more hypothetical estimates of the total number of malnourished people broadly confirm the view of a universal decline in the prevalence of undernutrition over the 1970s, with a net, if modest, increase in the number of malnourished people because of population growth (table 2).

THE 1980s

Health and nutritional trends have changed dramatically in the 1980s. Empirical data on infant mortality for the 1980s are available for only a few developing countries and years. The 1980-1985 estimates included in table 1 were calculated in 1984 by extrapolating past trends. They could not therefore take into account the effects of the 1984-1985 drought, the AIDS epidemics and the severe economic dislocations of the 1980s. For these reasons, the further decline in IMR shown between 1975-1980 and 1980-1985 for all regions by table 1, including Africa, does not appear realistic and needs to be reassessed in the light of the empirical evidence that has become available in the meantime.

Empirical data from national sources support the view of declining IMR for several countries in Asia such as India, Indonesia, the Republic of Korea and Thailand. In India, for instance, sample registration data show that IMR dropped from 124 in 1980 to about

163

104 in 1984, a larger decline than that recorded throughout all of the 1970s. In contrast, the empirical information from Latin America seems to point to a pronounced slow-down or, in some cases, to significant increases in IMR during the 1980s. Indeed, IMR increased in Brazil (where about 32,000 more infants younger than one year of age died in 1984 as compared to 1982), Guatemala, Guyana and Uruguay, while stagnating in Costa Rica, Panama and others (United Nations, 1985; Cornia and others, 1987). These were all countries which in the 1980s faced considerable economic problems and were generally slow to introduce low-cost measures to protect the poor. Empirical evidence on IMR for the 1980s is totally missing for Africa. Hospital records from Zambia, a country that suffered severe economic dislocations during most of the 1980s, point to a sharp increase in infant and child mortality. Generally speaking, it is plausible that IMR rates may have increased or stopped declining in a considerable number of African countries. The implication is that a substantially larger number of infants and children died in Africa in 1985 than in 1980.

The available evidence on nutritional status points to continued improvement over the 1980s in many parts of Asia, with the possible exceptions of the Philippines, Sri Lanka and a few others. In Thailand, for instance, the incidence of first-, second- and third-degree malnutrition declined from, respectively, 28.5, 5.9 and 0.8 per cent in the final quarter of 1983 to 21.0, 2.6 and 0.1 per cent in the final quarter of 1986. The reasons for such improvements are discussed in greater detail in the following sections. By contrast, in Latin America no further improvement was realized, possibly owing to the severe drop in real wages and food consumption, especially among the poor. Empirical evidence of increasing prevalence of malnutrition among children (measured by means of anthropometric indicators) is available for Barbados, Bolivia, Brazil, the Dominican Republic, Guyana, Jamaica, Mexico, Peru and Uruguay (Cornia and others, 1987). While the duration and extent of such deteriorations vary substantially from country to country, this general trend indicates that progress in the nutritional status of Latin American children probably ceased in the 1980s.

In Africa, the long-term decline in food production per capita was exacerbated in the 1980s by a sharp drop in household income and by drought. Despite recourse to food aid and imports, there was a substantial fall in average dietary energy supply, from about 2,150 Kcals in 1979-1981 to 2,050 Kcals in 1983-1985. Prevalence of under-nutrition rose from 22 to 26 per cent of the total population over the same period, while for children under five the increase was from 23 to 25 per cent (United Nations, ACC Sub-Committee on Nutrition, 1987). Empirical evidence of increases in child malnutrition during the 1980s is available for African countries as different as Botswana, Burundi, Cameroon, Ghana, Guinea-Bissau, Kenya, Leso-

164

tho, Madagascar, Rwanda, United Republic of Tanzania and Zaire (Cornia and others, 1987).

In conclusion, the 1980s witnessed a marked polarization of health and nutritional trends in the third world. Malnutrition and/or mortality have increased in most countries of Africa and Latin America. In contrast, progress has continued, or even accelerated, in the majority of the South and East Asian countries. A good overall economic performance is at the base of this success, which can be explained largely in terms of the greater insularity and low level of indebtedness of the large Asian economies and of the ability of the fast growing exporters of manufactured products of East Asia to take advantage of any expansion in world trade. However, sectoral policies emphasizing the need for accelerating agricultural production in formerly food-importing countries and for expanding cost-effective, wide-coverage, programmes in health, nutrition and water supply have been important contributory factors. The next section examines in some detail the nature of such programmes.

New approaches in health, water supply and nutrition

MAIN HEALTH AND NUTRITIONAL PROBLEMS

At the risk of considerable simplification, the main health hazards faced today in developing countries, particularly in countries with medium and high mortality, can be schematically classified as follows:

(a) *Birth-related problems,* such as tetanus neonatorum, trauma and asphyxia;

(b) *Digestive tract infections,* such as diarrhoea, gastroenteritis and cholera;

(c) *Infectious diseases,* type A (vaccine-preventable) including measles, meningitis, whooping cough, diphtheria, TBC and poliomyelitis;

(d) *Infectious diseases,* type B (non-vaccine-preventable) including hepatitis;

(e) *Infections of the respiratory tract* such as pneumonia, pharyngitis and otitis;

(f) Insect-borne diseases, i.e., malaria, onchocerciasis, trypanosomiasis and yellow fever;

(g) Intestinal parasites, such as hookworms and others.

The relative extent of these diseases varies enormously from place to place. Tetanus neonatorum, diarrhoea, measles, malaria and acute respiratory infections (with malnutrition often as an associated cause), however, account for about 90 per cent of the 14 million deaths of children under five in the developing world (UNICEF,

1987a). Diarrhoea, common in all developing regions, is the single most important cause of infant and child mortality.

As far as nutrition is concerned, the main problems are:

(*a*) Protein-energy malnutrition—particularly chronic under-nutrition—which currently affects an estimated 400 million people (World Bank, 1986b). It successively leads to reduced activity, weight loss, stunted growth and, during acute episodes, starvation. In addition, WHO (1980) estimated that every year there are approximately 120 million low birth weights (about 17 per cent of total births world-wide);

(*b*) Iron-deficiency anaemia, found in about half the women and one third of the population of many developing countries. It leads to sluggishness, reduced work and cognitive performance and diminished resistance to infection;

(*c*) Iodine-deficiency disorders, which in the form of goitre and cretinism manifest themselves in approximately 190 million people, particularly in the Andes and the Himalayas. It is now recognized that iodine deficiency provokes reduced growth and reduced intellectual and neurological capacity in a larger section of these communities. Some 800 million people world-wide are believed to be at risk;

(*d*) Vitamin A deficiency, resulting in xerophthalmia (or night blindness) and in total blindness. It is the largest single cause of blindness among children and altogether affects an estimated 40 million people world-wide. Because of it, about 250,000 children become blind or partially blind every year. It is most often seen in children with severe protein-calorie malnutrition and measles.

HIGHLIGHTS OF THE NEW APPROACHES

For the first time in human history, economically and socially viable solutions to most of the problems identified above (including, to some extent, protein-energy malnutrition) are now available to all developing countries, including the poorest among them. Such solutions are listed below.

Health interventions

The main activities include:

(*a*) A simple pregnancy management programme consisting of periodic check-ups for pregnant women, supplementary feeding for malnourished mothers, vaccination against tetanus and training of traditional birth attendants;

(*b*) Oral rehydration therapy (ORT), which is the most appropriate treatment for most digestive tract infections, while improvement in water supply and sanitation and health education are the best forms of prevention. ORT consists of the administration of a simple mix of salt, sugar and boiled water, and can stop the dehydration which kills an estimated five million young children a year;

(*c*) Immunization, providing full protection to children against the six communicable diseases, measles, meningitis, whooping cough, diphtheria, TBC and poliomyelitis, and against tetanus neonatorum;

(*d*) An essential drug programme, covering about 15-20 basic products (WHO, 1983), provides efficient treatment (at the level of primary health care) to many health problems, including infectious diseases, respiratory diseases and insect-borne diseases. The bulk purchase of generic drugs, reliance on the communities for their transport and the use of village health posts for their distribution are important elements of the programme.

These and other key health activities are part of the broader approach to primary health care (PHC) adopted in 1978 (WHO, 1978) and gradually endorsed by a majority of the developing countries that have accepted the objective of Health for All by the Year 2000. Such an approach aims at providing basic care to all citizens through a three-tier health system manned at the first level by village health volunteers and paraprofessionals. It places strong emphasis on community involvement, preventive action, the broadening of health interventions so as to include basic education, proper nutrition, safe water and sanitation. For some of the PHC components, specific targets, such as universal child immunization by the year 1990 and universal awareness of oral rehydration therapy, have also been established by WHO.

Water supply programmes

Economically, socially and culturally appropriate technical solutions include handpumps, rainwater collectors and gravity-fed systems with public standposts. Handpumps in particular are well-suited for improving the quality and quantity of water supply in rural and peri-urban areas as they can provide between 20 and 40 litres of pure water per day to about 250 people. They are of simple design and can be manufactured in developing countries. The Indian Mark II model is currently being produced in thousands of units in a few developing countries and is also relatively easy to install, operate and maintain.

The efforts at increasing coverage of safe water (and sanitation) throughout the developing world are integrated in the common framework of the International Drinking Water Supply and Sanitation Decade 1981-1990, which spells out targets, technical and social approaches and estimates of the financial requirements. As of 1986, 76 developing countries had committed themselves to the Decade and set full or partial targets.

The reduction of malnutrition is possibly the most complex and thorny issue in development. Basically, people are hungry because they lack the resources such as land, water and inputs to grow enough food for themselves or they lack the purchasing power to acquire food in the market. Therefore, the basic long-term solution to this problem involves fundamental changes in the area of assets ownership, agricultural extension, employment and income distribution. These changes, often difficult to bring about and requiring time to materialize, can be complemented by nutrition interventions aimed at mitigating the worst symptoms of malnutrition or at dealing with specific nutritional problems such as those due to micro-nutrient deficiencies.

The most frequent interventions adopted to tackle the problem of protein-energy malnutrition are food subsidies and direct feeding (including the promotion of breast-feeding). Other approaches (not dealt with here) include nutrition education, home gardens and improved food commercialization. Consumer food subsidies or food coupon programmes aim at transferring a certain amount of income or consumption (normally 20-30 per cent of the daily requirement) to population groups (such as the very young, the very old, pregnant women, the disabled) that cannot be integrated into employment-based, poverty-alleviation programmes or that are simply very poor. Supplementary feeding (either on-site or at home) provides nutritional supplements (normally for a limited amount of time) to malnourished children and to pregnant and lactating women. Beneficiaries are often identified through an assessment of health status or of weight for age. Monitoring the growth of small children by means of growth charts is in most cases an effective way of detecting the early, otherwise invisible, stages of malnutrition. Most supplementary feeding schemes are administered through health centres or the school system.

Most micro-nutrient deficiencies can now be dealt with through food fortification or supplementation. A breakthrough in food technology by Indian and Guatemalan scientists has made it possible to fortify a country's salt supply with iron. Similarly, salt can be fortified with iodine to control endemic goitre and reduce cretinism and deafness. If salt is not centrally processed or deficiencies are severe, an alternative is an intramuscular injection of iodized oil with protection lasting three to five years. Vitamin A capsules or fortified sugar can substantially reduce the incidence of nutritional blindness and the severity of measles. In Bangladesh, for instance, wide distribution of capsules has prevented an estimated 2,500 cases of blindness each year.

A global policy framework integrating these and other interventions, setting overall nutritional objectives and mobilizing resources for this purpose has not yet been established. The United Nations ACC Sub-Committee on Nutrition, however, has discussed the goal of reducing the prevalence of severe malnutrition to below 0.8 per cent, while the International Council for the Control of Iodine Deficiency Disorders has recently been formed with the objective of mobilizing world opinion on the control of these disorders.

IMPACT ON HEALTH AND NUTRITION

In 1974, the World Health Organization established the Expanded Programme of Immunization (EPI). Steady, but slow, progress was realized until the early 1980s when efforts intensified substantially. Between 1981 and 1985 rates of coverage increased by almost 15 per cent for the developing countries as a whole, and almost doubled in the case of measles. The results have been noticeable. The reported incidence of measles, poliomyelitis and tetanus (per 100,000 population), which had almost levelled off during the 1970s, declined dramatically between 1982 and 1985, that is, by about 60 per cent for measles and poliomyelitis and by over 30 per cent for tetanus (UNICEF, 1987c). However, the number of reported cases of poliomyelitis increased by 11 per cent between 1985 and 1986 in Latin America (*ibid*).

The 1983 WHO Interim Progress Report on the Programme for the Control of Diarrhoeal Disease showed that in eight surveyed hospitals in selected developing countries the admission of diarrhoea patients dropped 56 per cent after the introduction of oral rehydration therapy, while the overall hospital case-fatality rate dropped 48 per cent.

An example of success at the micro level of the new overall health approach is offered by the Cheraga district of Algeria, with a population of 150,000. At the beginning of the project, in 1976, IMR was 103. Simple measures such as breast-feeding, immunization, vitamin D supplements, growth monitoring and education about home-based oral rehydration therapy have reduced IMR to 43 over a five-year period, a staggering improvement by any standard. The project, moving away from the centralized hospital tradition, established a network of 18 local health centres close to the homes of the population (UNICEF, 1985).

Gwatkin and others (1980) have evaluated the overall effect of integrated health and nutritional interventions in 10 projects for which accurate data on infant and child mortality, nutritional status and costs could be assembled. While cautioning against overly simplistic conclusions, the authors note that ". . . mortality declines were notably more rapid in a clear majority of the ten project sites than they would have been in the projects' absence" (pp. 11-12). Indeed, in seven out of nine cases for which comparison was possible, infant and child mortality fell rapidly (on average between 30 and 50 per cent over five to seven years) and at a substantially faster pace than in control areas. Five of the six projects that sought to stimulate physical growth and that collected anthropometric data also appear to have achieved somewhat more rapid weight gains than in control areas.

The health and nutrition impact of water (and sanitation) programmes can be assessed in terms of the incidence of diarrhoeal diseases. A 1985 review of 67 studies from 28 countries (Esrey and others, 1985) indicates that, although the extent of the improvements varied substantially from project to project, improved water supply had indeed a significant impact in reducing diarrhoea morbidity rates (besides proving effective in controlling cholera, typhoid, amoebiasis and other parasitic infestations). Improvement in water quality and availability, in particular, reduced the incidence of diarrhoea by nearly 40 per cent (table 3).

TABLE 3. PERCENTAGE REDUCTIONS IN DIARRHOEAL MORBIDITY RATES ATTRIBUTED TO WATER SUPPLY IMPROVEMENTS

Type of intervention	Number results	Percentage reduction	
		Median	Range
Improvements in water quality	9	16	0-90
Improvements in water availability	17	25	0-100
Improvements in water quality and availability	8	37	0-82

Source: Esrey and others (1985).

A recent review of World Bank-assisted nutritional programmes comes, on the whole, to positive conclusions, namely, that substantial progress can be made even during periods of economic decline (Berg, 1987). The review describes the significant nutritional impact of one food subsidy programme in Colombia and of the Tamil Nadu Integrated Nutritional Project. The project, which started in 1980, concentrated exclusively on children from 6 to 36 months old and on expectant and nursing mothers. It employed growth charts to identify children who were nutritionally at risk (about 25 per cent at any point in time) and administered to them and to mothers at risk short-term (three months) supplementary feeding. All mothers were involved in the process through a comprehensive communication programme. The effects of the programme appear to have been dramatic. According to monitoring data for 9,000 villages, even in a year of drought and economic difficulties, serious and severe cases of malnutrition dropped from a baseline of 19 per cent to 12 per cent, while they rose from 16 per cent to 30 per cent in control areas. The latest data (1987) confirm that in the project area there was a 58 per cent decline in serious and severe malnutrition.

170

Health Programmes

One of the common characteristics of the health interventions illustrated previously is the use of low-cost inputs. The cost of supplying vaccine doses against measles, diphtheria, pertussis, polio, BCG and tetanus is estimated at about $1.20 per child even when allowance is made for transport cost and 50 per cent wastage (Parker, 1985). The per capita cost, including transport, of 15 essential drugs needed at the village health post level amounts to 50-60 cents a year (*ibid.*). Finally, a sachet of oral rehydration salt is commercialized in most developing countries at 15-20 cents (it can be procured by UNICEF at 8-10 cents). Even assuming four episodes of diarrhoea per child per year, the expenditure involved is at most the equivalent of 60-80 cents, and probably less, particularly if the solution is prepared at home by the mother.

The cost of these health interventions is substantially higher when including expenditures on personnel, supervision, capital formation and others. Even then, however, unit costs remain relatively low. Costs per capita vary substantially from country to country and, in particular, with the scale of the service delivered and with the cost concept adopted. An analysis of immunization programmes suggests total yearly costs for a fully immunized child in the $1.70 to $16 range, with a median of about $5 (Creese, 1986). On a per capita, rather than per child, basis these costs are, of course, much lower, possibly a sixth of that. A study of seven primary health care projects offering a variety of maternal and child health services found that annual operating costs per capita were in the ranges $0.60-$2.70 for large-scale programmes and $6 to $15 for small demonstration projects (Grosse and Plessas, 1984). Monetary costs per capita of less than one dollar a year were found for the PHC programme in Kasongo, Zaire (Kasongo Project Team, 1984). An analysis of a very comprehensive programme in Indonesia, covering about 9 million children and including growth monitoring, supplementary feeding for energy and micro-nutrients, immunization, oral rehydration, training of traditional birth attendants and family planning, estimated a yearly average cost per child (0-5) effectively protected by all these interventions of $11 to $12 (Cornia, 1984). On a per capita basis the cost was $2.

Water programmes

Table 4 illustrates the installation and recurrent cost of low-cost water supply projects. For small diameter wells total cost per capita per year ranges from under $0.50-1.50 (in Asia) to over $5 in many parts of Africa where the water table is located at up to 100-120

TABLE 4. COST PER CAPITA OF SELECTED WATER SUPPLY INTERVENTIONS
(US dollars in 1987 values)

Type of system	Description	Country or region	No. of Users	Capital cost per unit		Operation and Maintenance	Total cost
				Total	Annualized per capita[a]	Annual per capita	
Small-diameter wells (drilled or sludged)							
Shallow ground water	Suction handpump (cast iron)	Bangladesh	50	150	0.20	0.04	0.24
Intermediate	Low-lift (Tara pump) (plastic)	Bangladesh	50	250	0.30	0.04	0.34
Deep ground water	High lift (steel) (e.g., Mark II or Afridev pumps)	India	250	2 450	1.20	0.20	1.40
		Uganda	250	3 300	1.65	n.d.	..
		Burkina Faso	250	11 600	6.80	n.d.	..
Large-diameter well (excavated)							
With handpumps	Cast iron pump	Thailand	250	540	0.70	0.95	1.65
	Steel pump	Malawi	250	720	0.70	0.20	0.90
No handpumps	Platform and protected margin	Sahel	1 000	15 000	1.00	n.a.	1.00
Rainwater catchment							
Tanks (low rainfall)	Ferro-cement, 10 cu m	Indonesia	10	approx. 310	approx. 3.50	n.d.	..
Jars (high rainfall)	Ferro-cement, 2 cu m	Thailand	10	approx. 150	approx. 1.75	n.d.	..
Piped water with standposts (public taps)							
Protected springs with gravity feed	Estimate	Guatemala	100	850	4.95[b]		4.95
Power pumps	Estimate	Nepal	500	10 000	3.10	1.90	5.00
		Yemen	50	23 000	6.75	3.75	10.50

[a]The value of capital inputs amortized over the working life of the installation, adjusted for interest rate and other factors.
[b]Including operation and maintenance.
n.d. = no data; n.a. = not applicable.

metres of depth. Large-diameter wells have total costs of $1-2 per capita per year. Rainwater catchment and piped water with stand-posts—the latter to be found mostly in urban areas—are more expensive, with total costs in the range of $2-5, although they represent a very appropriate technology in many areas.

Potable water can thus be made available in most parts of Asia at a total (annualized capital plus recurrent) cost of $1-2 per capita per year and, where circumstances are favourable, as in river deltas, for instance, at well below that cost. Costs increase to the $2-5 range in other parts of the developing world with less favourable conditions. As a point of comparison, annualized per capita costs of conventional urban water supply typically run up to approximately $ US 100 per year in western European countries, with operation and maintenance per capita costs of about $60 (UNICEF, 1987b).

Nutrition interventions

Table 5 provides a tentative assessment of the per capita total costs of selected interventions in food subsidy, child nutrition and of other nutritional programmes combining nutritional surveillance, nutritional supplementation and some health care services. The figures in table 5 indicate that such programmes can be extended at relatively modest costs, that is at $4 to $5 per capita of population in the case of food subsidies and $1 to $2 for child feeding and nutritional surveillance. These costs are generally a fraction of those incurred for similar services in hospital settings or for untargeted food subsidies.

TABLE 5. COST PER CAPITA OF FOOD SUBSIDY AND FEEDING PROGRAMMES

Project	Type of intervention	Population served (thousands)	Cost per capita ($US)	Cost per capita as a per cent of income per capita
Colombia	Food subsidy	960	4.4	0.3
India Tamil Nadu ...	Comprehensive nutrition and health services for children)	8 250	1.0	0.4
Indonesia, NIPP	Weighing and feeding prog. (for children)	194	1.0	0.2
Imesi, Nigeria	Nutritional surveillance	6	1.5	2
Narangwal, India	Nutrition supplements and medical services	10.5	0.8-2.0	1-2
Jamkhed, India	Nutrition supplements and education medical services	40	1.25-1.50	1-1.25

Source: Gwatkin and others (1980) and Berg (1987).

In all these cases, targeting on the needy (one tenth to one third of the total population) contributed to the cost-effectiveness of the programmes. The last three projects presented in table 5 are somewhat more expensive in relative terms, partly because of their limited scale of delivery. These expenditures—for targeted subsidies, feeding and nutritional surveillance cum health care—compare quite favourably with those of more conventional interventions such as generalized food subsidies.

Finally, the cost of combating three serious micro-nutrient deficiencies is very low. Vitamin A capsules cost $ 0.10 per person per year, iodizing salt costs $0.05 and providing iron via fortification of salt or centrally processed grains costs between $0.05 and $0.09 (Berg, 1987).

FINANCING LOW-COST BASIC SERVICES

In the previous section it was shown that comprehensive and high-impact PHC services can be provided at a cost of $2 to $5 per capita per year, while equally critical water and nutrition interventions would require another $2 to $5. An overall expenditure on these programmes of $4 to $10 per person per year would therefore allow for substantial gains against the double scourge of high mortality and hunger.

Are these costs excessive for the financial resources of developing countries? In 1981/82, total (i.e., government and private) per capita expenditure on health care averaged $9 in low-income countries, $31 in middle-income and $670 in developed countries (World Bank, 1987). Public expenditure per capita taken alone ranged between $0.80 and $16 in 29 low-income countries, with about half of them spending $3 or less, while for 39 lower middle-income countries it ranged between $4 and $67, with about half of them spending $12 or less (Jespersen, 1987).

The implications are clear. Even if the recession and adjustment effort have cut government expenditure on health, water and food subsidies, existing private and public resources would be able to support an expansion of the above programmes in the majority of developing countries. The exceptions would be those low-income countries still facing a severe resource constraint. But in the majority of middle-income countries, basic services in health, water and nutrition could be financed largely out of the present government and private expenditure in such sectors.

In most countries the allocation of public (and, often, also of private) resources suffers from severe distortions. WHO estimates that approximately three quarters of all health spending in the developing world is being used to provide expensive medical care for a relatively small urban minority. Examples of glaring misallocation

174

abound. In the Congo, for instance, the Ministry of Health's 1987 annual budget foresees no expenditure on preventive care, while about $15 million are being spent on the refurbishing and extension of one urban hospital. In the Philippines, in the early 1980s, government subsidies to sophisticated private hospitals for heart, kidney and lung diseases, catering to upper-income groups, were five times as great as the total allocation for primary health care (Cornia and others, 1987). National biases are often reinforced by the preferences of aid-givers for modern hospitals and costly medical technology which absorb a large proportion of health-related aid. The absence of a comprehensive analysis of aid flows to the health sector in developing countries prevents us from quantifying the extent of this bias.

Misallocation of resources is not only to be found in the health sector. Despite their far greater cost-effectiveness, low-cost water programmes receive only about 20 per cent of the investment of the water sector (UNICEF, 1987b). And of the total World Bank lending to water projects, only 8 per cent was allocated to low-cost activities in 1986.

Given the present allocation of resources, the goals of the International Drinking Water Supply and Sanitation Decade, of Health for All by the Year 2000 and of reducing third-degree malnutrition to less than 0.8 per cent will not be met even under optimistic assumptions about economic growth and budgetary resources. For most countries, particularly when the world recession and Draconian adjustments are reducing available resources, the only way these goals can be achieved is through the reallocation of part of public (as well as private) expenditure towards the low-cost, high-impact measures described above. Where hospitals and large water systems are given a lower priority they consume considerably less public resources. In China, for instance, hospitals absorb 42 per cent of recurrent expenditure on health (Barnum, 1986) as compared with 70-80 per cent for many developing countries.

Until recently there were few signs of significant changes in this gross misallocation of resources. According to the 1987 evaluation of the PHC strategy (WHO, 1987a), however, some countries are now allocating a greater share of resources to underserved populations and there seems to be a slow-down in the construction of new hospitals. Algeria, India and Pakistan are attempting to restrain expenditures on hospitals while stepping up immunization programmes and other low-cost measures. In Brazil, possibly the country with the most unequal distribution of health resources, in 1981, 6 per cent of the total expenditure of the National Health Insurance system was allocated to renal dialysis, coronary bypass and similar operations for 12,000 people, more than the amount spent on basic health care and communicable disease control for 41 million people in north and north-eastern Brazil (World Bank, 1987). The newly elected Brazilian

175

administration intends to withdraw incentives to highly specialized medical services (WHO, 1986). There is also evidence of countries such as Indonesia, which, in spite of severe fiscal adjustments, have increased expenditure on low-cost health approaches and shifted expenditure towards the financing of recurrent costs (Gani, 1987). Botswana and Zimbabwe expanded their primary health care, child feeding and drought relief programmes when overall government expenditure was being restrained (Cornia and others, 1987).

The restructuring of health, water and nutritional expenditure requires important changes. These changes, however, are "affordable" in most circumstances. The percentage share of hospitals in total health expenditure would have to decline from the 70-80 to the 45-50 range, while that of large water programmes should decline from 80 to 60 per cent of total expenditure on water. The same holds for expenditure on health training. In Latin America, for instance, the medical schools are expected to produce an additional 200,000 fully qualified doctors between 1985 and 1990. For the same cost, it would be possible to train 150,000 doctors plus 1 million primary health care workers (UNICEF, 1985).

For practical purposes, it may be useful to set specific targets concerning the minimum share of resources to be allocated to PHC, low-cost water and targeted nutrition to be allocated in government and aid budgets. Or, with Segall (1987) one could propose, for instance, that the growth rate of expenditure in low-cost programmes should be twice as large as that of the overall sector.

In very low-income countries, even a radical restructuring of government expenditure would not generate the $4 to $10 per capita per year needed to finance key interventions in health, nutrition and water supply. For these countries, the solution lies in the mobilization of additional resources from the beneficiaries of the services and from the international community. For instance, doubling concessional aid flows to the least developed countries, in line with the United Nations target of transferring 0.15 per cent of the industrialized countries GNP to the least developed countries, would generate an additional $1 billion to $1.5 billion a year. Greater aid to low-cost, high-impact programmes could be used for policy-based lending with the purpose of facilitating the reallocation of budgetary resources in developing countries towards PHC and similar programmes.

User charges could also generate part of the funds required for health and water. Because of their potentially regressive nature, however, user charges should be mean-tested for preventive health services and installation of public water points. In contrast, a large portion of the full economic cost should be recovered from all income groups for higher-income services.

Over the past 20 years, a number of contributions to economic analysis have focused on human needs and on the human factor in development. Most prominent among them are the "basic needs" and the "human capital" approach. In spite of these advances, health, nutrition and education have remained peripheral to the theory and practice of most academics, policy makers and development planners. Indeed, while it is generally accepted that nutrition and health programmes are desirable because of their contribution to the welfare and happiness of the population, most conventional and radical economists still do not see them as a *sine qua non* of development. For the former, health and nutrition programmes represent a form of lower-priority consumption which ought to give precedence to investment in infrastructure and industry. For many radical economists, most of these measures can be dismissed as "welfaristic", unable to bring more than superficial and temporary relief to the structural problems faced by the poor.

Both views have elements of truth. Some expenditure on health, such as excessive treatment with drugs and cosmetic or unnecessary surgery, is not productive and can, in fact, be deleterious. It is also true that public expenditure has often been used in an attempt to placate the poor. Both views, however, are fundamentally flawed as they ignore the important contribution of appropriate interventions in health, nutrition, water supply and education to economic performance and to redistribution.

To be sure, there are fundamental ethical and humanitarian arguments for advocating better and increased investments in human resources. There are also solid economic arguments and growing empirical evidence to support this view. One can identify short-term, long-term and intergenerational effects on economic development of human-focused interventions, as well as redistributive effects.

(a) Short-term effects

Effects on labour productivity

Dietary improvements have been shown to have an immediate effect on performance of adult workers. An energy supplement of 650 calories a day provided to plantation workers in Guatemala, for instance, was found to produce significant results in terms of greater work intensity, energy expenditure and productivity (Viteri and others, 1975). A survey of the literature confirms this conclusion for a variety of countries (Maturo, 1979). Productivity gains were found to be even more staggering in the case of supplementation of micronutrients. A study on rubber plantation workers in Indonesia (Basta and others, 1979) found that treatment of anaemic workers with iron tablets for a period of 60 days (at a total per capita cost of about

$0.08) resulted in an increase in productivity of 15-20 per cent as compared to control groups. The benefit-cost ratio of the intervention in terms of increased latex production alone was estimated at 260:1. It has recently been estimated that output increases in the 10-20 per cent range for every 10 per cent rise in haemoglobin level (Levin, 1986). Using cost data on iron fortification and supplementation programmes, it was shown that the benefit-cost ratio of such interventions varied between 7 to 70 for fortification and 4 to 38 for supplementation (*ibid*).

Effects on reduced work losses

Poor nutrition and health of workers are responsible also for substantial losses of output owing to increased absenteeism from work. It is estimated, for instance, that millions of workdays are lost every year to malaria alone. In addition, children's illness adversely affects adult productivity and family production, particularly in agriculture, as parental time is shifted from productive activity to nursing care or to the pursuit of health care. It has been estimated, for instance, that at least 140-280 million workdays are lost annually to the care of the approximately 140 million malnourished children alone (McGuire and Austin, 1987). Substantial reductions in work loss could thus be achieved through an improvement in the health status of the population as a whole.

Effects on resource savings

The establishment of a capillary network of primary health care posts has been shown to have immediate beneficial effects on the demand for expensive hospital staff, inputs and infrastructure. The savings so realized would be expected to more than offset the costs incurred for the establishment of a primary care system. Good data on costs are difficult to find. A recent survey covering several developing countries, however, shows that hospitalization is more expensive than outpatient care by a factor of 2 to 20 (Robertson, 1985). Similar results have been obtained for the United States of America by Kennedy and Kotelchuck (1984) and by the House Select Committee on Children, Youth and Families, which reported, for instance, that each dollar spent on child immunization saves 10 dollars in later medical costs (see *The New York Times,* 6 September 1987, p. E14).

The provision of cost-effective basic services generates substantial savings for household budgets, too. Where there are no primary health care posts, drugs and health services are purchased by the poor from private providers at prices up to 20 times higher than those charged by village health posts. UNICEF (1987c), for instance, considers that the introduction of oral rehydration therapy in developing countries would not only prevent unnecessary deaths and reduce occupancy of hospital beds, but would also generate savings of as much as $US600 million on private and public purchases of often inappropriate and misused anti-diarrhoeal drugs. Similarly, the installation of handpumps in peri-urban areas can save those households forced to purchase water from private retailers up to 6 per cent of household income. In these and similar cases a reduction takes place in the monopoly profits and position rents of private providers, together with a net increase in the income and consumption of the poor.

Another positive, but more subtle, effect is on the time-use of the poor. Closer and more efficient services can greatly reduce the time necessary for carrying out given tasks such as fetching water or taking an infant to a health post. Women, the main beneficiaries of these programmes, can often use the time saved for more productive purposes. However, some of the health and nutritional activities advocated in this paper, such as, for instance, oral rehydration therapy, place additional claims on women's time (Leslie and others, 1986). While this issue deserves further investigation, it is likely that the implementation of the measures described previously would result in a net saving of parents' time.

Effect on the mobilization of idle resources

In many cases, low-cost basic services are provided with the active participation of the communities that provide free labour and local inputs. A substantially greater volume of output can thus be achieved with the same monetary expenditure. In this way, production factors with low or zero (monetary) opportunity cost, but with intrinsic production potential, are being brought into the stream of production. In Indonesia, for instance, the monetary cost per child of an integrated health-nutrition programme was reduced by approximately 30 per cent through the provision of free labour from village health volunteers (Cornia, 1984).

(b) *Long-term effects*

Effects on long-term labour productivity via alleviation of physical and mental growth retardation

Malnutrition at an early age, caused by dietary deficiency, infection or lack of sensory stimulation, leads to severe impairment of cognitive capacity and physical performance. There is now indisputable evidence of the positive relation between body size, aerobic capacity and endurance. Shorter people (generally with a history of chronic undernutrition since childhood) have less muscle mass and, therefore, a lower aerobic capacity. Aerobic capacity has been found to influence labour productivity among lumberjacks, sugar-cane cutters, construction workers and other adult and adolescent manual workers in countries as different as Australia, Brazil, Colombia, Ethiopia, Guatemala and India (for a survey of the literature, see Scrimshaw, 1986 and McGuire and Austin, 1987). In Guatemala, the analysis also showed that the present value of lifetime earnings of stunted sugar-cane cutters was 16 per cent lower than for taller cutters (Immink and others, 1984). Substantial gains in the productivity of manual workers could be obtained through appropriate health and nutrition measures aimed at reducing physical growth retardation during childhood. At times, the reduction in work performance can be extreme. A World Bank review of public work programmes in developing countries mentions that 30 per cent of those invited to participate in a food-for-work programme in Bangladesh had to decline the offer as they were too weak to carry out any meaningful physical work (Burki and others, 1976). While consuming some, albeit modest, food resources, these individuals were unable to contribute to the production process. Besides being tragic from a humanitarian perspective, this situation also makes no economic sense.

Long-term economic growth is even more markedly affected by the severe effects of early protein-energy malnutrition on the cognitive performance and mental development of the child. The link between education, labour productivity and economic growth is well established in the literature (Schultz, 1980 and Hicks, 1980). Undernutrition and insufficient sensory stimulation, however, affect brain growth, attention span and short-term memory, all factors having a negative influence on school performance. The loss of intelligence in growth-retarded young children thus reduces their later ability to learn and acquire skills required for productive activities. Although there is a total lack of longitudinal analyses examining adult capability and economic performance in relation to early child malnutrition, a few studies have attempted to quantify the benefits of nutritional interventions in favour of the young child through indirect methods. For instance, a well known study (Selowsky and Taylor, 1973) using Chilean data on differential I.Q. of normal and undernourished children and differential earnings of construction workers ranked by I.Q. level, comes to the conclusion that providing nutritional supplements during the first two years of life to the 25,000 or so children becoming malnourished in Chile every year would generate additional benefits in excess of 1 per cent of GNP.

Effects on cognitive capacity similar to those produced by protein-energy malnutrition can be produced also by specific nutritional deficiencies, such as iodine and iron deficiency. In Indonesia, it was found (Pollitt, 1984) that iron deficiency anaemia negatively affected attention span and school performance. A three-month programme of iron supplementation raised concentration and scores of the anaemic children to the level of the control group.

Effects on long-term resource savings

Lack of adequate nutrition and health care at an early age can cause greater demand for health services and substantial outlays in the longer term, as early interventions are more cost-effective as well as more efficacious from a health perspective than subsequent treatments in adolescence and adulthood (Lechtig and others, 1980). For instance, the often large costs borne for the care of permanent impairments such as blindness, deafness, mutism, cretinism and paralysis of the lower limbs could in many cases have been avoided by modest investment earlier in child immunization or supplementation. In addition to immediate savings, therefore, substantial expenditures can be avoided in the longer term. Low-cost preventive measures would thus have a favourable impact on the intertemporal allocation of resources from both the individual and the societal perspectives.

Effects on population growth

There is abundant evidence that in the longer term, better health and nutrition are conducive to a reduction in fertility larger than the corresponding decline in infant mortality, thus lessening population pressure on resources (see, for instance, Bulatao, 1984).

(c) Intergenerational effects via the reduction in the incidence of low birth weights

Perhaps the most negative, and most often overlooked, effect of poor intra-uterine growth and of poor health and nutrition at an early age for female infants is that on reproductive efficiency during their adult life. In recent studies a positive relation was found between low birth weight and poor nutrition in the mother's childhood and her later bearing of low birth weight infants or of infants with birth defects (Hackman and others, 1983). In this way, maternal malnutrition is passed on to at least the two successive generations, and studies show that several generations may be required to wash out the deleterious effects of poor intra-uterine growth and early child malnutrition (Martorell and Gonzalez-Cossio, 1987).

Studies from around the world (*ibid*) demonstrate conclusively that, despite the strong association between birth weight of the mother and birth weight of the newborn, maternal supplementation during pregnancy does make a difference in terms of birth weights. For the United States, Kennedy and Kotelchuck (1984) found such interventions to be highly cost-effective, since for every dollar spent on prenatal supplementation and health care, three dollars were saved on hospital care of low-birth-weight infants.

(d) Redistributive impact

Low-cost, high-impact and wide-coverage interventions also have an important redistributive impact, as they make widely available to the poor scarce resources such as good health, working potential and cognitive capacity while freeing part of their monetary and time resources for other purposes. In this way the provision of proper nutrition, potable water in sufficient quantity and basic health care not only promotes development but also strengthens the relative position of the poor in society, thus possibly facilitating more fundamental changes in the distribution of assets and incomes.

The political economy of the new approach

THE NEED FOR A FAVOURABLE OVERALL POLICY FRAMEWORK

The preceding discussion has focused on those sectoral interventions that can help improve health and nutritional standards even during periods of economic decline and adjustment. Successful examples of such interventions do exist. In Zimbabwe, for instance, despite the strong recession of 1982/83 and a most severe drought which lasted from 1981/82 to 1984, the infant mortality rate continued to decline while malnutrition did not rise during the same period. These results were due to the Government's decision to sustain expenditure on primary health care and to expand immunization and diarrhoeal disease control programmes in spite of severe budgetary restrictions. With the support of non-governmental organization and foreign donors, a cost-effective children's supplementary feeding programme was instituted, providing food, at the peak of the drought, to over a quarter of a million children, while the expansion of the rural water-supply programme continued on schedule (Cornia and others, 1987).

Over the long term, however, it would be illusory to try to pursue continued improvements in health and nutrition through sectoral interventions alone. Their success crucially depends on a global policy framework aimed at supporting the incomes of the poor and promoting growth with equity. In Zimbabwe, for instance, credit and procurement policies favouring poor farmers, continued, albeit lessened, efforts at land reform and a broadly equitable distribution of the burden of adjustment contributed to the creation of an economic environment supportive of health and nutrition, while the long-term reforms initiated after independence contributed to the resumption of growth in 1984 and 1985 (*ibid*).

ELEMENTS OF INNOVATION OF THE NEW APPROACH

The previous discussion identifies the main elements of the new approach which, possibly, make low-cost basic services a viable political proposition in a number of developing countries. There are four interrelated new elements.

(*a*) Technological breakthroughs have facilitated the replacement of expensive solutions by cost-efficient ones (e.g., sturdier handpumps, easy to operate and maintain, and new PVC pipes have

182

replaced traditional piped water systems), or have substantially improved the efficiency of existing ones. New vaccines are heat-resistant, cheaper, easier to transport and less subject to waste. Similarly, breakthroughs in the understanding of the interrelationships between water use, waste disposal and disease transmittal have led to more efficient project design. All these breakthroughs substantially reduce the unit costs of production of basic services.

(b) Greater reliance on community participation and social mobilization in the design, delivery and monitoring of these activities has ensured, in the first instance, a greater internalization of the programmes' benefits by the poor. Secondly, the adoption of less skill-intensive approaches leads to substantial cost containment and improvement in overall efficiency. For instance, the introduction of village health workers has allowed substantial savings on personnel costs and a more rational allocation of qualified staff to complex tasks. Considerable advances in training, providing basic skills at very low costs and over short periods of time (from a few days to a month), have been a key to the success of this approach. World-wide, the cost of basic training for a community health worker is in the range of $100 to $500. By contrast, the cost of training a fully qualified doctor is at least $60,000. Thirdly, community participation facilitates the mobilization of additional resources such as labour and locally available materials which have low opportunity costs but intrinsic productive value.

(c) The use of mass communication and education aimed at the diffusion of appropriate health and nutritional practices is another approach. It has been estimated that at least 75 per cent of all health care takes place at the family or individual level, with women having the greatest responsibility for its promotion. Providing women with appropriate knowledge about these practices is therefore essential. Long-term efforts at increasing literacy among women can be complemented by specific educational messages on health, nutrition and sanitation practices delivered through face-to-face demonstrations, simple printed material, radio and/or TV, now available even in many very poor communities. A concrete example is that of diarrhoea. Until recently it was treated at considerable cost in clinical settings using expensive intravenous feeding. The new strategy emphasizes home treatment by the mother. The key element is, thus, the transmittal of information on the home-based therapy to mothers.

(d) Targeting of interventions on the poor is a powerful way of reducing programme costs and increasing the equity of social expenditure, particularly on food subsidies and supplementary feeding. In the past, targeting was rare. This shortcoming substantially increased costs, limited coverage and produced adverse distributional effects. In contrast, some form of targeting appears feasible today. In Colombia, for instance, a highly effective distribution of food coupons was concentrated on families with children under five and pregnant women of the poorest 30 per cent of municipalities. In direct feeding programmes targeting is now facilitated by the use of growth-monitoring charts, illustrating over time the weight gains of the child against a given standard, and is an effective instrument for identifying children in need.

THE MUTUAL INTEREST ARGUMENT

Class interests, privileges and bureaucratic inertia represent formidable obstacles to the reallocation of resources towards low-cost, wide-coverage, health-nutrition programmes and to a better targeting of such interventions on the poor. On the whole, however, the expansion of low-cost basic services appears an attractive proposition both for Governments and the poor for a number of reasons.

In view of the decline in resources provoked by the recession and the ensuing austerity of the 1980s in Africa and Latin America, many Governments might be forced to abandon the traditional Western-based, high-cost approaches in order to provide a modicum of services to the entire population and to reduce social tensions. In conditions of heightened scarcity, waste and misallocation may become politically less tolerable. Data on the expansion of some cost-efficient, high-impact programmes during the 1980s tend to support this interpretation. Immunization rates against the six vaccine preventable child diseases increased for the developing countries as a whole (excluding China) from 23 to 41 per cent between 1981 and 1986. Similarly, the proportion of the population covered by potable water supply increased on average by about 5 per cent between 1980 and 1985. The main task now is to accelerate the expansion of such programmes.

In view of their positive impact on growth and human welfare, the implementation of such programmes may well generate political support for existing Governments among those in poverty, an important consideration in the old or newly established democracies of Latin America, Africa and Asia. While in countries characterized by severe political repression the argument of "mutual interest" loses applicability, there have been cases of benevolent or populist dictatorships genuinely promoting, possibly for some of the same reasons, health and nutrition programmes in favour of the poor.

From the perspective of the poor, these new approaches to health and nutrition present two advantages. First, they not only generate better health and nutrition, but also they can improve income-earning potential both in the immediate and, even more, in the longer term. Secondly, the heavy reliance on social mobilization and community participation in the design and delivery of these new programmes results in better organized, self-reliant and dynamic communities with greater collective bargaining power and with an increased ability to take advantage of economic and political opportunities. This greater bargaining power may be an important asset when discussing other key components of the social contract.

THE ROLE OF THE INTERNATIONAL COMMUNITY

Three main lines of action can be identified.

(*a*) There is a case for increasing the flow of concessional aid earmarked to cost-efficient, high-impact interventions to low-income countries, particularly Africa south of the Sahara, and, more important, improving the quality of existing aid flows to health, water and nutrition, which now often finance high-cost foreign expatriates or urban-based, infrastructural expenditure with little or even negative impact on the poor.

(*b*) These concessional and semi-concessional resources should be used for policy-based assistance with a strong emphasis on human resources development. External assistance can be extremely useful for facilitating the process of restructuring national resources towards low-cost, wide-coverage, high-efficiency interventions favouring the poor.

(*c*) The United Nations system can play an important catalytic role in mobilizing political consensus for these new initiatives, in co-ordinating the aspects related to policy and technical assistance and in channelling a growing share of this assistance to the recipient countries. The recent successful attempts at mobilizing the necessary political consensus and financial resources for universal child immunization by 1990, the renewed political resolve for Health for All by the Year 2000 and the International Drinking Water Supply and Sanitation Decade and the discussion on the possible reduction of severe malnutrition below 0.8 per cent are all encouraging signs. Planning for the achievement of these and similar objectives within a common, consistent framework and helping countries put them into operation could in fact represent one of the main, if not the main, thrusts of the fourth United Nations development decade.

REFERENCES

Barnum, H. N. (1986). Issues in the allocation of health sector resources to hospitals. Washington, D.C.: World Bank.

Basta, S. and others (1979). Iron deficiency anemia and the productivity of adult males in Indonesia. *American Journal of Clinical Nutrition,* vol. 32, No. 4, pp. 916-925.

Berg, Alan (1987). *Malnutrition, What Can be Done? Lessons from World Bank Experience.* Baltimore: Johns Hopkins University Press.

Bulatao, Rodolfo (1984). Reducing fertility in developing countries: a review of determinants and policy levers. World Bank Staff Working Paper, No. 680. Washington, D.C.: World Bank.

Burki, S. J. and others (1976). Public works programmes in developing countries: a

185

comparative analysis. World Bank Staff Working Paper, No. 224. Washington, D.C.: World Bank.

Cornia, Giovanni Andrea (1984). A cost analysis of the Indonesian experience with GOBI-FFF, 1979-1982. New York: United Nations Children's Fund.

Cornia, Giovanni Andrea, Richard Jolly and Frances Stewart, eds. (1987). *Adjustment with a Human Face: Protecting the Vulnerable and Promoting Growth.* Oxford: Oxford University Press.

Creese, Andrew L. (1986). Cost-effectiveness of potential immunization interventions against diarrhoeal disease. *Social Science Medicine,* vol. 23, No. 3, pp. 231-240.

Economic Commission for Latin America and the Caribbean (1986). *Economic Survey of Latin America and the Caribbean 1986.* United Nations publication, Sales No. 88.II.G.2.

Esrey, S. A., R. G. Feachem and J. M. Hughes (1985). Interventions for the control of diarrhoeal diseases among young children: improving water supplies and excreta disposal facilities. *Bulletin of the World Health Organization,* vol. 63, No. 4, pp. 757-772.

Gani, Ascobat (1987). Adjustment with a human face: Indonesian experience. Paper presented at the First International Conference on Tropical Pediatrics, Bangkok, 7-13 November 1987.

Grosse, R. N. and D. J. Plessas (1984). Counting the cost of primary health care. *World Health Forum,* vol. 15, No. 3, pp. 226-230.

Gwatkin, Davidson R., Janet R. Wilcox and Joe D. Wray (1980). Can health and nutrition intervention make a difference? Monograph No. 13. Washington, D.C.: Overseas Development Council.

Hackman, E. and others (1983). Maternal birth weight and subsequent pregnancy outcome. *Journal of the American Medical Association,* vol. 250, No. 15, pp. 2016-2019.

Hicks, N. (1980). Economic growth and human resources. World Bank Staff Working Paper, No. 408. Washington, D.C.: World Bank.

Immink, M. and others (1984). Micro-economic consequences of energy efficiency in rural populations in developing countries. In *Energy Intake and Activity,* vol. 11, *Current Topics in Nutrition and Disease,* E. Pollitt and P. Amante, eds. New York: Alan R. Liss, Inc.

Jespersen, Eva (1987). Restructuring social expenditures towards the poor: a review of options. New York: United Nations Children's Fund.

Kasongo Project Team (1984). Primary health care for less than a dollar a year. *World Health Forum,* vol. 5, pp. 211-215.

Kennedy, E. and M. Kotelchuck (1984). The Effects of WIC supplemental feeding on birth weight: a case-control analysis. *American Journal of Clinical Nutrition,* vol. 40, pp. 579-585.

Lechtig, A., M. Irwin and R. E. Klein (1980). Social implications of early protein energy malnutrition: prevention in childhood of specific adult health problems. Geneva: World Health Organization.

Leslie, J., M. Lycette and M. Buvinic (1986). Weathering economic crisis: the crucial role of women in health. Washington, D.C.: International Center for Research on Women.

Levin, H. M. (1986). A benefit-cost analysis of nutritional programmes for anemia reduction. *World Bank Research Observer,* vol. 1, No. 2, pp. 219-245.

Martorell, R. and T. Gonzalez-Cossio (1987). Maternal nutrition and birth weight. *Yearbook of Physical Anthropology,* vol. 30. New York: Alan R. Liss, Inc., pp. 195-220.

Maturu, N. Rao (1979). Nutrition and labour productivity. *International Labour Review,* vol. 118, No. 1 (Jan.-Feb.), pp. 1-12.

McGuire, J. and J. Austin (1987). Beyond survival: children's growth for national development. *Assignment Children,* vol. 2.

Parker, David (1985). The cost of GOBI activities within primary health care: an estimation of external resource requirements. Final report to UNICEF. New York.

186

Pinstrup-Andersen, Per, Maurice Jaramillo and Frances Stewart (1987). Impact on government expenditures. In Cornia, Jolly and Stewart, eds. (1987), pp. 73-89.

Pollitt, E. (1984). Nutrition and educational achievement. *Nutrition Education Series,* issue 9. Paris: United Nations Educational, Scientific and Cultural Organization.

Robertson, R. L. (1985). Review of literature on costs of health services in developing countries. Report prepared for the World Bank, Population, Health and Nutrition Department.

Schultz, W. (1980). *Investing in People: The Economics of Population Quality.* Berkeley: University of California Press.

Scrimshaw, N. (1986). Nutritional and health consequences of economic adjustment policies that increase poverty. Paper for the North-South Round Table on Development, Salzburg, September.

Segall, Malcolm (1987). The primary health care approach is viable with slow economic growth. Paper delivered at the Fifth International Congress of the World Federation of Public Health Associations, Mexico City, 22-27 March 1987.

Selowsky, M. and L. Taylor (1973). The economics of malnourished children: an example of disinvestment in human capital. *Economic Development and Cultural Change,* vol. 22, No. 1, pp. 17-30.

United Nations (1985). *Demographic Yearbook,* Sales No. E/F.86.XIII.1.

_____ (1986). *World Population Prospects. Estimates and Projections as assessed in 1984.* Population Studies No. 98. Sales No. 86.XIII.3.

_____ , ACC Sub-Committee on Nutrition (1987). *First Report on the World Nutrition Situation.*

United Nations Children's Fund (1985). *The State of the World's Children 1985.* New York: Oxford University Press.

_____ (1987a). *The State of the World's Children, 1987.* Oxford: Oxford University Press.

_____ (1987b). UNICEF co-operation in water supply and sanitation: a review and perspective. A draft Board paper, 29 September 1987.

_____ (1987c). Progress review of the child survival and development revolution 1983-86. *Assignment Children.*

Viteri, F. E. and others (1975). Interaction between nutrition and productivity of agricultural labourers. Washington, D.C.: Pan American Health Organization.

World Bank (1986a). *World Development Report 1986.* Washington, D.C.: Oxford University Press.

_____ (1986b). *Poverty and Hunger, Issues and Options for Food Security in Developing Countries.* A World Bank policy study. Washington, D.C.

_____ (1987). *Financing Health Care in Developing Countries. An Agenda for Reform.* A World Bank policy study. Washington, D.C.

World Health Organization (1978). *Alma-Ata 1978: Primary Health Care.* Health for All Series, No. 1. Geneva.

_____ (1980). The incidence of low birthweights: a critical review of available information. *World Health Statistics Quarterly,* No. 33, pp. 197-224.

_____ (1983). The use of essential drugs. Report of a WHO Expert Committee. Technical Reports Series No. 685. Geneva.

_____ (1986). *Evaluation of the Strategy for Health for All by the Year 2000,* vol. 3. *Region of the Americas.* Washington, D.C.: WHO/Pan American Health Organization.

_____ (1987a). *Evaluation of the Strategy for Health for All by the Year 2000.* Seventh Report on the World Health Situation, vol. 1. Global Review. Geneva.

_____ (1987b). Global nutritional status anthropometric indicators. NOT/ANTREF/3/87.

8

RURAL DEVELOPMENT AND LOCAL RESOURCE INTENSITY: A CASE-STUDY APPROACH

Jacques Gaude* and Steve Miller**

CONTENTS

Introduction

The use of local resources for developing rural infrastructure has been a subject of interest to the International Labour Organisation (ILO) for several decades. Through both its research and its project work, ILO has sought, along with other development organizations, to devise ways and means of mobilizing local resources and using them in an efficient and cost-effective manner in the construction of rural infrastructure. The importance of local resources as an input in this development process has increased as the availability of external resources, especially foreign exchange loans and grants, has diminished. The growing financial problems of developing countries are forcing Governments to reallocate their budgets in order to meet increasing debt-service requirements and to develop export-oriented industries. As a result, the pace of development of rural infrastructure is expected to slacken unless local resources are substituted for imported resources.

The concept of local resources is both obvious and, because it is so all-encompassing, complex. For the purposes of this paper, local resources refer specifically to the array of human capacities—individual, institutional and corporate—manufactured products and raw materials, finance, tools and equipment that are locally produced or locally available within a particular area of the country concerned.

---

*Senior Officer, Infrastructure and Rural Works Branch, International Labour Organisation.
**Officer, Infrastructure and Rural Works Branch, International Labour Organisation.

While an increase in the use of local resources may be the most promising alternative, it is sometimes seen to be less attractive because it requires substantial changes in the way many development programmes and aid donors currently operate. Furthermore, the institutional and technical requirements for using local resources are not always well understood. There are uncertainties about how they can be mobilized and there are doubts about their cost-effectiveness. However, this alternative is not new and there is mounting evidence of the feasibility of increasing the use of local resources to support future development. In fact, the basic issue is: Is there any alternative to increased and more effective use of local resources to development? The answer is clearly no, at least for low-income countries with limited export potential; any other development path would not be sustainable.

The purpose of this article is to explore the way in which ILO, in collaboration with with the United Nations Development Programme (UNDP), other aid donors and the developing countries, has tried to promote the use of local resources in carrying out the labour-intensive special public works programmes (SPWPs) now under way in some 26 countries. These programmes have two main advantages for developing countries. First, by forgoing the equipment-intensive technology typical of conventional investment programmes, they can produce a rapid and much needed increase in the volume of employment since many essential infrastructure works do not necessarily require heavy investment in equipment. Secondly, they can be a means of redistributing income and/or basic needs benefits in favour of the most needy sections of the population and of areas hitherto neglected in the development process.

SPWPs are designed to develop the infrastructures and land and water resources in rural areas in order to boost agricultural production, protect the environment, open up communications and provide the populations with basic community facilities. The works are carried out, wherever possible, using methods that favour the intensive use of local resources and, in particular, unskilled labour. These programmes are implemented locally by means of small-scale projects geared to the capacities of the villages involved. This limited scale makes it easier to adjust the programme quickly to unforeseen factors that might require changes in its nature, content and duration.

During the first generation of pilot programmes (1975-1984), the principal objectives were employment creation and the distribution of income with a view to reducing the massive unemployment in the most disadvantaged areas. Subsequently, these objectives were reviewed in the light of the results achieved and the accent has now been placed on the following longer-term effects the SPWPs are expected to have at the end of the pilot phase:

(a)   Durable sources of employment and income for the benefit of the poorest inhabitants (target groups) of the project area;

(*b*) Expanded agricultural production and marketing capacity through the construction of productive infrastructures using labour-intensive methods;

(*c*) Better protection of the environment and improved living conditions through the construction of basic facilities in the most disadvantaged rural areas (water supply, afforestation, health centres, schools etc.);

(*d*) Participation of the local population in the selection, construction and routine maintenance of infrastructures;

(*e*) Enhanced capacity of local government, through appropriate institutional and financial arrangements, to identify and implement infrastructures and maintain and develop those created;

(*f*) Strengthened national managerial capacity to replicate labour-intensive programmes on a larger scale.

As can be seen, these objectives centre on the basic development criteria of sustainability. In applying these criteria, it is important to consider a programme's ability not only to sustain itself over time, but also to develop supporting institutions, to broaden its scope and to be replicated in other parts of the country.

The reader will see below how far these objectives have been achieved shortly following the construction phase with the aid of examples (Martens, 1988; Guichaoua, 1987; and ILO, 1987) taken from forestry schemes in Burundi, Mali and Rwanda and from irrigation schemes in Nepal and the United Republic of Tanzania. These types of infrastructure are representative of most ongoing or completed SPWP projects. Owing to space limitations, however, emphasis will be placed here on the project instead of the programme approach (Gaude and others, 1984 and 1987), and on the linkages between project design and conditions for its sustained exploitation. It is argued that these conditions are partially met if the technology used is well adapted to the local environment and if the population is associated right from the design stage with decision-making and with project implementation.

Design

Deficiencies in project design are frequently cited to explain poor project performance; project design comprises here the objectives, phasing, scope and components, community participation, management structure, and financing and work plans. At first, SPWPs were somewhat hastily prepared, at times to satisfy donors' time limits and financial constraints. Projects were consequently financed on the basis of only a preliminary appraisal, and very quickly implementation pressures precluded adequate feasibility studies from ever being carried out. With hindsight, of course, it is easier to trace weaknesses of early SPWP projects back to the design stage. Despite the strong interest shown by Governments and donors, these early projects have not always been backed up by solid technical data or sufficient knowledge of the local situation and its antecedents.

Based on this experience, the process of identifying new programmes has been spread over a longer period, with a more flexible transition from the design stage to that of implementation. By considering a range of possible projects, project designers attempt to reconcile the general objectives of the Governments concerned with the wishes of the local populations. To avoid planning and technical shortcomings, priority is given to a limited number of small complementary projects requested by the local population but not exceeding their absorptive capacity. The most successful projects use simple techniques, are limited in geographic scope and offer obvious advantages to the future beneficiaries. Unfortunately, such precautions were not always taken before launching the SPWP projects examined here.

In SPWP forestry activities, faulty design was primarily responsible for failure to establish project sustainability, popular participation, maintenance arrangements and appropriate institutions, with inadequate design itself being a reflection of pressure to achieve quick results. This pressure clashes with a feature of forestry projects which is that, in comparison with other SPWP projects, they require a longer preparation phase (12 to 18 months) before large numbers of workers can be employed productively. Activities to be carried out in the preparation phase include technical advice, negotiations with beneficiary communities and with the Government, and the construction of nurseries. In particular, assurance of long-term, reliable maintenance must be obtained before operations develop on a large scale. This necessitates the negotiation of maintenance responsibilities and the identification, before actual planting activities begin, of those who will have the right to long-term benefits.

The Mali project, located in a zone with 700-800 millimetres of rainfall per annum, sought to protect three natural forest reserves in the Kayes and Segou regions with a total area of 13,650 hectares. These forests were overexploited and their existence threatened by encroachment of cultivators and by bush fires. However, initial output targets had to be revised downward in order to take account of the absence of adequate preparations, logistical complications and the need to undertake restoration in addition to protection *per se.*

Projects in Burundi and Rwanda are located in Ruyigi Province and Gitarama Prefecture, respectively. They have focused on afforestation of eroded hilltops at altitudes of about 2,000 metres. In this case, as part of a much larger multi-sectoral pilot programme, unit costs were in fact hugely overestimated, leading to much higher achievements than those foreseen in initial, tentative output targets.

In irrigation projects, the Bhorletar site, a 155-hectare command area for the irrigation canal in Nepal, was chosen after the villagers, having tried in vain to dig a canal themselves, asked the regional authorities for help. After carrying out a feasibility study, ILO and the Nepalese Department of Irrigation agreed to support the completion of the project. In the United Republic of Tanzania, the Mto wa Mbu site, which entailed irrigation of 1,300 hectares and flood control of 1,950 hectares as targeted command areas, was chosen in response to requests from the local population and the Government.

As a general rule, popular participation was limited in all projects to the voicing of opinions by designated spokespersons who were village or party representatives. Whatever the nature of the contacts or the perspicacity and experience of the spokespersons, the beneficiaries, and in particular the target groups, seldom had any real say in the matter.

The two main weaknesses observed in the design stage, which carried the seeds of the shortcomings noted in the implementation of the projects, were overambitious output targets in relation to logistical capacity and insufficient popular participation. The first weakness is explained by the fact that the beneficiary Governments often try to satisfy diverging interests and are thus led to select project areas that are too widely scattered in relation to the logistical and managerial capacities available. The lack of prior consultation with the local populations, particularly concerning land issues and the assessment of their real needs, the second weakness, arose primarily from haste in preparing the programme. In this connection, SPWP-type projects aimed at favouring the use of local resources should be designed on the basis of solid background information and data collected within the area, e.g., surveys of locally available raw materials and tools, assessment of labour availability, cost-efficiency of alternative techniques already tested, and local management and technical capacity.

Technical issues

While it is necessary to make optimal use of local resources, account should also be taken of the actual availability of materials, tools and equipment, the time allowed for the work, taking into consideration seasonal factors, the existing labour legislation and possible cultural obstacles. In addition, technical choices are sometimes imposed from outside, depending as they often do on the financial conditions laid down by the donors, on the one hand, and the higher cost of technical assistance compared with the investment cost if the work takes too long to complete, on the other hand.[1] Moreover, the efficiency of labour-intensive methods varies from case to case and, owing to the lack of reliable or comparable data, it is difficult to compare projects from one country to another or even from one project to another within a country.[2] Finally, the notion of cost, which is certainly important in itself, only becomes meaningful,

TABLE 1. FORESTRY ACTIVITIES: A COMPARISON OF CONSTRUCTION COSTS
(Current United States dollars)

	Total expenditures (thousands of United States dollars)[a]	Direct employment created (thousands of work-days)	Cost price of work (dollars per hectare)	Cost price of work (dollars per thousand seedlings planted)	Labour cost per hectare	Labour use (work-days per hectare)	Labour cost per work-day (implicit cost of labour)	Potential long-term employment created at full development (work-days per hectare per year) Maintenance	Potential long-term employment created at full development (work-days per hectare per year) Operation
Protection/restoration of forest reserves									
Mali (1981-1986)[b]	596.3	197.7	-	-	-	-	-	..	..
Protection in Kayes/Segou regions (13,650 hectares plus 300 hectares restored)	378.7	168.2	plant/prot. 520/ 20	-	plant./prot. 258/ 10	(see text)	1.67	3[d]	9[d]
Village afforestation (606,500 seedlings—main species: neem)	217.6	29.5	-	359	-	48.6/1 000 seedlings	1.20	..	..
Large-scale plantation									
Burundi (1979-1986)[c]	972	645.7	-	-	-	-	-	..	..
Muramvya province (1979-1981) (1,761 hectares planted—91 per cent callitris)	361.4	268	204	185.6	136	152	0.89	9[f]	..
Ruyigi province (1981-1986) (4,966 hectares planted—80 per cent callitris)	610.6	377.7	123	158.9	74	76	0.97	..	..
Rwanda									
Gitarama (1981-1983)[g] (2,342 hectares)	807.6	552	329.3	299.3	250	188	1.33	12[h]	6[i]

194

NOTES: The Mali data are tentative owing to the absence of real expenditure data broken down by type and item of activity, inconsistencies between different sets of figures and lack of a reliable key for the attribution of overhead costs, i.e., transport, supervision, technical assistance, training etc. It follows that only global indicators based on a mixture of actual and anticipated figures and on a number of assumptions can be calculated. The data relative to Burundi and Rwanda afforestation projects are relatively more accurate because they are based on an in-depth impact study.

a Direct costs.

b Average weighted rate of exchange for the period: 691.1 CFA francs = $US 1 (from 1981 to August 1984, maximum variations: 537 to 827 CFA francs). As of 1 September 1984: 417 CFA francs = $US 1 (maximum variations: 347 to 458 CFA francs).

c Exclusive of costs of supervision, technical assistance and overhead. The unit costs increase to $US 752 inclusive of such costs.

d Including surveillance, one permanent warden per 500 hectares, one weeding per annum during the first 14 years for firebreaks, plantation and restoration sites, together accounting for 10 per cent of total area per work-day; after the fifteenth year felling and cutting: 2 m3 of wood per hectare per year, with 1 m3 per work-day; carbonization by reversed-draught kiln: 750 m3 wood per 450 work-days, or by dismountable kiln: 285 m3 wood per 250 work-days.

e Average weighted rate of exchange for the period: 84.55 Burundi francs = $US 1 (stable from 1980 to 1983).

f Including annual clearing of firebreaks at 100 ml per work-day, assuming 75 ml of firebreak of 15 m width per hectare of forest: surveillance (one forest warden per 130 hectares), pruning in the sixth to eighth year (27.5 work-days per hectare), spot weeding at 11 work-days per hectare, thinning, cutting, felling etc. as of the tenth year, with assumed annual average of 10 m3 per hectare per year at 1.5 work-days per m3.

g Average weighted rate of exchange for the period: 92 Rwanda francs = $US 1 (stable from 1980 to 1983).

h Including clearing/weeding in the third year (18 work-days per hectare), pruning in the sixth to eighth year (46 work-days per hectare), surveillance (one forest warden per 130 hectares), maintenance of the 54.5 kilometres (approximately 1 kilometre per 43 hectares), of service roads (year 10 to 40) with major road maintenance in the twentieth, thirtieth and fortieth years; periodic annual maintenance during the other years.

i Including, on the one hand, the construction of service roads (ninth year: 5,000 work-days per kilometre for unskilled labour and 500 work-days per kilometre for skilled labour; on the other hand, operating costs (felling and skidding) in the tenth, twenty-fifth to thirtieth and the fortieth year.

195

particularly in the case of locally supported infrastructure works, once costs are compared with expected benefits.

Tables 1 and 2 contain some basic data on each project, by principal type of infrastructure.

FORESTRY

Since afforestation activities require large numbers of workers, these projects are frequently undertaken in the context of SPWPs.[3] The Mali forestry programme (1981-1986) comprised two components: the protection of natural forests and village afforestation. The former, through the creation of firebreaks and regular guarding, aimed at protecting 13,650 hectares, while some 300 hectares of degraded forests were replanted or restored using a total of about 250,000 seedlings (see table 1). A weighted average of the labour-use per hectare of the different operations of clearing firebreaks, destumping, planting and restoration comes to 100 work-days. Planting alone is the most labour-intensive of these operations requiring, on the basis of the density of 1,100-1,200 plants per hectare, a total of 220 work-days per hectare. Costs[4] per hectare planted, exclusive of staff salaries, allowances and technical assistance, amounted to $US 520. Labour costs, with a daily wage of 500 CFA francs ($US 1.60), amounted to about 50 per cent of total costs only, in view of high transport, equipment and running and maintenance costs. The total cost per hectare protected but not restored amounted to $US 20, increasing to $US 30 if restoration was included.

The second component consisted of various support activities to achieve afforestation in Sahelian villages. The main support was for the creation and operation of three nurseries distributing, at no cost to the recipients, about 200,000 seedlings, mainly neem, to individuals as shade or protection trees or to schools and other public institutions for decorative planting. Production required a total of 29,500 work-days (i.e., 48.6 work-days per 1,000 seedlings). Assuming that all seedlings are eventually distributed and that 50 per cent of the seedlings survive, the cost per tree, excluding labour for watering, would be $US 0.72, which is about 10 times more expensive than data currently observed. The nurseries are reportedly receiving continued donor support. Other support activities consisted of organizing two training seminars and producing management plans for six natural forests covering a total of 33,750 hectares.

Moreover, 6,727 hectares were planted in Burundi (mostly callitris c.) and 2,342 hectares in Rwanda (41 per cent pinus p.). Overall costs, including nursery work and government staff, but excluding technical assistance, are difficult to compare as they are expressed in current United States dollars, which has the effect of making dollar costs somewhat higher for earlier projects as opposed to those for projects undertaken in 1985-1986. Cost comparisons for

196

TABLE 2. IRRIGATION PROJECTS: A COMPARISON OF CONSTRUCTION COSTS
(1985 United States dollars)

	Total expenditures[a] (thousands of 1985 United States dollars)	Cost price of works (dollars per hectare)	Local resources intensity ratio[b] (percentage)	Direct employment created (thousands of work-days)	Labour use per unit of irrigable area (work-days per hectare)	Potential long-term employment created at full development (work-days per hectare per year)	
						Maintenance	Operation
Nepal[c]							
Bhorletar (1980-1983)							
Irrigation 155 hectares with 5 kilometres of canals	811.5	5 236 [162]d	65	257	1 657	8	215
United Republic of Tanzania[e]							
Mto wa Mbu (1980-1986)							
Irrigable area at present developed: 300 hectares	2 069.2f	6 900	72	350g	470h	..	..
Potentially irrigable area subject to additional investment: 1,300 hectares	..	..	..	..	..	23	206

aIncluding ILO overhead costs: 20 per cent in Bhorletar and 25 per cent in Mto wa Mbu.
bPercentage of labour and locally available or locally produced materials in total expenditures (excluding government and ILO agency costs).
cAverage rate of exchange for the period: 12.76 Nepalese rupees = $US 1.
dCost per linear metre of canal.
eAverage rate of exchange for the period: 8.64 Tanzanian shillings = $US 1.
fA part of expenditures corresponds to not yet operational infrastructures; however, these could be exploited through additional investment expenditures likely to reduce the cost price to $US 6,000 for a command area of 1,300 hectares.
gThe official number of work-days was 557,000. However, in order to attract enough workers to the project, the management had to lower the productivity standards so that the work set out (the piece-rate) could be done in less than a full work-day; the workers could then either carry out two jobs in one day or work on their farmland in the afternoon. The figure mentioned here would represent the actual number of full days involved, reducing the official figure by about 37 per cent.
hSome 40 per cent of labour use was for irrigation (300 hectares) and 60 per cent for flood protection.

non-SPWP projects in Burundi show that projects funded by the European Economic Community (EEC) in Ruyigi in particular achieved a cost figure of $US 158.90 per 1,000 seedlings planted against $US 185.60 for the SPWP (or even $US 299.30 in Rwanda). A major reason cited for the lower cost figures is the greater volume of EEC activities which tended to reduce fixed overhead costs per unit of output. Besides, the cost per hectare and the labour use were markedly higher in Rwanda than in Burundi where the topography is more favourable, with its gentler slopes, less isolated planted areas and its sites easier to organize.

Most of the cost of large-scale planting is labour, making up two thirds of the total cost, with abundant use of locally available or locally produced materials. Basic yield indicators as displayed in table 1 show considerable fluctuation in labour costs primarily because of differences in labour use (work-days per hectare), which may be related to dispersion of sites and/or to varying levels of work organization. High productivity figures were achieved in Ruyigi (Burundi) where afforestation work was concentrated in a few sites and where the SPWP staff directly undertook site organization, management and payment. In other cases in Burundi and Rwanda, communes were made responsible for site organization and payment. In all, over 90 per cent of the young plants have survived and their growth, which varies according to the quality of the soil, has been satisfactory. Very little replanting has been necessary.

IRRIGATION

Table 2 shows wide variations between cost indicators, revealing substantial differences in the construction technology used for the projects. In Bhorletar, nearly the entire canal is cemented and most of it had to be dug out of rocks on steep hill slopes. In Mto wa Mbu, nearly all canals are simple earthwork constructions dug out of loose soil, a technique that was not feasible in Bhorletar.

In Nepal, some agencies have built irrigation infrastructures without cement or steel constructions, applying a so-called "farmers' technology". The Bhorletar farmers had tried several times to build a new canal themselves but failed because of technical problems. The improved technology applied in the Bhorletar project is therefore a well-balanced solution: it makes as much use as possible of local resources and techniques while applying improved inputs only if and when necessary. To do so, diverse techniques were used, combining traditional elements (field channels in simple earthwork) and modern elements (main canals using concrete and plastic tubes). The use of local resources such as manpower, stone and sand for construction can be regarded as satisfactory (the local resource intensity is 65 per cent, see table 2). Only cement, iron, plastic tubes and explosives had to be imported; these materials are also manufactured in Nepal, but they are not produced in sufficient quantities. The main technical constraint was the rugged terrain, which, in effect, favoured labour-intensive methods. Tractors and heavy machines could not be used owing to the lack of roads, therefore all the equipment and materials had to be carried in by porters.

In the United Republic of Tanzania almost all the resources used in the Mto wa Mbu project, particularly the manpower, were local except for a small input of reinforcement bars used in concrete works. The canal banks were made of earth and purely traditional techniques were used. This is reflected by the high local resource intensity, amounting to 72 per cent (see table 2). The use of traditional techniques in Mto wa Mbu meant that more labour was required for maintenance. The scale of the project caused such serious management and technical problems that it is not yet ready to be handed over. Only 300 hectares out of 1,300 are completed at present as a result of damage due to exceptional floods in May 1987, lack of funds, shortage of transport and construction materials, work planning not always in line with labour availability, insufficient technical assistance inputs and labour recruitment problems. In view of high expectations based on the possibilities of irrigation for generating higher incomes, farmers have preferred working for higher wages offered in agriculture than earning the minimum wage paid by the project. The cost per hectare amounts to $US 6,900, which is higher than the Nepal project despite Nepal's more difficult environmental conditions, but nevertheless lower than unit costs currently observed in the United Republic of Tanzania for sophisticated irrigation projects of similar scale: $US 15,000 using equipment-intensive techniques.[5] It can be argued that the latter involves a higher development potential; however, severe operation and maintenance problems make it extremely difficult for these schemes to be actually more efficient in the long run than a simple project such as Mto wa Mbu.

To achieve full development, a master plan study will be necessary after which further ILO involvement will be determined. Difficulties mentioned above show that planning and worksite organization are a key factor to the success of all local resource-intensive works.

Impact

When it comes to discussing the potential impact of the projects under review, we are entering a field of speculation. Nevertheless we shall attempt to outline some of the possible effects below.

EXPECTED SOCIO-ECONOMIC BENEFITS

Expected benefits should be spelled out at the design stage of the programmes and constantly kept in sight during their implementation, whether in identifying the most disadvantaged population groups, in choosing the sites and infrastructures, in assessing the capacity of the authorities to provide additional services in order to bring the works to fruition, or in negotiating property guarantees between the landowners (private individuals, communes and the State) and the future beneficiaries, before finally deciding on each location.

Traditionally, the impact of the viability of projects is assessed by a cost-benefit analysis which produces a single parameter: the internal rate of return which is designed to measure the financial and/or economic profitability of projects. In the former case of the financial internal rate of return (FIRR), projects are considered from the point of view of beneficiaries and local financial institutions are obliged to base investment decisions on prevailing, and usually imperfect, market conditions. The FIRR value is a necessary condition for project sustainability. In the latter case, projects are viewed from the social welfare viewpoint and the corresponding index is the economic internal rate of return (EIRR), essentially relevant for planning purposes and for Governments concerned. The EIRR value represents a necessary condition for project replicability on a larger scale.

In the economic context of most developing countries with scarce foreign exchange and often overvalued local currency, one would normally expect the EIRR of labour-intensive projects to be superior to the FIRR. On the one hand, SPWPs aim at effectively utilizing the energies of the unemployed and the underemployed without adversely affecting farming and other productive activities. The work must therefore be planned to take account of seasonal patterns of labour demand in these activities. The surplus labour force available for an SPWP is defined as those workers who compose the excess of labour supply over demand and who are willing to work at a given wage rate. Thus, a relatively low opportunity cost of labour, reflecting the scarcity or unattractiveness of alternative productive opportunities, should be the rule in SPWPs, especially in areas with abundant, otherwise idle, labour resources.

On the other hand, the cost of imported equipment and materials would usually have an economic opportunity cost higher than the financial cost that is typically subsidized by overvalued exchange rates of local currencies. However, this cost element, in practice, should be outweighed by the labour element, resulting in a net reduction in project construction costs when viewed in economic terms.

Finally, project benefits would tend to rise under an economic analysis since overvalued local currency means that farmers do not reap the full social opportunity costs from selling agricultural output. The higher social benefits of this agricultural production would result in a net increase in project benefits.

The overall results of lower costs and higher benefits should therefore produce a higher EIRR than FIRR. Table 3 displays sensitivity tests on a number of FIRRs and EIRRs in the three categories of projects which will be discussed below.

Forestry

Afforestation is expected to produce multiple benefits:

(*a*) Soil conservation to improve water retention, increase water reserves and control river flooding;

(*b*) Production of timber and fuelwood within a period of 5-15 years;

200

(*c*) Creation of permanent employment (maintenance personnel, forest wardens) or temporary jobs;

(*d*) Reduction of time spent in collecting firewood;

(*e*) Subsequent use of tree nurseries by the communities for extending communal or private plantings (including fruit trees).

These benefits depend basically on the quality of maintenance (clearing and pruning), the maintenance of firebreaks, the employment of permanent forest wardens to detect fires, organize fire-fighting efforts and guard against unwanted intrusions from live-stock, and, during the felling or gathering period, the construction and maintenance of access roads through the forests.

In Burundi and Rwanda the International Labour Organisation has now managed to include in projects donor funds covering most of the costs of clearing and of building and maintaining firebreaks, tasks that have direct consequences for the development and hence future profitability of the afforestation works. However, the longer-term problems of maintenance and guarding have not yet been resolved since land ownership and the future use of the planted trees raise difficulties.[6] Furthermore, there is no organization as yet capable of logging the trees, pre-processing the timber locally and hauling it out. While communal afforestation poses few problems, since the demand for fuelwood and timber by local craftsmen could suffice to absorb future production, the large state forests require a semi-industrial approach which has not yet even been defined.

For the logging of the trees planted in Rwanda, it would be necessary to construct some 50 kilometres of forest tracks and skidding trails. Over a period of 40 years maintenance would guarantee an average of some 12 work-days per hectare per year, while logging itself (felling and skidding) would allow approximately 6.1 to be created (see table 1).

The afforestation works in Rwanda appear to be viable since the FIRR is approximately 10 per cent and the EIRR above 20 per cent, even if operating costs are doubled (see table 3). However, if service roads were not constructed, the resulting assumed 70 per cent decrease in expected benefits would reduce the EIRR to 12.4 per cent, making the project barely acceptable.

In Mali, where forest protection aims at increasing productivity of forest reserves, creating long-term employment and protecting or rehabilitating the environment, maintenance requirements are estimated at three work-days per hectare per year. Exploitation is envisaged at the rate of clear felling every 15 years for the purpose of firewood and charcoal (25 m3 per hectare in year 15, assuming an initial volume of 15 m3 per hectare), or thinning every year (3 m3 per hectare) on a continuous basis from year 15 onward. Total employment, over a 30-year period and inclusive of requirements for felling, cutting and carbonization, would amount to approximately 139 or so

TABLE 3. INTERNAL RATE OF RETURN FOR SELECTED SPWP PROJECT COMPONENTS
(Percentage)

	Financial internal rate of return (FIRR)	Economic internal rate of return (EIRR)
Large-scale plantings		
Rwanda		
Gitarama (1981-1983)[a](2,342 hectares)	9.5	21.3
Scenarios		
Operating costs doubled	..	20.4
Benefits reduced by 25 per cent	..	18.3
No construction of 55.6 kilometres access roads with resulting 70 per cent decrease in benefits	..	12.4
Irrigation		
Nepal		
Bhorletar (1980-1983)[b]	15.6	22.3
Scenarios		
Benefits reduced by 25 per cent	..	20.2
Total costs increased by 25 per cent unexpected landslides and ensuring higher repair and maintenance costs)	..	20.4
United Republic of Tanzania		
Mto wa Mbu (1980-1985)[c]		
Scenarios		
The combined projects	45.2	32.4
The completed sub-project with full development achieved by 1990)	46.5	33.7
Maintenance costs doubled	..	33.3
Benefits reduced by 30 per cent	..	26.6
The remaining sub-project	19.6	19.9
Construction costs doubled	..	12.2
Additional maintenance costs tripled	..	18.3

[a]The opportunity cost of unskilled labour has been set equal to zero for forestry works, for clearing/weeding and for pruning carried out in the slack agricultural season. As for skilled labour employed for the exploitation of forests and for forest wardens, the conversion factors for shadow pricing are 0.8 and 1.0, respectively. Similar conversion factors have been applied for the construction and maintenance of service roads. Other conversion factors are: 1.2 for equipment/materials imported and 1.0 for other local inputs. As for the marketed timber, the conversion factor is set equal to 1.2. See table 1, notes h and i for other details (Guichaoua, 1987, pp. 167-178).

[b]Agricultural labourers are supposed to be fully employed during the short peak seasons (March, July, October); the peak season market wage (25 rupees per day) is assumed to reflect the marginal productivity of unskilled labour, which equals the shadow wage rate. For off-season agricultural labour, the corresponding opportunity cost is taken at one tenth of the full employment market wage rate in agriculture (Rs 2 per day). For skilled labour, the shadow wage rate is set equal to the market wage rate (Rs 40 per day). A standard conversion factor for exchange rate of 1.1 has been applied (the actual 1985 rate of Rs 18 per dollar has been revised to Rs 20 per dollar). For agricultural outputs: paddy, maize and wheat, the following conversion factors were applied: 1.37, 2.24 and 1.73, respectively, including transportation costs. For further details, see Martens, 1988b, pp. 76-107.

[c]The Mto wa Mbu project has been split up into two sub-projects: the completed infrastructure as it now stands with some 300 irrigable hectares and the complementary infrastructure which should be implemented to reach the 1,300 hectares targeted command area. For unskilled labour in construction, the shadow wage rate has been set equal to an average of 50 per cent of the market wage rate (35 Tanzanian shillings) for both peak and slack seasons. For skilled labour in construction as well as in agriculture, opportunity costs have been set equal to market wage rates as skilled employment is presumed to be scarce. For agricultural labour, the shadow wage rate has likewise been set equal to the going wage rate since 85 per cent of all agricultural labour is carried out during peak seasons when full employment is reached. A shadow exchange rate of TSh 65 per United States dollar has been applied for the fiscal year 1985/1986. For further details, see Martens, 1988b, pp. 155-164.

202

work-days per hectare (see table 1) with annual averages of 2.9 (years 1-14) and 6.2 (years 15-30) work-days per hectare. These averages are close to those achieved during the project period, which did not, however, include exploitation.

Irrigation

Irrigation projects usually have a threefold effect: on agricultural production through the direct increase in the irrigated area; on cropping patterns; and on yields. For example, in 'Mto wa Mbu the irrigated area increased from 776 hectares of arable land in 1980 to 1,080 hectares in 1987 and the cropping intensity index rose from 122 in 1980 to 138 in 1987. In Bhorletar in Nepal this index rose from 128 before the project had started (1980) to 212 in 1985, only two years after the works had been completed.

As far as employment is concerned, it is estimated that the Bhorletar project should eventually help to provide about 8.4 work-days per hectare per year for maintenance and some 215 work-days per hectare per year for operation/cultivation, including local multiplier effects. The indirect long-term effects, at both the local and the macro-economic levels, are much greater than the direct effects of the use of the infrastructures. The additional income generated by the project in both the short and the long term is either consumed, hence the multiplier effects on demand, or reinvested, hence the multiplier effects not only on investment but also on production capacity and job creation. In principle, it is the poorest people who should benefit most from job creation: thus, the increase in job offers in Bhorletar is helping to reduce out-migration. Finally, simulation exercises have shown that significant variations in labour intensity have only a modest influence on long-term employment and incomes.[7] However, this result, although valid for a project in isolation, would be erroneous if the project were to be replicated on a larger scale. In effect the multiplication of alternative foreign resource-intensive projects would give rise to a development cul-de-sac.

In the short term the distribution of income barely changes since it is linked to the distribution of land on which the project has had no influence. The average income per inhabitant increased by 273 per cent over three years (1984-1986) and could rise by 347 per cent by 1990. However, even with this spectacular increase, the incomes of the poorest peasants may only reach the subsistence level. On the other hand, the rise in the incomes of the less poor will allow them extra funds for investing in other sorts of enterprises which could bring in additional income. It is then that inequalities in the distribution of income owing to indirect effects will appear and the Government should be encouraged to reduce these inequalities through tax measures. In the short term a progressive maintenance tax might help, but in the long term it would be better to establish an effective system of income tax.

The cost-benefit analysis (see table 3) reveals that the FIRR amounts to 15.6 per cent (in 1985 prices) over 20 years, enough to consider funding the project on a loan basis. As for the EIRR, it is significantly above 20 per cent, even with sensitivity tests assuming total costs increase (heavy repairs and ensuing higher maintenance costs) or, alternatively, benefits decrease by 25 per cent.

In the United Republic of Tanzania three major factors account for the jobs created: intensified cropping, enlargement of irrigated areas and flood protection, resulting in the creation of more important sources of durable employment than direct construction employment. At full development, some 23 work-days per hectare per year should be created for maintenance of the infrastructures, while about 206 work-days per hectare per year should be used in agriculture. Hence, the direct long-term employment created is higher than during the construction phase (the same in Nepal); the full development labour-to-land ratio in agricultural production would be about 210 work-days per hectare.

The long-term effects on incomes tend to be the same as for Nepal, but the income distribution runs the risk of being even more unequal because the relatively well-off peasants will have easier access to modern inputs (fertilizer, improved seed etc.). The Government, assisted by other co-operation bodies downstream from the project, could assist the poorest peasants in distribution and loans for the procurement of these inputs in order to reduce the inequalities.

The cost-benefit analysis (see table 3) shows that the Mto wa Mbu project (completed sub-project) is financially and economically profitable. However, we note that the EIRR is lower than the FIRR, which deserves explanation. The financial analysis carried out is based on evaluating the project as a private investment undertaking of the beneficiaries. Therefore, certain costs that are included in the economic analysis, such as ILO technical assistance and overhead support, and unpaid agricultural labour in cultivation, have been excluded altogether in the financial analysis, thereby increasing the FIRR. Also, although construction was indeed labour-intensive, the lowering of labour costs through shadow pricing is outweighed by the increase in costs of imported materials or equipment. This is due to the fact that shadow pricing has more than doubled the economic costs of equipment, materials and tools, whereas opportunity costs of labour, in the case of Mto wa Mbu which has only a limited labour surplus, are only marginally lower than their financial costs.

The overall result of the above factors is a significantly higher economic rate of return as compared to the financial rate of return. Finally, sensitivity tests to allow for a major increase in investment costs necessary to achieve the potentially irrigable area of 1,300 hectares (remaining sub-project in table 3) would lead to EIRRs ranging from 12 to 20 per cent depending on varying assumptions made on construction or maintenance costs.

PROJECT SUSTAINABILITY

Sustainability is a key criterion in evaluating the success or failure of rural development projects. This means that projects should, within a reasonable period of time, become self-supporting, independent of international assistance and rely only on the normal services of local institutions and of beneficiaries. Consequently, sustainability depends very much on:

(*a*)   Design and preparation of the projects;

(*b*)   Participation and interest of the local people in the projects right from the selection stage;

(*c*)   Methods adapted to the local environment (from the drawing up of work plans to maintenance), including training and maximum use of local resources;

(*d*)   Capacity of the beneficiary community, with the support of national and local government services, to administer, use and maintain infrastructures.

Given the relatively short period during which SPWP planning and construction is carried out, these projects often are not able to create, in and of themselves, the local institutional capacity necessary to make projects sustainable. Therefore, SPWP projects have been most successful when identified in collaboration with a community already possessing the necessary cohesion and dynamism. This brings us back to the issue of popular participation.

Sustainability depends above all on local factors directly related to the project and its immediate environment. The basic issue lies in the initial choice of the target groups and of organizational arrangements that help the infrastructures to operate efficiently.

There can be no doubt that productive infrastructures, provided the beneficiaries are clearly identified, are best able to guarantee project sustainability. Short-term upkeep and the exact identification of the beneficiaries (peasants, communes, or possibly the State) nevertheless call for special attention. Moreover, the viability of the works may be jeopardized if the State seeks to appropriate the future revenue from exploitation of the plantings.

The Mali project is expected to achieve financial profitability from about the fifteenth year onward provided that regular maintenance and guarding do take place and that bush fires are effectively controlled. Given the uncertainty that these conditions will be met, it is equally uncertain that financial autonomy will be achieved after the fifteenth year. Cost-benefit analysis based on tentative data also indicates that the financial internal rate of return is low. This points to the desirability of testing cheaper methods of planting-restoration, e.g., through taungya and agro-forestry systems, and of reviewing price policies of charcoal. Alternative methods of fire protection such as cultivation along firebreaks, controlled burning and granting of forest exploitation rights to private companies or local groups also deserve further investigation.

The Bhorletar (Nepal) project appears sustainable since the local population has a vital stake in it and the technology is suited to local conditions. The peasants are capable of maintaining the canals and financing their upkeep without government subsidies. The financial benefits that the peasants derive are high enough to envisage a system of private funding for the upkeep of the infrastructures. The legislation on decentralization provides for establishing such a system for the upkeep of all the irrigation schemes in Nepal. The village councils will fix the amount of the tax on the use of the infrastructures to finance their maintenance. By and large, the project has fulfilled the expectations of its designers since most of the wages paid have gone to the poorest people in the area. However, if no corrective measures are taken, inequality in the distribution of income is likely to increase because of the initial inequality in the distribution of land, with a greater proportion of the benefits going to the richest peasants in the area at the expense of the poorest.

The Mto wa Mbu project (1,300 hectares at full development) in the United Republic of Tanzania is intended to meet the needs of several villages. Although the construction methods are simple, the management and running of such a complex system clearly exceeds the capacities of the local population and requires the presence on site of qualified personnel. The lack of consultation at the design stage was one of the major reasons for this unsatisfactory result. Furthermore, inadequate field drainage structures may lead to increased salinity and may seriously compromise the expected benefits. However, on the condition that these problems are resolved, the irrigation projects, in particular at Bhorletar, seem so profitable that private funding might even be envisaged if people holding capital were prepared to invest. Moreover, even if these projects are financed by the Government, the peasants should have few problems, from a purely financial point of view, in taking charge of the running and upkeep of the infrastructures.

REPLICABILITY

Replicating a programme on a larger scale depends not only on the degree of success achieved in sustaining an SPWP but also on external factors, such as the political determination of the authorities and national managerial capacity. Both these factors are closely linked to the question of resources since political will (influenced by the economic results of the project) means regularly earmarking national funds for financing the programmes and making available human resources (in the form of competent and motivated national counterparts) with a view eventually to replacing technical assistance.

That being said, let us examine briefly the possibilities of replicating the SPWP projects considered here. In Burundi and Rwanda there are no plans at the moment to diversify the sources of funding (bilateral or development banks), for which the support of the Government would of course be indispensable. Only such a diversification would guarantee the durability of a national SPWP structure capable of filling the gap left by technical assistance and presenting projects to potential donors. In the event of technical assistance coming to an end, the competent ministry would terminate the activities of the SPWP unit which, in its eyes, duplicates the work of existing institutions or competes with them. Only the communes, if they had the means, would be interested in a decentralization of powers, which, at the local level, are not yet very effective or are only fragmentary. The communes would not be capable of envisaging an endogenous effort using their own resources unless they made production and employment the prime targets.

In Burundi the SPWP has been confronted with technical and political misgivings about the continuity of the programme as originally planned. The Government did not appear to be converted to a multi-sectoral approach and the works did not produce convincing results, particularly those intended to increase production. It nevertheless retained a functional interest in the SPWP unit, which served only for afforestation and rural road construction works in the enlarged phase. For its part, the Rwanda Government, though won over to the SPWP formula, has not been convinced to the extent of envisaging a country-wide replication despite an estimated 21.3 per cent EIRR on afforestation. The partners at the commune and prefecture levels are enthusiastic, but they have few means and skills at their disposal. A multi-purpose and country-wide SPWP organization is scarcely conceivable, particularly because of the strong presence of aid furnished by non-governmental organizations, whose structures could prove to be more flexible and better adapted in the field than those of the SPWP, and the opposition of other technical services, owing to the duplication of posts.

In Mali, the principal long-term objective of the protection and rehabilitation of natural forests is taken to be the generation of productive employment. Conservation and protection of environment are taken to be important but secondary objectives. The project has successfully demonstrated the possibility of implementing medium-sized forestry protection/restoration activities on a local resource-intensive basis. Replanting with labour-based methods subsequent to complete clearing was found to be significantly cheaper than equipment-based methods.[8] There are also further indications that lessons learned from the project are applied in the design of similar projects and that local resource-intensive methods are more widely used than before, in part also as a result of training courses held for field staff of the Forestry Department. Wider application of the principles and methods is, however, constrained by a low return on investment. Replicability, for that reason and because financing of maintenance between the fifth and fifteenth years is far from being assured, remains doubtful.

In Nepal, the multiplication of projects of the Bhorletar type on a country-wide scale is possible from both the technical and the administrative points of view, since this type of project is similar to those drawn up and carried out by the Department of Irrigation. Furthermore, these projects are viable in most cases (with an EIRR of about 15 per cent). Nevertheless, there is no multi-sectoral approach or extension of the SPWP on a wider scale and there is a lack of political support at the moment: the Government prefers that the major projects be funded by loans or external donations. If it were to secure the agreement of the Government for such a programme on a country-wide scale, the Agricultural Development Bank of Nepal could well finance projects of the Bhorletar type.

In the United Republic of Tanzania there are few irrigation projects of this type since the Government does not yet see their social or technical advantages. Moreover, it considers that this type of project is too costly to be developed on a larger scale although its profitability has been demonstrated, provided complementary infrastructures, upkeep and market outlets are ensured. In the light of these results, ILO technical advisers are endeavouring at the moment to convince the Government that it should expand the programme, subject to the national capacity to administer it being greatly increased. At the local level, few civil engineers have the necessary experience to complete such projects successfully.

Even where the initial political impetus has been given, the projects, more often than not, have proved successful because of the direct intervention of ILO technical assistance and the efforts of national counterparts who derive some motivation from their association with the project, either financial or in terms of career prospects. The whole point of the pilot phase is to demonstrate the effectiveness of its approach to the Government, and it can be assumed that the latter will base its judgement on the results of this phase where the aim is to ascertain whether there are good possibilities for following up the project. During the preparation of most pilot projects, direct impact and institutional support objectives have often been superimposed without always bothering to determine whether, in the specific circumstances, they were compatible. In most cases, concern about meeting delivery targets, both in terms of infrastructure built and budgetary disbursements, took precedence over the long-term objectives. Experts frequently are faced with a programme that receives only a minor part of its financing from counterpart sources, apart, of course, from the contribution of the beneficiary populations, through their labour, and local resources. In these conditions the expert becomes less an adviser than a simple implementor, with the institutional support provided to the Government being reduced more often than not to financial inputs in the form of salary support, running costs, various allowances etc., designed to oil the administrative wheels.

This produces a paradoxical situation where, on the one hand, the national institutional structures function because they receive external resources and, on the other, the dependence thus created reduces the possibilities of replication on a larger scale. Moreover, as matters now stand, the relationship between the expert and his counterpart, according to our experience, is seldom propitious for achieving the hoped-for results in terms of transfer of responsibilities and powers. This is due to the sometimes injudicious choice of the national counterparts by the Government, and of experts by ILO, or to frequent changes in appointments that do not give the counterparts sufficient time to acquire the skills needed eventually to replace the technical assistance team. By skills we do not necessarily mean technical knowledge but rather organizational and management capacities that are lacking, if only because the time factor, at least for the productive infrastructures, is appraised differently by each of the parties involved. These include the technical assistance team, national counterparts or Government, local communities and peasants. All of this leads to errors in planning and to misunderstandings.

In view of the problems involved in reinforcing independent institutional structures, most SPWPs increasingly fall back on the direct impact objective to the detriment of institutional support objectives. As a result of the experiments described here, the aspirations of SPWPs have inevitably become much more modest and are now limited to taking the necessary steps to ensure that the works are carried out by local resource-intensive methods, are of good quality and are maintained and utilized by the beneficiary populations.

Conclusions

In this paper an attempt has been made to take stock of the main results obtained in designing, implementing and operating local resource-intensive development projects. From this review, there is little doubt that, at least for the projects examined here:

(a) A notable part of local resource development was addressed to strengthening local institutions. Successful SPWP projects made effective use of local resources by encouraging bottom-up planning and implementation with the co-operation of recipients, and by stimulating outside funding and technical support on the basis of local initiatives;

(b) Where there was little prior experience in using local

resources, including labour-intensive techniques, it was necessary to start small and gradually increase the scope of projects as local institutional capacity was being built up;

(c) Prospects for project sustainability and replicability were increased when local resources were used and developed;

(d) Use of local resources could be economically efficient, although the notion for efficiency should be reconsidered for SPWP-type slow-yielding projects.

The initial choice of target groups and areas as well as adequate structures to ensure the proper functioning of the SPWP-type projects is decisive since their duration is insufficient to generate their own momentum. Too much stress cannot be laid on the need to devote enough time to their preparation: the choice of personnel, infrastructures and sites, and precise identification of the potential beneficiaries. Despite the considerable experience now amassed by SPWPs, the diversity of the national and regional contexts requires that, for each new project, detailed preliminary studies be carried out. There is no universal formula for mobilizing and providing incentives to local people during the construction of the infrastructures. This is all the more true when it comes to handing over to the beneficiaries responsibilities such as organization, management, maintenance and additional investment.

Ideally, what should be done is to launch an SPWP project only when sufficiently detailed information is available to obtain funding for a preparatory assistance project for a period of approximately one year in order to carry out more in-depth studies, to link up with a simple institutional structure within a single technical ministry, to plan projects in collaboration with future beneficiaries and to carry out small-scale and inexpensive works in order to try out various technical alternatives. In addition, the project should include various guarantees relating to land ownership and organizational matters to permit the local people to take charge of the infrastructure, and should anticipate development possibilities. From this point of view, the technology used to carry out the works should be harmonious with those that will be used by villagers to maintain them so that maintenance costs match the capacities of the village or commune.

While, on the whole, the time needed to construct the infrastructures was compatible with the three or so years a pilot project lasts, it appears very difficult in such a short time to ensure both the active participation of the populations concerned and the creation of the human and organizational resources needed for management and above all for the replication of the infrastructures. For this reason it would be advantageous if, during the pilot phase, which would follow a year of study and testing, the SPWP were to concentrate on the direct impact on the target groups, improving their employment situation and living standards and demonstrating the viability of local resource-intensive techniques. Institutional support objectives, therefore, would be carefully limited during the pilot phase to strengthening local capacities and, at the national level, to making sure appropriate co-ordinating mechanisms exist.

An enlarged phase would be mounted only when the grass-roots institutional structure needed to foster the use of locally supported techniques had been created. This phase would then give priority to institutional development aimed towards both the continuing development of project sustainability and replicability at the local level and institutional support at the national level. The staggering of objectives over time would enable the experts to liberate themselves to a certain extent from the time-consuming management functions inherent in all large-scale direct support infrastructure projects. Thus, through the experience acquired during the pilot phase, they could provide more support for the national technical services in favouring the use of local resource-intensive methods in the context of these services' regular programmes.

In the long run, the institutionalization of the SPWP approach and its structural integration into national development policy are vital elements in judging the success or failure of the projects. The direct construction by an SPWP of some infrastructures using low capital inputs is not in itself a sufficient justification, if only because SPWPs do not have a monopoly on this type of approach. Beginning with the mobilization of local resources, most of the non-governmental organizations, and some other aid agencies as well, encourage local resource-intensive methods on work sites. The specific goals of SPWPs in this enlarged phase would therefore be to ensure technical credibility, to specify the capacities and limits of this approach and to persuade the local and national authorities to establish a permanent set-up responsible for promoting and supervising these works within the context of the normal investment programmes of the beneficiary Governments.

These pilot schemes are in fact demonstration projects of an experimental nature. Therefore, a modest or uncertain profitability of a planned scheme should not necessarily imply that future funding will be jeopardized. Although SPWP projects must be profitable to be replicable, profitability is by no means sufficient in itself since actual replication depends largely on political will and consistent planning at the local, regional and national levels. What is more, the classical notion of profitability faces certain limitations for SPWP-type projects which take time to mature and produce long-term, and often intangible, benefits. Conventional project appraisal techniques assume a specific project life and discount future benefits using a discount rate often in excess of 10 per cent. Thus, they tend heavily to discount long-term benefits such as environmental improvements from afforestation and soil conservation, or the gradual build-up of institutions leading to a sustainable and replicable development activity. Over-preoccupation with internal rates of return tends to

211

favour quick-yielding projects and place a premium on techniques that can produce benefits early in the project rather than later on. Hence, the feasibility of such slow-maturing projects depends intrinsically on sustained interests by users, appropriate extension services and long-term upkeep. The notion of efficiency goes beyond the conventional notion of cost-efficiency, which remains more appropriate for equipment-intensive, quick-yielding projects.

To conclude, it seems obvious that SPWP-type projects, intended to satisfy the majority of the rural population's basic needs in the long run, should receive the highest political, hence financial, priority from Governments conscious of the aspirations of the poorest sections of their rural populations, particularly landless workers, small farmers and women. However, in actual fact, few such projects are being implemented on an annual basis and only a tiny fraction of them can be considered sustainable, which leads to an alarmingly low impact on the socio-economic environment on a national scale. Since sustainability is a necessary condition for replicability, we are far from the massive effort so badly needed to reverse the dramatic rise in rural poverty, urban underemployment and unemployment, inequality of incomes and wealth, and foreign indebtedness in most least developed countries. To move one step in the right direction, a co-ordinated effort should be made at three different levels in order to achieve a better match between good projects and the ample funding available. At the project level, criteria should be developed for combining sustainability objectives (self-reliance, self-management and organization of target groups) with short-term production and employment creation objectives to allow better appraisal of projects with long-term objectives. At the national level, a synergy of international aid and executive agencies is required in order to siphon financial flows into well designed projects, particularly those favouring the use of local resources and the direct involvement of rural communities. And last, international aid, particularly bilateral aid, should tone down its politico-economic egocentricity (which in the present context takes the form of selling or granting expensive equipment or plant ill suited to the setting) and restructure its collaboration in a manner more harmonious to local conditions and constraints.

ACKNOWLEDGEMENTS

*This paper is largely inspired by – and updates – an article (Gaude *et al*, 1987). Reference is also made to S. Hertel *et al* (1987) and ILO (1987). The authors are indebted to H. Watzlawick, P. Egger, J. Majeres, S. Hertel, J. Payen and P. Poschen from the ILO, and B. Martens and M. van Imschoot, ILO Consultants, for their helpful comments on an earlier draft.

[1] In fact, when the work is being carried out by labour-intensive methods largely unfamiliar to technical services and the workers, the projects are sometimes obliged to move ahead slowly; hence, because of the high cost of technical assistance, these works can prove more expensive than when carried out under state or local government control. However, it is a mistake to assume that the projects are more permanent if they are carried out by a large number of workers rather than by means of heavy machinery. Once they have reached cruising speed, these labour-intensive works are, in practice, often completed sooner than those carried out using capital-intensive methods because of the inherent delays in working with heavier equipment in developing countries (breakdowns, lack of spare parts, lack of qualified mechanics etc.).

[2] There have been attempts to make some comparisons in the field of costs between various projects, but with limited success. The technical ministries responsible for supervising the projects do not have global data since they have neither the time nor the means to collect them and because the frequently fragmentary and irregular information sent to them from the projects is not at all comparable. In fact, the methods of presenting and breaking down costs are almost never spelled out.

[3] Since the launching of SPWPs, total investment in forestry activities has risen to $US 8.7 million, or only 12 per cent of total investment. In view of the enormous need for afforestation works and soil protection, the proportion should be increased considerably in future programmes.

[4] Corresponding unit costs in Burkina Faso amount to $US 1,060, including the first four-year maintenance costs (see Kapp, 1987); another study (United States Agency for International Development, 1982) provides unit costs in the range of $US 680-1,100 (including the first two-year maintenance costs) in the Sahelian region. These two studies do not refer specifically to labour-intensive methods, which tends to explain the higher unit costs observed as compared to those estimated in SPWP projects in Mali, and particularly in Burundi and Rwanda.

[5] The project was evaluated in July 1987 and reassessed in February 1988 (ILO, 1987b; Payen and van Imschoot, 1988).

[6] In fact, although the forestry codes clearly define the criteria for the respective classification of communal and state land, no classification or actual demarcation has been made. Communes that are prepared to make the necessary effort, jointly with external financial support, to bring in considerable returns in the long run, quite justifiably make such an official demarcation a pre-condition for their participation in the maintenance activities.

[7] This is mainly due to the fact that the long-term economic effects are far greater than the immediate effects of the project. Even a large variation in the employment/materials ratio, in a range of efficient operations, has only limited effects on the long-term benefits.

[8] A case study undertaken in Mali concluded that labour-intensive plantings are between 30 and 50 per cent less expensive and use 13 times more labour than capital-intensive plantings (Pletscher, 1984).

REFERENCES

Daniel, P., R. H. Green and M. Lipton (1985). A strategy for the rural poor. *Journal of Development Planning*, No. 15, pp. 113-136. United Nations publication, Sales No. E. 85.II.A.6.

Gaude, J. and others (1987). Rural development and labour-intensive schemes: impact study of some pilot programmes. *International Labour Review*, vol. 126, No. 4 (July-August), pp. 423-446.

Gaude, J., N. Phan-Thuy and C. van Kempen (1984). Evaluation of special public works programmes: some policy conclusions. *International Labour Review*, vol. 123, No. 2 (March-April), pp. 203-219.

Griffin, K. and R. Ray (1985). Problems of agricultural development in Socialist Ethiopia: an overview and a suggested survey. *The Journal of Peasant Studies,* vol. 13, No. 1 (October).

Griffin, K. and J. James (1981). *The Transition to Egalitarian Development— Economic Policies for Structural Change in the Third World.* London: The Macmillan Press Ltd.

Guichaoua, A. (1987). Paysans et Investissement-Travail au Burundi et au Rwanda. Geneva. International Labour Office.

Guichaoua, A. and C. Thérond (1984). Entretien et Mise en Valeur des Infrastructures Réalisées dans la Province de Muramvya—Burundi. Geneva: International Labour Office (April).

Hertel, S. and others (1987). Promoting and sustaining the use of local resources in development projects. Washington, D.C.: World Bank Transportation Department, in collaboration with ILO (provisional draft).

International Labour Organisation (1987a). Review of SPWP forestry and soil conservation activities. Item 4 of the agenda for the Ninth Joint Meeting for Support to Special Public Works Programmes. Geneva.

———— (1987b). Principal Findings and Recommendations of the Joint Donor Evaluation of the Tanzania Labour-intensive Public Works Programme. Geneva.

Kapp, G. (1987). Agroforstliche Landnutzung in der Sahel-Sudanzone (Agro-forestry land use in the Sudan-Sahelian region). Munich: Weltforum Verlag, GTZ.

Martens, B. (1988a). *Sustainability of Economic Development through Irrigation Projects: Case Studies in Nepal and Tanzania.* Geneva: International Labour Office.

———— (1988b). Modelling the impact of irrigation projects. An experimental micro-macro approach to the Bhorletar project—Nepal. World employment research working paper No. 26. Geneva: International Labour Office.

Payen, J. and M. van Imschoot (1988). Technical assessment of Tanzania LIPWP irrigation projects. Geneva: International Labour Office (internal report).

Peek, P. (1988). How equitable are rural development projects? *International Labour Review,* vol. 127, No. 1, pp. 73-89.

Pletscher, R. (1984). Création d'emplois, mécanisation des travaux et problèmes de formation dans l'économie forestière du Mali. Geneva: International Labour Office.

Tiffen, M. (1987). Dethroning the internal rate of return: the evidence from irrigation projects. *Development Policy Review,* No. 5, pp. 361-377.

United States Agency for International Development (1982). Proceedings of Workshop on Energy, Forestry and Environment. Bureau for Africa.

World Bank (1987). World Bank experience with rural development 1965-1986. Review draft report No. 6883 (July). Washington, D.C.: Operations Evaluation Department.

9

PARTICIPATORY DEVELOPMENT: SOME PERSPECTIVES FROM GRASS-ROOTS EXPERIENCES

*Dharam Ghai**

CONTENTS

Introduction

In recent years, especially since the early 1970s, there has been an increasing interest in participatory approaches to development.[1] This interest is manifested at both the national and the international level and appears to be shared by individuals and institutions of widely divergent ideologies and backgrounds. At the international level, most multilateral and bilateral agencies have recognized the importance of participation both as a means and as an objective of development. Likewise, national plans in many countries pay a great deal of attention to the need for a participatory pattern of development. However, as tends to happen in situations of this sort, the growing consensus owes much to certain ambiguities in the concept of participation. Different authors and organizations give different interpretations to this concept. Often, these differences are a reflection of differences concerning the concept of development itself.

The notion of participation may be examined from different levels and perspectives. One distinction relates to participation in the public domain, the workplace and at home. The first aspect refers to all matters discussed and decided in public institutions—local organizations, national Governments, parliaments, parties etc. The

---

*Director, United Nations Research Institute for Social Development.

215

second concerns factories, offices, plantations, farms and other workplaces. The third dimension refers to family relations and work at home. The latter is largely neglected in most discussions on participation. Yet, in relation to the time spent in different places, "home democracy" is at least as important as "work democracy" and is a crucial determinant of the welfare of some members of the family, especially the women and children.

A different but slightly overlapping distinction concerns participation at the local, national and international levels. Although there has been a good deal of discussion of participation promotion at the local and national levels, much less attention has been given to the implications of a participatory approach at the global level.[2] In view of the linkages and interrelationships between developments at these different levels, a satisfactory analysis of participation should be based on a recognition of interdependence among the different levels of aggregation. This is, however, a complex and daunting undertaking. This article has a more limited and modest purpose: to shed some light on the participatory approach to development through a study of selected grass-roots initiatives in a few Asian and African countries. This is done in the belief that these experiences yield fresh and exciting perspectives on the meaning and processes of development and contain within them elements of a self-reliant, egalitarian and participatory approach to development. They, therefore, offer a rich field from which to draw lessons with a view to strengthening the quality of development efforts in rich and poor countries alike.

In the light of the preceding remarks, the paper begins with a discussion of some alternative concepts of development and participation. This is followed by a brief description of nine grass-roots initiatives whose experiences are used subsequently to illustrate some aspects of participatory approaches to development. The paper then examines the themes of participatory processes and institutional framework, and of self-reliance and the role of outside assistance. There is then an analysis of these initiatives as economic enterprises, agencies of social reform and schools for democracy. The concluding section focuses on their strengths and limitations as alternative development models. The gender issues are discussed in various sections of the paper.

Alternative concepts of development and participation

The notion of development is an ambiguous one and is subject to different interpretations.[3] We may distinguish three interpretations. First, development is often treated synonymously with economic growth and is thus interpreted to mean increases in labour productivity, declining share of agriculture in total output, technological progress, and industrialization with the consequent shift of population to urban areas. While these structural changes are generally associated with economic growth, equating them with development shifts the focus to economic aggregates and away from living standards and human dimensions.

The second interpretation of development seeks to remedy this deficiency by concentrating on such indices of living standards as poverty, income distribution, nutrition, infant mortality, life expectancy, literacy, education, access to employment, housing, water supply and similar amenities. This way of looking at development brings it closer to the common-sense view and endows it with greater human reality. Nevertheless, the emphasis continues to be on economic and social indicators and individual human being and social groups tend to be off-stage passively supplied with goods, services and materials.

In contrast, the third view of development puts the spotlight on human potential and capabilities in the context of relations with other social groups. According to this view, development is seen in such terms as greater understanding of social, economic and political processes, enhanced competence to analyze and solve problems of day-to-day living, expansion of manual skills and greater control over economic resources, restoration of human dignity and self-respect, and interaction with other social groups on a basis of mutual respect and equality. This notion of development does not neglect material deprivation and poverty but the focus shifts to realization of human potential expressed in such terms as human dignity, self-respect, social emancipation, and enhancement of moral, intellectual and technical capabilities.[4]

The three ways of looking at development are not, of course, mutually exclusive. Indeed, the optimal pattern of development should embody elements of all three: the growth of human capabilities and potential must be accompanied by progressive reduction of material deprivation and social inequalities which, in turn, should flow from structural change and modernization of the economy. But in practice, these aspects of development seldom evolve in a harmonious relationship and typically emphasis on one or the other would have different implications for organization of economic activities, patterns of investment and design of programmes and projects.

As with development, the concept of participation is also riddled with ambiguities. Once again, it may be useful to distinguish between three different interpretations. One common usage of the term refers to "mobilization" of people to undertake social and economic development projects. Typically, the projects are conceived and designed from above and the people are "mobilized" to implement them. Their participation thus consists of their contribution of labour and materials, either free or paid for by the authorities. The projects, which generally tend to be of an infrastructural nature, are meant to benefit the rural poor. But in many cases the benefit may accrue mainly in the form of employment generated during the construction phase. The distribution of the benefits from the assets and facilities created would depend upon a variety of factors such as the patterns of ownership of productive resources, the distribution of political power among social groups and the nature of the project. At their best, such projects may result in a widespread diffusion of benefits both in the construction and the subsequent phase. At worst, "participation" may result in free provision of labour and materials by the poor to create facilities that benefit primarily the affluent groups.

The second interpretation equates participation with decentralization in governmental machinery or in related organizations. Resources and decision-making powers may be transferred to lower level organs, such as local officials, elected bodies at the village or county level or local project committees.[5] While this may make possible local-level decisions on the choice, design and implementation of development activities, there is no presumption that this need imply any meaningful participation by the rural or urban masses. Indeed, the distribution of political and economic power at local levels in many countries is such that decentralization may well result in allocation of resources and choice of development activities that are less beneficial to the poor than when such decisions are taken at the central level.

The third view of participation regards it as a process of empowerment of the deprived and the excluded (Gran, 1983; Oakley, 1987; Oakley and Marsden, 1984). This view is based on the recognition of differences in political and economic power among different social groups and classes. Participation is interpreted to imply a strengthening of the power of the deprived masses. Its three main elements have been defined as "the sharing of power and scarce resources, deliberate efforts by social groups to control their own destinies and improve their living conditions, and opening up of opportunities from below" (Dillon and Steifel, 1987). Participation in this sense necessitates the creation of organizations of the poor which are democratic, independent and self-reliant (Advisory Committee on Rural Development, 1979; International Labour Organisation, 1976).

One facet of empowerment is thus the pooling of resources to achieve collective strength and countervailing power. Another is the enhancement of manual and technical skills, planning and managerial competence and analytical and reflective abilities of the people. It is at this point that the concept of participation as empowerment comes close to the notion of development as fulfilment of human potentials and capabilities. This view of participation and development may best be illustrated through the experience of some grassroots initiatives, to which we now turn.

218

Some grass-roots participatory initiatives

In recent years, there has been a huge expansion of small-scale development projects focusing on the rural and the urban poor and involving some sort of group action (Commission on the Churches' Participation in Development, 1981; Economic Commission for Latin America, 1973; Food and Agriculture Organization of the United Nations, 1979; Hirschman, 1984; United Nations, 1981; Wasserstrom, 1985; World Health Organization, 1982). These projects show a great deal of variation with respect to activities, organizational framework, financing arrangements, the sponsoring agencies, the role of outside assistance and the nature and extent of popular participation. They range from outstanding to disastrous judged by the criterion of participation as empowerment of the people. In this section we give a brief description of nine grass-roots experiences which, while displaying a great deal of diversity in respect of some aspects mentioned above, nevertheless share some characteristics as participatory initiatives. The nine initiatives considered here are the Grameen Bank (GB), the Small Farmers' Development Project (SFDP), the Self-employed Women's Association (SEWA), the Working Women's Forum (WWF), Sarilakas, Participatory Institute for Development Alternatives (PIDA), Se servir de la saison sèche en savane et au Sahel (Six-S), the Organization of Rural Associations for Progress (ORAP) and Action pour le développement rural intégré (ADRI).

Although they have several points in common, it is convenient to group them into four categories in accordance with their central characteristics. The first category, comprising GB and SFDP, illustrates innovative programmes to extend credit to the rural poor. SEWA and WWF represent pioneering efforts to organize poor women working in urban slums as vendors, home-based workers and casual labourers into trade-union type associations. The third category, illustrated by Sarilakas and PIDA, comprises initiatives to promote peasant groups and rural workers' organizations to struggle for their rights and to undertake collective initiatives to appropriate a larger share of the surplus generated by their economic activities. The fourth category, comprising Six-S, ORAP and ADRI, represents efforts to promote social and economic development through mobilization and pooling of labour and other resources, drawing inspiration from traditional self-help and mutual aid groups.

PROMOTING PARTICIPATION THROUGH CREDIT PROGRAMMES

The Grameen Bank was started in 1976 by a professor of economics at Chittagong University in Thailand as an experiment to provide credit to poor landless men and women in rural areas (Fuglesang and Chandler, 1986; Chai, 1984a; Hossain, 1984; Yunus,

1982). Initially supported by funds from some commercial and nationalized banks, it became an independent bank in 1983. At present, the Government has 25 per cent of the initial paid-up share of the capital with the remaining 75 per cent being held by borrowers of the bank. The GB, has received funds from a number of donor agencies, including the International Fund for Agricultural Development (IFAD), the Asian Development Bank and the Ford Foundation. Membership is restricted to the poor, defined by a net-worth criterion.

Members organize themselves into groups of five persons and 10 such groups constitute a circle. The loans, which are quite modest in size, are given for a one-year period and the principal is repaid in weekly instalments over this period. The banking operations take place in weekly meetings held in the locality of the groups. The loans are granted for a wide range of economic activities such as trading, transport, processing, handicraft, cattle raising and simple manufacturing. There are separate groups for men and women, with the latter now accounting for two thirds of the total. The bank has experienced a rapid expansion in its activities, with the number of members increasing from fewer than 15,000 in 1980 to nearly 250,000 in 1988. The members have established a variety of social programmes such as family planning, schools, nutrition, sports and music, and have sought to promote social reforms.

The SFDP in Nepal is also a credit programme for the rural poor but, unlike the GB, it extends loans to small and marginal farmers (Agricultural Projects Services Centre, 1979; Ghai, 1984b; Ghai and others, 1984; Mosley and Prasad Dahal, 1987; Rokaya, 1983). It evolved from a pilot project launched in 1975 by the Agricultural Development Bank of Nepal (ADB/N) with financial and technical support from the Food and Agriculture Organization of the United Nations (FAO) and the United Nations Development Programme (UNDP). The basic objectives of the project were to increase the incomes and standard of living of the rural poor, promote participation and self-reliance and adapt local delivery mechanisms of government agencies to the needs of the rural poor. The approach adopted was to encourage the rural poor to organize themselves in small groups with the assistance of a group organizer to receive credit for individual and group activities. The credit was provided on a group guarantee basis without any collateral.

Membership has expanded from about 440 in 1976 to about 25,000 in 1984 and perhaps 50,000 in 1988. It has attracted funds from a number of bilateral and multilateral sources. The programme comprises a wide range of economic, social and community activities, which are supported by an expanding training component. Economic activities include cultivation, livestock, horticulture, irrigation, cottage and rural industries and marketing. Social activities comprise health, education, family planning, maternal welfare, child care and sanitation. Community projects comprise construction of roads, bridges, schools, meeting halls, water facilities, irrigation, biogas and social forestry. The bulk of economic activities are undertaken on an individual basis with, however, growing importance of group ownership and management in cottage industries, orchards and irrigation.

ORGANIZING SELF-EMPLOYED POOR WOMEN IN URBAN SLUMS

SEWA represents a pioneering effort to organize self-employed poor women in urban slums in Gujerat, India, into a trade-union type organization (Self-employed Women's Association, 1984). Until they formed a trade union in 1972, self-employed women were not recognized as workers by legislation or by society. Thus, their struggle related as much to their desire for recognition as legitimate workers as to improvements in income and working conditions. The initiative in forming SEWA was taken by an experienced woman trade unionist who had previously worked with a long-established textile labour association. Its membership is drawn from three categories of women workers: petty vendors and hawkers, home-based producers, and providers of casual labour and services. Started primarily as a movement for poor urban women, it has now spread to include women agricultural labourers and home-based workers in rural areas.

As a trade union for self-employed women, SEWA has worked to secure higher wages for casual workers, for those on contract work such as home-based workers and for suppliers of services such as cleaning and laundering. There has been a gradual extension to such workers of the protection and benefits provided by labour legislation to organized workers in modern enterprises. It has also instituted a credit scheme for vendors, hawkers and home-based workers to finance working capital and to purchase raw materials and tools. Credit was originally arranged through nationalized commercial banks but soon the women decided to form their own savings and credit co-operative. The co-operative has expanded rapidly in terms of shareholders, deposits and loans.

Further benefits have accrued to vendors, craftswomen and home-based workers through the formation of producers' co-operatives for vegetable and fruit vendors, bamboo workers, hand-block printers, spinning-wheel and handloom operators and dairy workers. The economic capacity of the members has also been enhanced by the provision of training courses in a wide range of skills such as bamboo work, block printing, plumbing, carpentry, radio repairs, simple accounting and management. Finally, SEWA has sought to solve some of the urgent social problems of its members through a maternal protection scheme, widow's benefits, child care and training of midwives.

The Working Women's Forum was started in 1978 at the

initiative of a woman activist with considerable previous experience in social and political work. It operates in the southern Indian States of Tamil Nadu, Andhra Pradesh and Karnataka (Arunachalam, 1983; Azad, 1985; Chambers, 1985; Chen, 1982). Its membership of nearly 50,000 is drawn largely from poor urban women but there is also increasing representation from rural areas. It covers similar occupational groups as SEWA such as street hawkers, craft producers, home-based workers, and fisherwomen and dairy workers in rural areas. It also arranges loans for members from the commercial banks and increasingly from the Working Women's Co-operative Society, the savings and credit scheme set up by the members themselves. The repayment rates are above 95 per cent.

The WWF has also initiated a wide range of training schemes. It has organized extensive family planning and public health programmes, group insurance schemes, night schools for working children, campaigns against caste prejudice and discrimination, petty harassment and bureaucratic abuse suffered by its members, and educational sessions on workers' rights and minimum wages.

PROMOTING PEASANT GROUPS AND ORGANIZATIONS OF RURAL WORKERS

Sarilakas in the Philippines evolved out of an attempt by the Rural Workers' Office, Ministry of Labour, to organize rural workers. The initial attempts to promote rural workers' organizations suffered a series of setbacks owing to inadequate preparation, faulty approach and excessive economic expectations engendered by the "facilitators" (Rahman, 1983). With assistance from the International Labour Organisation (ILO) and exposure of the organizers to participatory initiatives in Sri Lanka, India and Bangladesh, the project adopted a different approach, with emphasis on group discussions and analysis of their socio-economic situation, reflection on the sources of their impoverishment and identification of feasible initiatives in a self-reliant framework. The new approach proved more successful in establishing durable participatory organizations in several villages resulting in a series of different initiatives such as the institution of collective savings schemes for purchase of inputs by marginal farmers, joint ownership and operation of agricultural machinery and rice mills, rehabilitation of irrigation facilities, enforcement of legislation on change from sharecropping tenancy to fixed-rent liability, protection of the fishing rights of small fishermen, land rights of sugar-cane growers etc.

PIDA in Sri Lanka was established in 1980 as a non-governmental organization for the promotion of grass-roots participatory groups. It is an action research collective with a membership of 15 or so animators working in 40 villages in various rural locations (Tilakaratna, 1985). It grew out of a UNDP-sponsored rural action research and training project initiated in 1978. Its main objective is to promote participatory and self-reliant organizations of the rural poor which in turn can become the main vehicle of their economic and social advance. The key role in this process is played by animators who encourage villagers with similar background to come together for informal discussion of their socio-economic situation, the problems they face and the steps they might take to improve their living standards and working conditions. After initiating the process of group discussion and reflection, the animator attempts progressively to reduce his or her role, leaving it to the villagers themselves to conduct their inquiries, form groups and take initiatives to strengthen their economic position.

The initiatives can take a variety of forms. Some groups focused their attention on possible savings from purchases of consumer goods in village stores. They expanded their activities to procure and distribute a wide range of basic consumer goods and start thrift and credit societies, thus evolving co-operatives of the rural poor. The groups, which started from the production front, cut down their cultivation costs through a series of collective efforts, used their spare time to cultivate a common plot of land as a means of increasing their collective fund, initiated action to develop irrigation facilities and diversify crop patterns, established links with banks and obtained bank credit by demonstrating their credit-worthiness, thus eliminating their dependence on usurer credit, and bargained for improved access to public services.

Some groups began activities in produce marketing. They devised collective marketing schemes, explored and discovered new market outlets, delinked from village traders and intermediaries and retrieved the surpluses hitherto extracted by them, stored a part of the crop to take advantage of better prices and increased the value of the produce by processing. In the case of wage labourers, attempts were made to check leakages from their income streams by forming informal co-operatives for consumer, credit and thrift activities, and to obtain access to land or other productive assets, thus switching over from the sale of labour to farming either on a part-time or full-time basis.

MOBILIZING RESOURCES THROUGH SELF-HELP AND CO-OPERATIVE EFFORTS

Six-S was started in 1974 in Burkina Faso at the initiative of a local agronomist working with some foreign volunteers. The original motive was to take advantage of the long dry period from October to May to undertake a series of self-help social and economic activities to improve the living standards of the rural people (Egger, 1987a; Rahman, 1988; Sawadogo and Ouedraogo, 1987). The practice until then had been for the young people to migrate to urban areas and to neighbouring countries in search of employment. One feature of this initiative was reliance on traditional Naam groups of mutual help and co-operation to promote a large-scale, self-help movement with numbers running into 200,000 and extension into other Sahelian countries such as Mali, Mauritania and Senegal.

The groups undertake a variety of income-generating, community and social activities. The first set includes vegetable gardening, stock farming, handicraft, millet mills, cereal banks, and production and sale of horse carts. Communal activities comprise construction of water dams and dikes, anti-erosion works, wells, afforestation etc., while social projects include rural pharmacies, primary health care, schools, theatres etc. Six-S provides credit to partially support such projects. Activities of communal benefit are subsidized through limited cash remuneration and food for work and free supply of the needed equipment. In turn, Six-S gets funds from member groups' contributions and external donors. All Six-S groups have a savings fund built with member subscriptions and receipts from income-generating activities.

There has been a rapid multiplication of groups in the region. The established groups assist new ones in a variety of ways. Farmer-technicians are employed by Six-S during the slack season to advise the groups and assist their activities. When some members of Six-S groups carry out an innovation or master a technique, they form a mobile school to transmit it to other groups. Thus, new ideas and innovations spread rapidly throughout the Six-S movement.

ORAP was started in 1981 by a group of concerned people in Matabeleland, Zimbabwe, to initiate a new approach to their development problems. It is essentially a support organization for self-reliant development in rural areas. Its first priority is to encourage and support autonomous organizations among rural people and to enhance their capability to analyse their own situation. (Chavunduka and others, 1985; Nyoni, 1986). As with Six-S, it also relied on traditional groups and practices of mutual help and co-operation. The basic units are village groups which federate into "umbrellas" and, higher up, to associations and finally to the Advisory Board of ORAP.

After a period of deliberation and analysis, the groups undertake a variety of economic and social activities, combining their skills and labour with material and financial assistance from external donors through ORAP. The activities include carpentry, netwire making, sewing, building, basketry, wood carving, livestock grazing, vegetable gardening, poultry-keeping, baking and grinding mills.

Considerable emphasis is put on training and development education activities. The prolonged drought in the region led ORAP to develop a food relief programme and subsequently to give priority to food production, with emphasis on recourse to traditional seeds and fertilizers, diversity of food produced, improved food storage and cereal banks in the villages and improved water storage and local irrigation schemes. Recently, new emphasis has been put on organizing activities at the family units—a collective of 5 to 10 families— to meet their immediate needs such as wells for drinking water, sanitary latrines, improved baths, improved kitchens, as well as cultivation, food production, harvesting and thrashing corn.

Another recent innovation has been the construction, on a self-help basis, of development centres. These are multipurpose centres for meetings, workshops, organization of training courses in various technical fields, such as bakery, building, blacksmithing and marketing outlets.

ADRI is an organization of peasant groups in Rwanda. It owes its origin to an initiative taken in 1979 by a local agronomist to undertake "animation" work with peasant women in the Kabaye district (Action pour le développement rural intégré, 1986; Egger, 1987b). As in Six-S and ORAP, the basis of organization was traditional groups of mutual help. Some other groups sprung up in the area leading to the formation of an inter-group organization, Impuzamiryango Tuzamuka Twese (ITT). Activities undertaken by the group include collective cultivation of cash crops, social forestry, grain storage, consumer stores, livestock rearing, furniture making, brick making, beer brewing and grain mills.

Dissatisfaction with the Banque Populaire led the peasant groups to form their own savings and credit society, the Caisse de Solidarité (Solidarity Bank). This society plays a particularly important role in the management of external funds for group activities. All the groups assume responsibility for these funds, which serve both as a guarantee to donors and to generate collective interest in the repayment of funds by each group. Several groups have evolved into multipurpose co-operatives covering farming, marketing, artisan production and collective savings schemes. In one area, several groups have come together to form a fund with contributions from peasants particularly at harvest time, in cash or kind. The fund serves as a social security scheme for members covering death, fire, natural disasters, accident, sickness and finance of secondary education.

ADRI was formed to stimulate the expansion of such peasant groups to all parts of the country. It is a development non-governmental organization which assists peasant groups and associations through animation work and exchange visits, promotion of a wider federation of associations and provision of direct support to base groups on funding and implementing collective social and economic projects.

Participatory processes and institutional framework

Contrasting conventional projects and participatory initiatives

A conventional development project is conceived and designed from outside by national and international experts, together with the paraphernalia of pre-feasibility and feasibility studies, appraisal reports, specification of inputs and outputs, calculation of internal rates and sophisticated cost-benefit analysis. The people for whom all this is supposed to be done exist only in the abstract as numbers whose output and productivity are to be enhanced and whose "needs" are to be satisfied. Their participation in the preparatory phase, if they are lucky, may, at best, consist of some hastily organized meetings with the experts and bureaucrats at which they are "briefed" about the objectives and activities of the planned projects. In the implementation phase they are expected to carry out their pre-assigned roles.

Participatory development is radically different in approach, methodology and operation. As implied earlier, its central concern is with the development of the moral, intellectual, technical and manual capabilities of individuals. A development project is, therefore, regarded as a process for the expansion of these capabilities. This implies that the initiative in establishing the activities must be taken by the people themselves who should also be firmly in charge of their implementation and evolution. This in turn calls for an entirely different methodology in initiating and sustaining development activities.

Social activists and leaders of grass-roots initiatives worldwide are working with many different approaches and methodologies for participation promotion. There is no single blueprint. Indeed, such a concept would be contradictory to the very spirit of participatory development whose central purpose is the awakening of people's dormant energies and the unleashing of their creative powers. The grass-roots experiences described in the preceding section likewise reveal the diversity of approaches to participation promotion. It may be useful to discuss separately two dimensions of this theme, namely, methodologies and institutional framework for participation promotion.

Methodologies for participation promotion

Whatever their differences, the nine experiences considered here have one aspect in common: the initiation of development activities is preceded by a preparatory phase involving interaction with and among the people concerned. The purpose, duration and intensity of

226

this interaction have tended to vary from one initiative to another. At one extreme, the interaction phase may consist only of understanding and accepting the basic objectives and operation of the project by the people before their enrolment as members. At the other extreme, this phase, extending over long periods, may involve intensive discussions and dialogue, analysis and reflection and conduct of field work and social inquiry, thus using the methodology of participation promotion associated with "conscientization" and "participatory action research".[6] Depending on its scope and intensity, the preparatory phase may serve to install discipline, build confidence, indoctrinate or socialize members to the underlying philosophy and objectives of the initiative, raise consciousness, develop critical and analytical abilities, and promote group solidarity and democratic practices. Furthermore, these processes of participation promotion are not considered one-time isolated events preceding the initiation of development activities, but rather an integral part of the style of work within the association.

The initial phase in the establishment of peasant groups in Rwanda consists of animation and conscientization (Action pour le développement rural intégré, 1986). It is only after this phase that the peasants decide to form associations. The process also generates the array of activities to be undertaken by the group. Likewise, the Six-S puts a great deal of emphasis on animation work and group meetings. The emerging pattern of activities is seen as a reflection of people's situation, knowledge, experiences, capabilities and wishes.[7] The WWF relies on spearhead teams and group organizers to initiate interaction with the potential members.

In ORAP, any material development work must be preceded and/or accompanied by continuous discussion and analysis of the reasons for undertaking a development activity. In principle, all groups must go through a discussion process to determine what their problems are, where they come from and how they can solve them. This approach is summarized graphically in the words of a member of a local group: "Before coming to ORAP, I didn't know how development started. Now I know that before development, there must be thoughts in mind" (Chavunduka and others, 1985).

SFDP and GB are first and foremost credit programmes. Before any activities are initiated, the group organizers in the former and bank workers in the latter undertake a socio–economic survey of the villages concerned. The target groups are then encouraged to come together for discussions among themselves and with the development workers. Out of this process emerge the groups which are the basic units around which the credit programme is organized. In GB, for example, the basic unit consists of a group of five landless persons. Before receiving loans, the groups go through an intensive instruction of one to two weeks on the philosophy, rules and procedures of the bank. The group members have to pass a test before they are granted recognition. During this test the members must satisfy the bank staff of their integrity and seriousness, understanding of the principles and procedures of the GB and ability to write their signatures.

The methodology of "conscientization" and "applied action research" is perhaps applied most systematically in the activities organized by PIDA. A brief illustration of the work of PIDA in a village may convey the flavour of its approach to participation promotion (Tilakaratna, 1984). In 1978, a four-member team of development workers visited a village to explore the possibility of initiating a grass-roots participatory development process. The first step was to make a preliminary study of the socio-economic conditions in the village. The workers visited all households and initiated discussions with the people individually, as well as in small informal groups, on the problems at the village level. The main poverty group was identified as betel producers. The development workers continued discussions about the source of their poverty. Soon, however, they reached the stage where further progress called for more information on production and marketing of betel than they possessed. Two village groups volunteered to undertake the investigations and collect information on the working of the betel industry—a women's group to examine production and a youth group to explore the marketing aspects.

This investigation enabled the peasants to see for the first time the reality of betel farming, in particular how an impoverishment process had been created by the loss of a sizeable economic surplus at the marketing stage to the village traders who in turn sold betel leaves to state exporting firms. A group of betel producers then met to explore alternative marketing possibilities. An action committee formed by the group spent two months visiting various traders in the vicinity and exporting firms. After a series of setbacks and negative responses, the committee found one exporting firm which was prepared to buy directly from them provided the sales were channelled through the registered village co-operative. This immediately resulted in a doubling of the prices received by peasants for their betel leaves and greater price stability. The group grew in number and the incomes of the members expanded threefold owing to better prices and higher production. Subsequently, they formed their own multipurpose co-operative.

The co-ordinator of PIDA has described the underlying approach of participatory development as follows:

"The central element of a participatory process was identified as conscientization which was seen as a process of liberating the creative initiatives of the people through a systematic process of investigation, reflection and analysis, undertaken by the people themselves. People begin to understand the social reality through a process of self-inquiry and analysis, and through such understanding, perceive self-possibilities for changing that reality . . .

Conscientization leads to self-organization by the people as a means of undertaking collective initiatives. Each action will be followed by reflection and analysis generating a process of praxis as a regular ongoing practice. These interactive elements . . . were seen as the heart and soul of a participatory process" (Tilakaratna, 1985).

A Sri Lankan peasant summed it all up in these simple words: "The rust in our brains is now removed" (Tilakaratna, 1985).

THE INSTITUTIONAL FRAMEWORK

While discussion, analysis and reflection constitute the methodology of participation promotion in most of the initiatives considered here, the institutional framework provides the vehicle for the practice of participation. As might be expected, there is a great deal of variation in the organizational arrangements devised by them to conduct their work. However, one common characteristic they share is that in all cases members are organized into base or primary groups. Participatory development is inconceivable in the absence of such groups. The process of conscientization presupposes the existence or creation of small groups with a homogeneous socio-economic background. Beyond that the organization of small farmers, rural workers and urban poor in groups serves a number of crucial functions. First, it provides a forum for dialogue, analysis and reflection, thereby contributing to the capacity of the members to understand and find solutions to their problems. Secondly, membership in a group reduces individual insecurity and dependence and builds confidence. This is a vital function especially in societies characterized by social oppression, economic polarization and status hierarchies. Thirdly, the groups provide a mechanism for discussion, choice and elaboration of social and economic activities to be undertaken on an individual or joint basis. Fourthly, they constitute appropriate structures for the launching, ownership, management and operation of some projects. Fifthly, the groups serve to increase the effectiveness of government social and economic services by acting as receiving mechanisms. Sixthly, the formation of groups enables the poor to transform their individual weaknesses into collective strength, thus enhancing their bargaining power *vis-à-vis* other economic groups and exerting countervailing pressure against local power structures.

The group structure of some of the initiatives discussed here illustrates these points. In the GB, groups and the centre hold weekly meetings for banking transactions as also for discussions on other social and economic activities. Although the loan is given to the individual and he or she has ultimate responsibility for it, it must be approved by the group chief and the centre chief. The groups, therefore, assume responsibility for its repayment. The choice of activity financed by the loan is left to the individual and the group. Group pressure plays an important role in ensuring the nearly perfect loan repayment record achieved by the bank. The group fund, consisting of personal savings and group tax for emergency and social security purposes, is operated by the groups. Joint enterprises such as shallow and deep tubwells, weaving and rice hullers are owned and managed at the level of individual groups, collection of groups, or centres. Construction, management and running of schools, community halls and other social activities would typically be organized at the level of individual or groups of several centres.

In the SFDP, the group plays a key role in investment decisions. The decisions on individual and joint loans are taken through group discussion and consensus, and the group provides the guarantee for the loan. The monthly meetings of the group also provide occasions for discussion and approval of annual and longer-term plans for social and economic activities.

In ORAP, the new emphasis is on base units comprising three to five families. A few of the family units come together to form production units. The activities to be undertaken emerge from discussions within these groups. Some of the projects are of a family nature such as cultivation and latrine and kitchen improvement, but others involve larger units such as irrigation, grain mills, food storage and community buildings. Mutual help and co-operation are organized through the family units or production groups. The Naam groups in the Six-S form the nucleus of a myriad of activities such as water catchment and storage schemes, reforestation, soil preservation, cereal banks, artisanal production and collective farming. They also operate credit and savings societies, provide guarantees for individual and collective loans, and organize a variety of welfare schemes and social activities. The peasant associations in ADRI constitute the core of the movement. A number of family, community and income-generating projects by peasant groups are gradually transforming themselves into multipurpose co-operatives.

The village groups promoted by PIDA and by Sarilakas seek to raise the living standards of their members through collective action designed to improve wages, secure access to land, reduce the burden of usury, and retain a larger share of surpluses through joint purchase, elimination of middlemen in marketing etc. In SEWA also exertion of pressure through collective power has been an important element in the benefits derived by its members. In addition to its function as a trade union of self-employed women workers, SEWA has organized members in co-operatives based on occupation. Social insurance, welfare and training programmes have also been organized.

While SEWA and WWF are exclusively women's organizations. GB and SFDP have separate groups for men and women, although SFDP also has a few mixed groups. In the other initiatives, on the other hand, while there may be some separate groups for men and women, the common pattern is to have mixed groups. This has served to break down sterotypes of gender roles and has promoted solidarity and co-operation between sexes and generations.

While participation of members in the activities of the organization through base groups is a feature common to all these grass-roots initiatives, there is a great deal of variation concerning higher-level entities. Sarilakas and PIDA essentially act as promoters of self-reliant participatory organizations of the rural poor. The organizations thus formed may co-operate in a variety of ways, including joint projects, exchange of visits, information etc. but so far no attempts have been made to federate them into regional or national associations, although federations have emerged at municipality levels and across villages in Sarilakas and PIDA respectively. The parent body of the SFDP is the Agricultural Development Bank, which does not have any representation from the small farmers in its policy-making organs. While the original intention was to encourage regional and national associations of SFDPs, this has not materialized, although individual groups co-operate in a variety of ways. Essentially, the same remarks apply to the GB with the crucial difference that now 75 per cent of the paid-up share capital belongs to members and the 12-member Board of Directors includes four persons, including (preferably) two women, elected by the borrower shareholders.

The other organizations have ascending layers of bodies with representatives chosen from lower-level entities. For instance, in ADRI, the peasant groups come together into regional associations which federate into a national organization. Likewise, the ORAP organizational structure moves up from village groups to "umbrellas" to associations and the Advisory Board. WWF and SEWA have representative or general assemblies at the apex. The higher-level bodies consist of representatives elected from the lower ones. Some activities and services may be carried out at higher levels, for example, the development centres in ORAP are operated at the level of associations and the Solidarity Bank in ADRI is run at the apex as are the savings and credit co-operatives run by SEWA and WWF. Thus, in all these cases the organizational structure provides for participation in decision-making by the rank-and-file members of the movement.

Self-reliance and the role of outsiders

These initiatives have a diversity of origins. SFDP, PIDA and Sarilakas originated as government programmes with the support of international agencies. But PIDA and Sarilakas moved away from their official links to convert themselves into development non-governmental organizations. SFDP continues to be run as an ADB project but the bank operates in an independent manner. Although

GB was started as an experiment by an academic, it has been converted into a bank with joint ownership by the Government and the borrowers. It is also run independently of the government ministries. All the other initiatives originated with concerned professionals and social activists independently of official agencies. It is noteworthy that the key figures in the initiation and consolidation of these initiatives were nationals of these countries. This is an aspect of self-reliance which already sets them off from the great majority of development projects which are often conceived and designed by outsiders.

A key characteristic of these initiatives, both in their establishment and subsequent expansion, is the role played by development workers variously described as social activists, change agents, facilitators, group organizers, catalysts and animators.[8] The success of these initiatives is in no small measure due to the approach and style of work adopted by these development workers. They do not possess any special technical skills but their human qualities are vital to the success of their mission. These include a deep understanding of the economy and society of the impoverished groups, compassion and sympathy with their plight, ability to inspire trust and confidence and to motivate and guide them, not in a paternalistic and authoritarian way, but in a manner to enhance their confidence and self-reliance. While many initiatives, such as for instance the GB, the SFDP and SEWA, continue to rely on a core of professional and administrative staff to run their activities, others such as PIDA and Sarilakas regard their primary objective as being the stimulation of self-reliant participatory organizations. The animators who perform this role are expected to be gradually phased out, and internal cadres and animators selected from within the village population to progressively take over their functions. Likewise, it is the policy of WWF to have members of that organization steadily take over as group and area organizers. It was noted earlier that Six-S increasingly relies on peasant-technicians and advanced groups to transmit knowledge and innovations to other members and groups.

Self-reliance has many other aspects and several of these are illustrated by the experiences of the participatory initiatives discussed here. In some ways, the most important element is growing control over economic resources and social environment resulting in greater confidence and reduction in insecurity and dependence, brought about on the one hand by the strength derived from membership of a group and on the other by a steady increase in individual intellectual, moral and technical capabilities. Indeed, it is this aspect of their experience that is repeatedly emphasized by members in discussions and evaluations of the impact of the initiatives. Another dimension of self-reliance concerns the mobilization of labour and other resources to launch income-generating

232

activities and infrastructural and service projects. This feature is common to all initiatives but is central to the African experiences.

Provision of credit is the cornerstone of GB and SFDP but plays a role of varying importance in other initiatives as well. It should be noted here that in most cases funds are made available on a loan basis to be repayable over a specified period and at commercial rates of interest, although the rates are lower than those charged by private money-lenders. It was noted earlier that in cases where a credit programme is a major component of their activities such as SFDP, GB, SEWA and WWF, the default rate is astonishingly low by any standards. This is eloquent testimony to the self-reliance with which these initiatives are undertaken.

Furthermore, almost all initiatives have engendered other schemes, which reinforces this self-reliance. The organization of collective savings for consumption and production loans and for emergency purposes is a common element in all initiatives. The Six-S, ADRI and ORAP have initiated various types of cereal banks to enhance food security. Some groups in ADRI have started schemes which represent the beginnings of a social security system. Similar schemes covering childbirth, death, widowhood, etc., have been launched by SEWA and WWF financed completely or partly by members' contributions.

The high rates of saving and accumulation achieved by many groups in these initiatives is further evidence of their self-reliant approach. In GB, for instance, together with interest payments, group fund and emergency fund, the members save a minimum of 25 per cent of the income generated by the bank loans. If to this is added savings for special projects and members' personal savings and investment, the savings rate in many cases may well amount to 50 per cent of the additional income. In an extremely poor community where meeting subsistence needs is an everyday struggle, such rates of saving can only be considered phenomenal.

Initiatives such as PIDA and Sarilakas push the concept of self-reliance to extreme limits. PIDA regards its role as assistance in the mobilization of efforts by the rural poor through animation work. It does not provide any technical assistance, extension services, grants or loans. The villagers themselves are expected to enhance their incomes and production and social welfare through collective actions of the type discussed earlier and through staking a claim for their share of resources from the commercial banks and government social and economic services. Even the animation and facilitation work done by external animators is for a limited period to be taken over at the earliest opportunity by internal cadres.

Most of the initiatives discussed here have been recipients of assistance from national, multilateral and bilateral sources. No conventional type of analysis has been undertaken of the effectiveness of this assistance. Except for the two major credit programmes, the assistance received has been relatively modest. It has consisted for the most part of funds to start loan schemes, grants for training programmes, financing of workshops and occasional grants for equipment for production or infrastructural projects. No foreign experts have been attached to these movements nor have they benefited from technical co-operation and consultancy missions. These initiatives thus represent truly authentic indigenous attempts at self-reliant development at the grass-roots level.

Participatory initiatives as economic enterprises

The initiatives we have been considering cannot be looked at as conventional development projects. They respond to the multifarious needs of their members. Efforts to improve the living standards of the members are certainly at the core of their concerns and often provide the motivation for the creation of the movement but both the leaders and the participants also stress objectives that go beyond material achievements. In this section, we discuss some economic aspects— leaving for later sections the social and political dimensions of the work of participatory initiatives. The pattern of economic activities undertaken by them has already been discussed. The intention here is to analyse briefly the nature of these activities and to make a rough assessment of their economic impact.

ECONOMIC BENEFITS TO MEMBERS

Provision of credit to individual members or to groups, directly or indirectly, plays an important role in all initiatives. Credit facilitates the purchase of stock in trade, raw materials, equipment, tools and agricultural inputs. Especially in densely populated poor countries, capital is an extremely scarce factor of production and carries high potential returns. Its value is further enhanced to the poor as institutional credit is largely unavailable to them and they must rely for urgent needs on money-lenders who impose 5 to 15 times the rates charged by commercial banks. The provision of credit thus contributes to increases in the incomes of the members by financing a higher turnover of their stock, improvements in tools and equipment, access to raw materials and inputs, and by the substitution of institutional loans for money-lenders' loans.

While detailed evaluation of economic activities of other initiatives is not available to the author, several surveys have attempted to quantify the economic impact of the credit programme of the GB and SFDP.[9] There is naturally a good deal of variation in returns on individual activities but overall the investment programme financed by loans generated rates of return in the region of 30 to 40 per cent. Apart from the factors mentioned earlier, the contributory factors in the GB have been that the activities undertaken are familiar to

234

members; the skills and technologies are known and are relatively simple; the clients are not dependent, except in a few cases, on extension services or inputs from the Government. Furthermore, the participants themselves select the activities for which they seek loans. It may be assumed that they select activities they are confident of carrying out successfully. Group dynamics, emulation, competition and peer pressure are additional factors which have played a positive role in all initiatives of the type considered here.

Similar factors have been at work in the SFDP with the additional point that high yields in its projects have been possible in part because the credit programme has brought within reach of small and marginal farmers the Green Revolution package of improved seeds, irrigation and fertilizers. Impressive income gains to women vendors, hawkers and home-based workers in SEWA and WWF have also been made possible essentially through access to credit. As indicated earlier, the mere substitution of institutional credit for that of money-lenders—even disregarding higher turnover, better prices and improved technology—is a source of substantial gains in income. Rough estimates made for SFDP members showed that income gains from this source alone equalled those brought about by increased production.

Another way in which these initiatives have helped increase incomes, production and employment is through the pooling of labour and other resources under collective projects such as irrigation and water catchment schemes, soil conservation, reforestation, construction of access roads, cultivation of common plots, mutual help in ploughing and harvesting, food storage, cereal banks, transport, marketing and joint purchase of agricultural inputs. The list of such efforts is long and impressive. In Africa especially, activities of this nature have contributed to stability and increases in income and production, reduction of food insecurity and generation of fuller employment through the breaking of infrastructural bottle-necks, overcoming of labour shortages and introduction of improved techniques. Co-operation in pooling resources facilitated by institutional innovations inspired by traditional practices has been at the heart of gains achieved through these initiatives.

The third and related source of gains has accrued from the exertion of collective pressure and power to secure higher wages for jobs and contract work, enforcement of land and tenancy reform, fishing and forestry rights, implementation of the provisions of labour legislation, improved prices for raw materials and for processed foods. These gains have been the result of stronger bargaining and countervailing power, as well as of institutional reforms such as service and production co-operatives, collective funds, credit and thrift societies, and consumer stores. These aspects have been especially important in the work of PIDA, Sarilakas, WWF and SEWA. This is a reflection of deep-seated social cleavages and economic polarization prevalent in many Asian countries.

Finally, some of these initiatives, especially in South Asia, have contributed to increased incomes through reduction of excessive expenditure on ceremonial occasions. These include dowries, birth and death ceremonies, and festivities of various kinds. Group discussions, solidarity and demonstration provide the necessary support for members to make the radical break from ancient practices. The gains accrue not only from direct reductions in expenditure but, even more importantly, from the savings in servicing of loans incurred by poor people at exorbitant interest rates from money-lenders and landlords, a debt trap from which they are unlikely to escape during their lifetime. Although no precise estimates are available of gains to disposable income from these sources, the rough estimates I made for SFDP members show that, even disregarding the interest charged by money-lenders, the average annual reduction in ceremonial expenditures was equivalent to 600 to 700 rupees—somewhat more than the gains realized from increases in income owing to production loans.

WIDER ECONOMIC IMPACT OF INITIATIVES

The final theme under this heading concerns the wider economic impact of the initiatives. It is possible for a programme to confer significant socio-economic benefits on its members while simultaneously generating strong negative efforts on other segments of the society. Likewise a project with a mediocre rating in terms of the direct impact on intended beneficiaries may nevertheless generate beneficial indirect and side effects for the poor. All the initiatives considered here are doubly blessed: they bring significant social and economic benefits to members, while simultaneously generating positive spill-over effects on the poorer segments of these societies. These wider economic effects may be considered under three headings: "macro-economic" impact of project activities, assistance given by members to the fellow poor in their area or "technical co-operation at the grass-roots level" and the impact on national programmes and policies.

Although in aggregate terms most of these programmes are of negligible importance, they exercise significant influence at the local and regional levels. The macro-economic effects may extend to markets for labour, credit and goods and services. As far as the labour markets are concerned, the impact of activities undertaken under most initiatives is to intensify the utilization of family labour and shift the labour allocation from wage to self-employment. This may be the result of more intensive cultivation, non-farming activities, access to land, work on infrastructural projects and participation in training and social programmes. The effect is that, while the demand for labour goes up, the supply of wage labour goes down. Other things being equal, this should contribute to an increase in wages for the poor and the unskilled. This indeed seems to have happened in the areas in which SFDP, GB, WWF and SEWA have been active.

Many of the activities launched under these initiatives result in the diversion of bank credit to the rural poor, the creation of new credit and savings schemes and the substitution of institutional credit for money-lenders' credit. Thus, by increasing the supply of institutional credit and reducing the demand for money-lenders' loans, these initiatives exercise a downward pressure on the terms for non-institutional credit. Since the rural and urban poor are the main clients and victims of credit from money-lenders, traders and landlords, this must be counted among the more important benefits to non-members generated by these initiatives.

Productive activities associated with these initiatives result in increased output and marketing of goods and services consumed by the poverty groups in rural and urban areas. These include such things as rice, maize, vegetables, fruits, meat, milk, eggs, cloth, household utensils, bamboo products, baskets, simple agricultural tools and services such as transport, storage, marketing and shopping. Typically, these are the goods and services of mass consumption and figure prominently in the expenditure patterns of the poor. Although the rise in the incomes of the members results in increased consumption of many of these goods and services, the net effect for most goods is to increase their availability. This in turn, by keeping the relative prices of such commodities lower than they might otherwise be, contributes to an increase in the real incomes of the poorer segments of the society.

The benefits from these initiatives also spread to other poor people through assistance rendered to them by members in a variety of ways. The pioneer groups must be looked upon as constituting a social vanguard whose impact radiates through the neighbouring communities. The members assist the fellow poor to form their own groups. This may happen at the initiative of the members of the established groups or at the request of the non-members who spontaneously wish to emulate their efforts. It is possible to quote instances from all the initiatives discussed here of the pioneer groups and animators being besieged by requests from others in the same or neighbouring villages for help in starting similar activities. This is perhaps the most important explanation of the rapid expansion of the membership of many of these organizations. Even where the entire set of activities is not replicated, some aspects of their valuable experiences are quickly disseminated to the neighbouring communities. Indeed the "bush telegraph" is the most effective vehicle of transmission of new ideas, techniques and practices among the peasantry and rural workers. To give some examples, SFDP members helped others with group formation, initiation of social activities and

237

community projects, credit and technical advice. In Khopasi and Jyamire villages, community irrigation projects were started at the initiative of the SFDP groups but non-members in the catchment area were invited to participate in the scheme through donation of labour and cash. The example of betel and coir yarn producers in establishing new marketing channels was swiftly followed by several neighbouring villages.

Likewise, the pioneering efforts of Six-S, ORAP and ADRI have spread rapidly to other parts of the country through demonstration effect and emulation. For example, the Groupement Naam de Somiaga in Burkina Faso helped set up 11 groups in six other villages. For their part, 42 villages assisted this group in the construction of a dam. Six-S has developed original methods for the transmission of skills through peasant-technicians who are paid by the organization to train other members and groups in new technologies, social innovations and management techniques. The principal vehicle for this is *chantiers-écoles* (training camps) organized on a regular basis during the dry season at the request of the groups. These range from soil conservation techniques to management of maize mills, from water pump maintenance to fenced livestock, and from cereal banks to nutritional centres. Each group assumes the responsibility of passing its special skills to others.

The impact of these initiatives is spreading farther afield. Six-S is already operating in four Sahelian countries and plans are afoot to extend its activities to the Niger and Chad. WWF is working in three States in southern India. Sister organizations to SEWA have been set up in about 10 other Indian cities such as Bhopal, Delhi, Lucknow, Mithila and Bhagalpur. Many international seminars, study tours and workshops have been organized around these initiatives. The South West Africa People's Organization (SWAPO) cadres have visited ORAP, the GB has attracted visitors from several Asian and African countries and has given technical assistance for the organization of credit programmes for the rural poor in Malaysia, Sri Lanka and Malawi. Perhaps the most dramatic example of the international impact of these initiatives is the role played by the managing director of the Grameen Bank in establishing small-scale credit schemes for the urban poor in Chicago and Arkansas, the latter at the request of the Governor of the State. That the leader of a credit programme for the impoverished masses of one of the poorest countries in the world should be advising on establishing similar programmes in the metropolis of one of the richest countries in the world is indeed a paradox of extraordinary proportions.

Each of these initiatives contains valuable lessons for official development programmes, projects and policies. It is one of the tragedies of the development efforts in our countries that these creative and original efforts at self-reliant development through mobilization of the limited resources of the impoverished groups should have had so little impact on official development thinking and practice, at both the national and international levels. Fortunately, there are glimmers of hope. By way of example, we may mention that in Nepal the basic concept of credit for the rural poor based on group guarantee has been extended by the ADB/N to other villages where the SFDP is not operating. Likewise, many elements of the SFDP— formation of groups, channelling of credit for individual and group activities through the group, investment decisions by the groups— have been partially incorporated in several integrated rural development projects in the country. Several women's programmes have also drawn upon the experience gained in the SFDP. Its existence has enhanced the effectiveness of some support services and has put pressure on other institutions such as co-operatives and the Agricultural Inputs Corporation to improve their performance.

As another example, we may mention the success achieved by SEWA in projecting the problems of poor self-employed women at the national level. The efforts of the organization have had some impact on thinking and action concerning self-employed workers. After prolonged pressure from SEWA, the Gujarat Government set up the Unorganized Labour Board in 1980. The National Planning Commission added a chapter on the self-employed in the Sixth Five-Year Plan and the Prime Minister has set up a Commission on Self-employed Women, which appropriately is chaired by the originator and leader of SEWA.

Participatory initiatives as agencies of social reform

The preceding sections have already touched on the role played by the participatory initiatives as instruments of social change. We discuss here four aspects of social progress: provision of social services and cultural amenities, change in family relations, emancipation of women and reform of antiquated and harmful customs and practices. Unlike many other development projects, the initiatives discussed here have integrated social and economic activities in their programmes. In this respect as in others, the leaders and organizers of these associations have simply followed the wishes of their members. ORAP, Six-S and ADRI have a wide range of social and cultural activities such as literacy, schools, nutrition, child care, help for the aged and the handicapped, village clinics, personal hygiene, music and dances. WWF organizes literacy classes, night schools for working children, family planning and nutrition education. SEWA has pioneered social assistance and welfare schemes for maternity, death, widowhood etc. The social activities of the GB comprise sanitation, health care, nutrition, education and family planning. The performance of the SFDP members has been superior to those of their neighbours in terms of literacy, education, family planning, sanitation and access to health services. It should be remembered that, except perhaps for SFDP, the bulk of these social services is organized by the members themselves with contributions in cash and kind.

The second aspect relates to the effect on family solidarity. As mentioned earlier, it is a collective of three to five families that contributes the base units for many ORAP activities. The involvement of all members of the family in projects of direct benefit to them serves to promote family unity and harmony. In Six-S, the traditional Naam groups have brought together the old and the young, thus reducing generational tensions and promoting harmony among members of different age groups.

All the initiatives provide for full participation by women in all their activities either in mixed or in their own groups. This is leading to slow but profound changes in the social status and economic position of women, especially in South Asia. Membership in SEWA and WWF has given women, long subjected to subordination and oppression, a new sense of pride, dignity, personal worth and economic independence. All the South Asian initiatives have enabled women to increase their incomes and acquire some organizational and management skills in planning and implementing group activities. In many households, the participation of women in income-generating activities has created a new division of labour and a new pattern of relationships. In some of the households with women members of the GB, it was found that the male members had begun to perform some of the tasks traditionally done by women, for example, looking after the children. It was also noted that the economic activities undertaken by women in turn created new opportunities for male members of the family. The women may, for instance, husk rice, make bamboo and cane products, or look after milch cows, while the husbands complement the household economy by buying raw materials, selling processed rice, handicrafts, milk or meat. This has enhanced women's economic independence and social status within the extended family. The husbands and other male members in the household have accepted the new situation willingly and, in some cases, even enthusiastically.

Finally, participation in these organizations is leading to a reform of ancient but antiquated customs and practices. Reference was made earlier to the role played by these organizations in reducing burdensome ceremonial expenditures. More impressive is the progress being made by the initiatives in South Asia in combating the age-old practice of dowry and child marriages, in caste and ethnic prejudice and discrimination. There is also evidence of decline in drunkenness, gambling, crime, wife-beating and similar types of anti-social behaviour. All this casts an interesting light on the determinants of social attitudes and behaviour. It may be noted that government policies and programmes in many countries have long sought to bring about precisely this type of change but without much apparent success. The experience of these initiatives shows that once the people are organized in voluntary, co-operative groups and are given the necessary motivation, they decide on their own to carry through social changes of far-reaching significance.

Participatory initiatives as schools of democracy

Grass-roots participatory organizations may be regarded as foundations of a democratic society. They promote the democratic cause in at least three ways. First, a representative and pluralistic democracy presupposes that all major social and economic groups in the country have a voice and a role in shaping national policies. For this to be possible, such groups should be able to articulate and press their views on vital issues of concern to them. Typically, in most poor countries, and in many rich ones for that matter, the weaker and more impoverished groups represented by the landless and marginal farmers in rural areas and the unemployed, casually employed and the poor self-employed in urban areas, have little voice and a limited role in influencing government policies on social and economic matters. Given their individual weaknesses, they can exercise pressure and influence only by forming their own organizations.

None of the initiatives considered here has articulated its role in political terms. But it is clear that in practice some at least have come close to representing the interests of their groups in the political and economic processes of their countries. SEWA and WWF have served as pressure groups in the struggle against certain vested interests that have opposed the reforms proposed by them. They have also sought to influence legislation on matters of interest to their members and have deployed their strength in relation to bureaucracy and political parties to promote the interests of their members. Likewise, Sarilakas and PIDA have enabled poor peasants, landless workers and fishermen to exercise their collective strength to enforce legislation, renegotiate contracts and generally enhance their bargaining power.

In some cases the members of these organizations are beginning to play a more direct political role. In Nepal, for instance, it is rare for the small farmers, tenants and sharecroppers to hold offices in co-operatives and ward panchayat (local government) bodies. It is, however, a common sight now in all project areas for SFDP members to participate in such organizations at the village level. To give just one example, in Khopasi, 32 SFDP participants served as ward members, 19 as panchayat members and 3 as members of the executive committee of co-operatives out of a total of 9. Likewise, in areas where the GB has opened its branches, there has been a perceptible increase in the influence and power exerted by its members in village affairs.

The second way in which these initiatives serve the democratic cause is simply by providing an example of an embryonic democracy

241

at work. In the section on the institutional framework of grass-roots initiatives, it was noted that base groups constitute the core of their organizations. These groups are generally run in an open democratic manner. The style of work is through discussions and dialogue and decision is reached through consensus. Some of the groups have devised original solutions to the problems faced by organizations as democratic entities at all levels, namely, those of accountability of leadership, prevention of concentration of power in the hands of office-holders and active participation by all members in the management of group activities. The betel producers, for instance, decided to limit the size of their membership to ensure that all members participate actively in and effectively control the economic activities of the group. The requests for additional membership were handled by assisting them to form new groups of their own. The insistence on keeping the members of the group to a manageable size is also characteristic of other initiatives. The Six-S and ADRI groups seek to prevent perpetuation of hierarchical division of labour by rotating the tasks among members. Office-bearers are chosen by election for limited periods. Some groups elect a different person to preside at each meeting. These organizations, therefore, promote the habit of group discussion, consultation, planning and implementation of group activities, and resolution of conflict through debate— qualities that constitute the foundations of a participatory democracy.

Thirdly, the grass-roots initiatives aid the democratic processes in poor countries by developing the intellectual, moral, managerial and technical capabilities of their members. This aspect has been discussed at length above. Suffice it to say here that in the last analysis it is these human capabilities that are the ultimate determinants of the vitality and creativity of a truly democratic society.

Conclusions

In this paper we have attempted to analyse the significance, processes and characteristics of participatory development through an examination of the experiences of a few grass-roots initiatives in Asian and African countries. In this concluding section we touch on the strengths and limitations of participatory grass-roots initiatives as models of development. But before addressing the issue, it is necessary to make some qualifying remarks on the initiatives analysed in this paper.

The analysis presented here has been necessarily selective, highlighting distinctive features and notable achievements of nine participatory initiatives. As such it has undoubtedly given an optimistic, perhaps idealistic, picture of the functioning of such initiatives. It is necessary to emphasize first that the initiatives considered here are among the most successful of numerous similar efforts under way in third world countries. Secondly, there is a great deal of variation in the quality of performance between and within the different units of the initiatives discussed here. Thirdly, the account presented above has not discussed the many difficulties, setbacks and frustrations suffered by these initiatives. It is necessary to point out that these movements had to overcome a wide variety of problems at some stage or another and continue to face difficulties of organization, finance, know-how, staff and opposition or indifference from certain vested interests.

Despite these difficulties, the grass-roots initiatives considered here have achieved a wide measure of success. It may be useful to summarize what appear to have been the major contributory factors to their success. There are three elements in the participatory character of these initiatives which probably have contributed strongly to their good performance: work in the preparatory phase prior to initiation of activities, an institutional framework that allows for an assertion of members' priorities in the unfolding of the activities undertaken and the formation of groups as a basic unit in the organization. These features in turn owe much to the approach and human qualities of the leaders of these movements and their band of dedicated development workers.

Relatively quick positive results in terms of the satisfaction of the psychological and material needs of the members have been important in sustaining interest and commitment. The material achievements in the Asian initiatives flowed in large measure from the provision of credit and the wresting of a larger share of surpluses through enhanced bargaining power and co-operative activities, and in African experiences from co-operation in the mobilization of internal resources and attraction of outside funds for production diversification, infrastructural development and technological innovations. The organizational framework adopted facilitates the mobilization of labour and other resources, the institution of schemes for collective savings and social security, and the provision of social and economic services. At the same time, it allows for the initiation of activities of different sizes and with different modes of production and systems of management. Finally, these experiences demonstrate that a pattern of development rooted in grass-roots participatory organizations, while giving full play to individual and group initiatives, promotes a relatively egalitarian distribution of incomes and access to common services and facilities.

Despite its promising potential, the participatory approach to development has made little headway in official programmes and policies at the national or international levels. Even among the non-governmental initiatives, the success rate is relatively low. A full discussion of this apparent paradox cannot be undertaken here, but some of the relevant considerations may be noted. In the first place, the participatory approach to development is relatively new and few in the "development establishment" have proper knowledge or full understanding of it. Secondly, as noted previously, many apparently participatory programmes provide little more than token representation of the beneficiaries and thus fail to arouse their interest or commitment. Thirdly, the participatory approach, especially in its empowerment version, tends to be mistakenly equated by the dominant groups with subversive or revolutionary doctrine. As such, many participatory initiatives have to contend with hostility, harassment and attempts at suppression. Certainly, relatively few attract resources of the type and amount reserved for more conventional development projects.

There are some additional difficulties which are perhaps inherent in a participatory approach. The pace and pattern of activities may evolve slowly and haltingly and in directions different from those envisaged initially. The initiatives are often of a limited size and dependent for their success on the leadership of an exceptional person and a small band of dedicated social activists. It is, therefore, difficult to replicate them on a nation-wide basis. Furthermore, while successful in handling simple operations, they lose their effectiveness when confronted with large-scale complex activities. Their expansion beyond a certain size is likely to provoke the antagonism of more powerful forces. There is some validity in these charges but the experience of some of the initiatives has refuted a few of them. It would, however, require a separate paper to do full justice to these issues.

NOTES

[1] This article represents an effort to introduce to a wider audience a little known but particularly interesting and promising approach to development. It is based largely on the work I initiated in ILO on participatory organizations of the rural poor (PORP), co-ordinated by Anisur Rahman. I acknowledge my debt to him and to colleagues who participated in the PORP programme, as also to numerous but anonymous peasants and landless workers, both men and women, leaders of peasant groups and of participatory initiatives, social activists and sympathetic officials who have deepened my understanding of the social reality of the impoverished masses in rural areas of the third world. For comments on an earlier draft, I am grateful to Mohiuddin Alamgir, Orlando Fals Borda, Philippe Egger, Keith Griffin, Albert Hirschman, John Knight, Peter Oakley, Anisur Rahman, Amartya Sen and Fredj Stambouli. I alone am responsible for the views expressed here.

[2] At least one author has made the brave effort to explore the implications of participatory development at all these different levels (see Gran, 1983).

[3] Among numerous treatments of this subject, three may be mentioned here: Dag Hammarskjöld Foundation (1975), Sen (1983) and Wahidul and others (1977).

[4] A more restricted definition but along similar lines has been given by Sen (1983): "The process of economic development can be seen as a process of expanding the capabilities of people."

[5] For an extended discussion of the role of local institutions in development projects, see Uphoff (1986).

⁶The classic work on conscientization is Freire (1972); see also Rahman (1985) and Fals Borda (1985).

⁷Sawadogo and Ouedraogo (1987) described this approach in these words: "C'est ainsi que nous animons les groupes-cibles en fonction de ce qu'ils *sont,* de ce qu'ils *savent,* de ce qu'ils *vivent,* de ce qu'ils *savent faire,* et de ce qu'ils *veulent.* "

⁸The issue of self-reliance in relation to animators is addressed in Tilakaratna (1987).

⁹These have been summarized in my evaluations of GB (Ghai, 1984a) and SFDP (Ghai, 1984b). All subsequent information on these initiatives is taken from these sources.

REFERENCES

Action pour le développement rural intégré (1986). La dynamique des organisations paysannes au Rwanda: le cas de l'intergroupement Tuzamke de Kabaya. Geneva: ILO.

Advisory Committee on Rural Development (1979). Rural employers' and workers' organizations and participation. Geneva: ILO.

Agricultural Projects Services Centre (1979). Impact study of Small Farmers' Development Project. Kathmandu.

Arunachalam, Jaya (1983). Alternative employment options for Indian rural women. Manila: IRRI.

Azad, Nandini (1985). Improving working conditions for rural women through creation of alternative employment options. *Rural Development and Women: Lessons from the Field,* Shimwaayi Muntemba, ed. Geneva: ILO.

Chambers, Robert (1985). The Working Women's Forum: a counter-culture by poor workers. Brighton: Institute of Development Studies.

Chavunduka, D. M. and others (1985). Khuluma Usenza: the story of ORAP in Zimbabwe's rural development. Bulawayo: ORAP.

Chen, Marty (1982). *Working Women's Forum: Organizing for Credit and Change.* New York: Seeds Publication.

Commission on the Churches' Participation in Development (1981). People's participation and people's movements. Geneva: World Council of Churches.

Dag Hammarskjöld Foundation (1975). What now? Another development. *Development Dialogue.* Uppsala.

Dillon, Bridget and Matthias Stiefel (1987). Making the concept concrete: the UNRISD Participation Programme. *Reading Rural Development Communications,* Bulletin 21. Berkshire: Reading University.

Economic Commission for Latin America and the Caribbean (1973). Popular participation in development. *Community Development Journal.*

Egger, Philippe (1987a). L'Association Six-S—se servir de la saison sèche en savane et au Sahel—et les groupements Naam: note sur quelques observations. Geneva: ILO.

———— (1987b). La leçon de Jomba: trois tableaux pour une conclusion sur l'emploi rural au Rwanda. Geneva: ILO.

Fals Borda, Orlando (1985). Conocimiento y poder popular. Siglo Veintiuno editores. Bogotá.

Food and Agriculture Organization of the United Nations (1979). *Participation of the Poor in Rural Development.* Rome.

Freire, Paulo (1972). *The Pedagogy of the Oppressed.* Harmondsworth: Penguin.

Fuglesang, Andreas and Dale Chandler (1986). *Participation as a Process: What We Can Learn from Grameen Bank, Bangladesh.* Oslo: Norwegian Agency for International Development.

Ghai, Dharam (1984a). *An Evaluation of the Impact of the Grameen Bank Project.* Dhaka: Grameen Bank.

———— (1984b). *Small Farmers' Development Project: Mid-term Evaluation.* Rome: IFAD.

Ghai, Dharam, Prakash Lohani and Anisur Rahman (1984). Small Farmers' Development Project of Nepal. *Grass-roots Participation and Self-reliance: Experiences in South and South-East Asia,* Anisur Rahman, ed. New Delhi: Oxford and IBH Publishing Co.

Gran, Guy (1983). *Development by People: Citizen Construction of a Just World.* New York: Praeger.

Hirschman, Albert (1984). *Getting Ahead Collectively.* Elmsford, New York: Pergamon Press.

Hossain, M. (1984). *Credit for the Rural Poor: The Experience of Grameen Bank in Bangladesh.* Dhaka: Bangladesh Institute of Development Studies.

International Labour Organisation (1976). Employment growth and basic needs. Geneva.

Mosley, Paul and Rudra Prasad Dahal (1987). Credit for the rural poor: a comparison of policy experiments in Nepal and Bangladesh. *Manchester Papers on Development* (July).

Nyoni, Sithembiso (1986). ORAP since "Khuluma Usenza": a review of self-assessment. Geneva: ILO.

Oakley, Peter (1987). State or process, means or end? The concept of participation in rural development. *Reading Rural Development Communications,* Bulletin 21. Berkshire: Reading University.

Oakley, P. and D. Marsden (1984). Approaches to participation in rural development. Geneva: ILO.

Rahman, M. A. (1983). Sarilakas: a pilot project for stimulating grass-roots participation in the Philippines. Geneva: ILO.

————— (1985). The theory and practice of participation action research. *The Challenge of Social Change,* Orlando Fals Borda, ed. London: Sage Publications Ltd.

————— (1988). Glimpses of the "other Africa". Geneva: ILO.

Rokaya, Chandra M. (1983). Impact of Small Farmers' Credit Programme on farm output, net income and the adoption of new methods. Kathmandu: Agricultural Projects Services Centre.

Sawadogo, A. R. and B. L. Ouedraogo (1987). Auto-évaluation de six groupements Naam dans la province du Yatenga. Geneva: ILO.

Self-employed Women's Association (1984). Self-employed Women's Association. Ahmedabad.

Sen, Amartya (1983). Development: which way now? *Economic Journal,* December. London.

Tilakaratna, S. (1984). Grass-roots self-reliance in Sri Lanka: organisations of betel and coir yarn producers. *Grass-roots Participation and Self-reliance: Experiences in South and South-East Asia,* Anisur Rahman, ed. New Delhi: Oxford and IBH Publishing Co.

————— (1985). The animator in participatory rural development: some experiences from Sri Lanka. Geneva: ILO.

————— (1987). The animator in participatory rural development. Geneva: ILO.

United Nations (1981). *Popular Participation as a Strategy for Promoting Community Level Action and New Development.* Sales No. E.81.IV.2.

Uphoff, Norman (1986). Local institutional development: an analytical sourcebook with cases. West Hartford: Kumarian Press.

Wahidul, Haque and others (1977). Towards a theory of rural development. *Development Dialogue.* Uppsala: Dag Hammarskjöld Foundation.

Wasserstrom, Robert (1985). Grass-roots Development in Latin America and the Caribbean. New York: Praeger.

World Health Organization (1982). Activities of the WHO in promoting community involvement for health development. Geneva.

Yunus, Muhammed (1982). Grameen Bank Project in Bangladesh: a poverty-focused rural development programme. Dhaka: Grameen Bank.

INDEX

Abemba, B. 110, 111, 125n
*Action pour le développement rural
   intégré* (ADRI) 219, 225, 227,
   230–1, 233, 238–9, 242
Adelman, Irma 39n, 57n
Adjustment with a Human Face (UN
   Children's Fund) 39n
Africa
   austerity in 34
   education: enrolment 124;
      expansion 61; government
      expenditure on 27, 62, 103;
      returns to investment 68–70
   GDP per capita 16, 160
   government expenditure on health, 62,
      159–60, 184
   health standards in 159, 161
   human development expenditure 30–3
   hunger 17
   industry 150–2
   infant mortality 14, 28–9, 162, 163–5
   level of productivity 16
   life expectancy 14
   malnutrition 164–5
   non-agricultural real wages 17
   participatory development
      initiatives 242–4
   water supply 171–3
   see also individual countries; other
      areas of Africa
Africa, East, education in 66
   see also individual countries; other
      areas of Africa
Africa, North
   malnutrition 163
   nutrition deficiency 18
   ratio of females to males 53
   see also individual countries; other
      areas of Africa
Africa, Sub-Saharan
   aid to 185
   education 15, 63, 64, 118
   GDP 140–1
   government expenditure on health 63
   industry 130, 133, 140–56:capabilities
      needed for 132–40, 146–50; lack
      of educated manpower 61;
      policies on industrial capability
      development 150–6; poor

performance of 143–6; structural
   characteristics of 141–3
   malnutrition 163
   nutrition deficiency 18
   see also individual countries; other
      areas of Africa
Ahluwalia, Montek S. 39n
Ahmed, Manzoor 74, 98n
AIDS 163
Algeria
   government expenditure on
      health 175
   infant mortality rate (IMR) 169
*Alternative strategies for Economic
   Development* (Griffin) 39n
America, Central and South
   malnutrition in 163
   see also individual countries; Latin
      America
Andes 17–18
   effect of education on farm
      productivity 73–97
   iodine-deficiency disorders 166
   see also Peru
Arab countries, infant mortality rate
   (IMR) in 162
Argentina
   government expenditure: defence 36;
      education 20–1, 62; health 20–1;
      public administration 20–1
   non-agricultural real wages 17
   per capita external debt 19
   per capita income 19
   urban unemployment 16
Aristotle 43, 44, 56n
armed forces 36–7
   see also defence expenditure
Asia
   education 27, 64, 68, 103, 124
   government expenditure on
      health 184
   human development expenditure 30–1
   level of productivity 16
   nutrition standards 164
   participatory development
      initiatives 242–4
   water supply costs 171–3
   see also individual countries; other
      areas of Asia

248

250

251

Rogers, E.   99n
rural development   217–18, 219
  forestry schemes   191, 192, 196–8,
    199–203, 205, 207–8
  irrigation schemes   191, 192–3, 197,
    198–9, 199–200, 202–6, 208
  special public works programmes
    (SPWPs)   190–212
  see also development, participatory
Rutter, M.   110, 127n
Rwanda
  *Action pour la Développement rural
    intégré* (ADRI)   219, 225, 227,
    230–1, 233, 238–9, 242
  child malnutrition   164–5
  forestry schemes   191, 192, 196–7, 201,
    202, 207

Sabot, R. H.   72n
Sahel countries   15–18, 238
  forest schemes   196
  water supply costs
  see also individual countries
sanitation   167, 170
  and human development   25
  see also water supply
Sarilakas   219, 222, 230–3, 235, 241
Schultz, T. W.   95, 99n
*Se servir de la saison sèche en savane et
  au Sahel* (Six-s)   219, 223–4, 225,
  227, 232–3, 238, 239, 240, 242
Self-employed Women's Association
  (SEWA)   219, 221–2, 230–3, 235–7,
  240, 241
Sen, Amartya   10, 39n, 40n, 56n, 57n,
  58n, 246n
Senegal
  per capita external debt   19–20
  per capita income   19–20
Sierra Leone, educational expansion
  in   60–1
Small Farmers' Development Project
  (SFDP)   219–21, 227, 230–41
Smith, Adam   43, 44, 56n
Social Policy Making During Adjustment
  (Cornia)   40n
Somalia
  educational expansion   60–1
  industry   148–9
Soto, Hernando de   40n
South Africa
  GNP per capita   42
  life expectancy   42
  racial discrimination   32
South West Africa People's Organisation
  (SWAPO)   238
Sri Lanka

credit programmes   238
debt crisis   160
educational expansion   60–1
GNP per capita   42
government expenditure; defence   36;
  education   20–1; health   20–1;
  public administration   20–1
infant mortality rates (IMR)   161–2
life expectancy   42
nutrition   164
participatory development
  initiatives   222
participatory Institute for Development
  Alternatives (PIDA)   219, 222–3,
  228–9, 230–3, 235–6, 241
State of the Worlds Children, The (UN
  Children's Fund)   58n
Stewart, F.   72n
structural adjustment   20, 22–3, 26, 31
*Subsistence Agriculture and Economic
  Development* 99n
Sudan
  educational expansion   60–1
  fiscal squeeze   62

Tanner Lectures. . .(Sen)   56n, 57n
Tanzania
  child malnutrition   164–5
  education   65–9, 110–11, 117, 124
  educational expansion   60–1
  government expenditure: defence   36;
    education   20–1; health   20–1;
    public administration   20–1
  industry   145, 148–9
  irrigation schemes   191, 193, 197,
    198–9, 202, 204, 206, 208
  non-agricultural real wages   17
  per capita external debt   19
  per capita income   19
  secondary education   15
*Technology, Employment and
  Development* (Sen)   40n
Thailand
  defence expenditure   36
  infant mortality rate (IMR)   163
  nutrition   164
  water supply costs   172
Theory of Justice, A (Rawls)   39n, 58n
Tokman, Victor   40n
*Transforming Traditional
  Agriculture* 99n
*Transition to Egalitarian Development,
  The* (Griffin and James)   40n
Tunisia, government expenditure
  in   20–1, 36, 62
Turkey, government expenditure
  in   20–1, 36

257

258